COMPLETE ENCYCLOPEDIA OF

Cricket

COMPLETE ENCYCLOPEDIA OF

Cricket

The definitive guide to the international game

JOHN STERN

Bath · New York · Singapore · Hong Kong · Cologne · Delhi
Melbourne · Amsterdam · Johannesburg · Shenzhen

68

105

135

167

CONTENTS

FOREWORD BY MARK NICHOLAS

My story starts in black and white. The batsman walking to the wicket at Lord's is Colin Cowdrey. His left arm is in plaster so he holds the bat in his right hand. It is the last over of the Test match and, unlikely as it sounds, all four results remain possible.

The bowler is Wes Hall, the ferocious West Indian who had broken Cowdrey's arm that afternoon. Cowdrey is lucky that he is not on strike though few people think that the uncelebrated batsman who is, the off-spinner David Allen, has a chance of survival. Wrong. Hall's Herculean effort is resisted and the match, played over five compelling days, is drawn. The year was 1963 and a five-year-old boy had fallen in love with the game of bat and ball. The scene repeats to this day as if a cast of life.

The players in this drama are worth review. In the leading role was the incomparable Garry Sobers. Co-starring were Ted Dexter, Fred Trueman, Ken Barrington and Brian Close on one side; Frank Worrell, Rohan Kanhai, Charlie Griffith and Lance Gibbs on the other. None was built the same, nor did they move alike or smile or snarl from a manual.

These were men cut from another, distant age. No gym, no huddles, no money, no cuddles.

Soon I am old enough to play out a similar scene on a small piece of turf in the back garden. First I cut and roll the grass, then mark a crease at each end with white emulsion. My friend arrives with little time to spare and the match begins promptly at 11:30 am.

I am England, he is West Indies. Put in to bat, his whole West Indian team is bowled out for 48. In the reply only six wickets are lost – two of those to six and outs, lost forever in the neighbouring garden – and Dexter makes a double hundred in a total of 502. West Indies muster 91 in the second innings. The friend never returned to play again.

When I say my mother was under instruction to serve lunch at 1:30, tea at 4:10 and supper at 6:30, I kid you not. Cricket had washed over me and has still not washed out. Its various forms have different appeal for they ask contrasting questions of both player and spectator. Pause for a minute to think of the Twenty20 game as a one-night stand. Then take a little longer to reflect on the 50-over game in the form of a three-week fling. It will not be long before the realization that Test cricket is a lifelong love affair.

> Cricket had washed over me and has still not washed out ... the best game ever created

As we look forward we must do so with an eye for the time and the mood. This will forever change, like the seasons, and demand that administrators are more alert and sympathetic than at present. Nowadays, we watch cricket in vast swathes of colour but the price for that is high, paid mainly by television networks. Too much of a good thing is the game's greatest threat, allied to the notion that it is a cash cow for the constituents. There I go, modern corporate speak. It is a game for goodness' sake. The best game ever created.

JOHN STERN is a former editor of *The Wisden Cricketer* magazine and writes on the game for various international publications including *The Times*, *Observer* and *Wisden Cricketers' Almanack*.

PATRICK EAGAR is the most admired and respected cricket photographer in the world. Since 1972 he has covered more than 300 Test matches, including more than 100 between England and Australia. He has produced 13 books.

MARK NICHOLAS is one of the world's leading cricket broadcasters. He is the presenter of Channel 9's coverage of Australian international cricket and in England he fronts Channel 5's highlights programme. A former professional cricketer, he captained Hampshire to four trophies in the 1980s and 1990s and also captained England A.

INTRODUCTION

Whether you are the sort of person who takes days off work to watch every ball of a Test match or whether you just like the odd Twenty20 match, this book is for you.

It is a guided tour of international cricket, focusing on the ten countries that play Test cricket. It's a distilled history of the game, leaning towards more recent events, with the major players and events discussed within their proper context. The words are enhanced by the world-class photography of the peerless Patrick Eagar who has been covering international cricket for over 40 years.

The first chapter, The Global Game, sets the scene and explains how international cricket arrived at where it is today from its late 19th-century roots and the birth of the Ashes. Each of the Test-playing nations has its own space and interspersed through the book are 32 player profiles, selected for their achievements, noteworthiness or their personality. In addition ten of the world's most famous cricket grounds are profiled.

Cricket is a game that adores its statistics so inevitably numbers are never far away throughout this book. Also inevitably some of these statistics date quickly though the value of them is to place individual players in their comparative context. Stats in the book are correct up to 9 February 2012. For up-to-date statistics and coverage of the game, I suggest visiting www.espncricinfo.com, the world's leading cricket website, which has been an essential research tool for this book.

Equally valuable has been *Wisden Cricketers' Almanack*, references to which are dotted throughout the book. *Wisden* is known as the bible of cricket and has been published every year since 1864, containing a vast spectrum of statistics, records, reports and authoritative journalism on the previous year in cricket.

Force for good: eight-year-old Abdullah plays a shot in Kabul. Afghanistan's rise has been one of the game's more uplifting and improbable stories of recent years. They competed in the 2010 World Twenty20 and in 2012 played Pakistan in their first full ODI.

THE GLOBAL GAME

While cricket may seem, to some unbelievers and the uninitiated, a cure for insomnia it is in fact the sport that never sleeps.

Rarely a day passes when somewhere in the world 22 men or women are not representing their countries in competition over five days, four, three, one or, in the case of Twenty20, three hours.

There is something to tickle everyone's taste buds. There is the gourmet banquet of a five-day Test match, the reliable fill of the 50-over one-dayer or the bite-sized 20-over format, the game's most recent addition to the menu. There are World Cups for the 50- and 20-over games plus the Champions Trophy, a 50-over tournament for the top one-day nations. Test and one-day international sides are ranked according to recent results while the whole calendar is arranged precariously by the governing body, the International Cricket Council (ICC), in what it calls the Future Tours Programme.

There is no doubt that at times international cricket's global schedule groans under its own weight, like Mr Creosote from Monty Python's *The Meaning of Life*, but there is also no doubting the colossal appetite for the game, especially in India and other parts of south Asia.

However, like the snow-capped West Indian quick bowler Curtly Ambrose, cricket has a long reach that takes it beyond its traditional boundaries. One of the most surprising statistics of the last decade is that the second biggest source of internet traffic for www.espncricinfo.com, the world's leading cricket website, is North America where mostly non-resident Indians, starved of their favourite sport through the traditional media of newspapers, television and radio, consume live scoreboards, reports and opinion with seemingly unstinting relish.

Only ten nations play the most ancient and revered form of the international game, the five-day Test, but by late 2011 the overall membership of the ICC stood at 105 countries. That might not have the universality of football's FIFA but it is still an impressive and surprising number of outposts that include spots on the map like the Pacific island of Vanuatu to the global behemoth of China and European giant-killers like Denmark and the Netherlands.

The game has taken hold in Afghanistan where players who learned the game in Pakistani refugee camps during the 1980s' Soviet occupation have now spread the word in their homeland.

The emerging nation in Europe is Ireland, whose stunning defeat of England in the 2011 World Cup, following on from their victory over Pakistan in the previous tournament

Dutch courage: Netherlands all-rounder Ryan ten Doeschate.

Giant-killers: Ireland's John Mooney (left) and Trent Johnston celebrate beating England at the 2011 World Cup.

of 2007, confirmed their status as the strongest nation outside the ten Test-playing countries.

So it was no surprise that Irish joy turned to outrage after the 2011 World Cup when the ICC announced that forthcoming tournaments would be reduced in size from 14 to 10, effectively eliminating the emerging nations. Such was the outcry that the ICC almost immediately ordered a rethink. The theory behind its original decision was that the growth of the World Cup had led to too many one-sided matches in the early stages and a protracted tournament that did little for

Cricket has a long reach that takes it beyond its traditional boundaries

No.1 Test Team

RELIANCE RANKINGS

The pinnacle: Andrew Strauss holds the ICC mace awarded to the top Test team after his side beat India 4-0 in 2011.

the image of the global game. In early 2012 Ireland unveiled an ambitious plan to become a Test-playing nation by 2020.

In Test cricket the ICC proposed a World Test Championship to add further context to the five-day game that, other than one or two unsuccessful experiments, has existed solely as series of bilateral contests. The context of these fixtures is derived almost entirely from national and professional pride and the tradition that develops over time.

And what a tradition. When England took on India at Lord's in July 2011 it was officially the

There is a uniquely thrilling narrative to a Test and more so a series

2,000th Test ever played. By the end of the four-match series England had demolished the world's No.1 ranked Test side 4-0, to claim top spot for the first time since the ICC's team-ranking system was introduced in 2003 complementing the existing player rankings.

But the pursuit of that goal, while highly prized and much discussed, is less significant than the simple pursuit of victory and excellence in the form of the game that is still regarded as the ultimate test of an elite cricketer.

The landscape is changing for sure, with the Twenty20 explosion and the commercial viability of the limited-overs game. Sadly, Test matches do not command sell-out crowds everywhere in the world.

However, there is a uniquely thrilling narrative to a Test and even more so to a series. No one who witnessed, say, the 2005 Ashes, where the sporting and human drama built over eight weeks, will forget the experience, nor would they be able to name a sporting contest that could offer such engaging theatre over such a sustained period.

Achieving greatness in the Test arena is still the aim for players and the aspiration for teams is to emulate the sustained period of dominance of the great West Indies sides of the 1970s and '80s or the magnificent Australians who usurped West Indies in 1995 and remained the global benchmark until August 2009 when their No.1 ranking was taken by South Africa.

Since then India held top spot until England beat them 4-0 in 2011. England's tenure looked set to be short-lived when they remarkably lost all three Tests to a resurgent Pakistan side in early 2012.

Australia have been the undisputed kings of the one-day game in recent years and, even though their outstanding run of World Cup triumphs – three successive titles from 1999 to 2007 – came to an end in 2011, they remained the top limited-overs side.

These rankings have become an accepted way of judging the relative strengths of the world's teams as they compete against each other on a bilateral basis through the year. The team rankings were born from the player ratings that were the brainchild of the former England captain Ted Dexter in the late 1980s.

The game's traditional statistics did not take into account playing conditions or the strength of the opposition, which is the strength of the complex player rankings. No lay person would claim to understand how they are calculated but most acknowledge their legitimacy, at the very least as a forum for debate.

The team rankings (*right*) are a rolling ladder rather than a league table. They take into account results over a four-year period and, like the player rankings, make allowances for factors like the strength of the opposition and gives extra weight to matches won away from home.

Gold standard: Australia's one-day side.

ICC Test team rankings
Positions in January each year

	2012	2011	2010	2009	2008
England	1	3	5	5	5
South Africa	2	2	2	2	4
India	3	1	1	3	2
Australia	4	5	3	1	1
Pakistan	5	6	7	6	6
Sri Lanka	6	4	4	4	3
West Indies	7	7	8	7	8
New Zealand	8	8	6	8	-
Bangladesh	9	9	9	9	9

ICC ODI team rankings
Positions in January each year

	2012	2011	2010	2009	2008
Australia	1	1	1	1	1
India	2	2	2	3	2
South Africa	3	4	3	2	4
Sri Lanka	4	3	6	4	3
Pakistan	5	6	7	6	6
England	6	5	5	5	5
New Zealand	7	7	4	8	7
West Indies	8	8	8	7	8
Bangladesh	9	9	9	9	9
Zimbabwe	10	11	10	-	-
Ireland	11	10	11	-	-
Netherlands	12	12	-	-	-
Kenya	13	13	12	-	-

MAHENDRA SINGH DHONI

One day he was a hard-hitting batsman and maverick captain with fashionably long hair. Twenty-four hours later, sporting a No.1 cut, a blazer and a gleaming trophy, he looked every inch the global cricket statesman.

The transformation had not, in truth, been that dramatic but that is what it felt like. On 2 April 2011, Mahendra Singh Dhoni had sealed India's home World Cup victory – their first since 1983 – with a straight six, the ultimate boyhood dream made real. Promoting himself above the in-form Yuvraj Singh in the batting order, he made 91 not out, a captain's innings if ever there was. He had not scored more than 34 in the tournament and had gone 16 innings for India without a fifty. If the true test of greatness is to perform when the pressure is at its most suffocating and the prize the most glorious, then Dhoni passed with honours.

'Dhoni showed himself to be one of the finest leaders of the last 30 years' – Ian Chappell on the 2011 World Cup win

In seven short years this small-town boy from the industrial, mineral-rich state of Jharkhand in eastern India had risen to challenge Sachin Tendulkar as the nation's sporting icon.

He is a wicketkeeper but it is his batting rather than his glovework that brought him his fame. In only his fifth one-day international he smashed 148 off 123 balls against Pakistan in April 2005. Six months later he hit 183 not out, with 15 fours and 10 sixes, against Sri Lanka.

His technique is simple and unconventional, inelegant even, with quick hands whipping and scything the ball to all parts. He is strong in body and mind and smart enough to skipper the highest-profile national team in the world, despite also having the responsibility of wicket-keeping. Such was India's injury crisis during their Test against England at Lord's in 2011 he even removed the pads and gloves and had a bowl during the Test at Lord's and was within a whisker of trapping Kevin Pietersen lbw.

Also during that series his sportsmanship was hailed when he withdrew a controversial run-out appeal against England's Ian Bell.

He is a winner. He captained India to victory in the first World Twenty20 tournament in South Africa in 2007 and led his club side, Chennai Super Kings, to the Indian Premier League title in 2010 and 2011, not to mention reaching the final of the inaugural competition in 2008 and the semi-final the following year. Under his captaincy India attained No.1 status in the world Test rankings, though they since endured 4-0 thrashings in England and Australia.

His talent and good looks have brought colossal marketability and wealth to rival any of the world's top sportsmen. In 2010 he signed a $42-m deal with a sports marketing agency to handle all his commercial affairs, an arrangement that puts even Tendulkar in the shade.

Full name: Mahendra Singh Dhoni
Born: 7 July 7 1981, Ranchi, Bihar (now Jharkhand)
International career span: 2004 –
Role: Right-hand middle-order batsman, wicketkeeper
Notable numbers: As of February 2012 he played 67 Tests and 201 ODIs scoring 3,509 and 6,866 runs, respectively; averages 51 in one-day internationals – of players who have appeared in 100 or more ODIs, only the Australian Michael Bevan has a higher average
Extras: Loves motorbikes and Manchester United FC, even missing a warm-up match on India's tour of England in 2011 to catch a game at Old Trafford

Where it all began: James Lillywhite's England team who toured Australia in 1876–77 and played the first Test at Melbourne in 1877.

TEST OF CHARACTER

The clothing might be all man-made fibres, rather than sturdy cotton, but it is still white. The bats might be bigger and super-powerful but they are still made from willow. The stumps might carry lurid sponsors' logos but they are still made of ash. There might be floodlights, Hawk-Eye, HotSpot and Snicko but the ball is still red and made of leather. In short, Test cricket has changed massively yet barely at all since its first match in 1877.

And that is a large part of its charm. It is a recognizable descendant of its early ancestors but it is not stuck in the past. An institution like the Ashes, which was born in 1882, is a continuous narrative of such depth and flavour that it needs no media hype (though there is plenty, of course) to sustain itself. Players and spectators know the meaning of an England–Australia contest. They can feel its importance. Likewise when India play Pakistan there is much more at stake than simply the result of a cricket match. Cricket has bonded the Caribbean region: different nationalities united beneath the majestic maroon cap.

The Anglo-Australian contests of 1877 were referred to as Test matches only retrospectively. The phrase had been used during the first cricket

At its best Test cricket offers endless possibilities for dramatic ebb and flow

Birth of a legend: the mock newspaper obituary that spawned the concept of the Ashes.

tour to Australia in 1861–62 but the significance of the 1877 tour of Australia by James Lillywhite's team of professionals was that the matches were played on level terms of 11 against 11.

When England lost at home to Australia in 1882 the *Sporting Times* published its famous mock obituary for English cricket and the legend of the Ashes was born.

For decades the tiny terracotta urn remained in the museum at Lord's regardless of which team held them. Then for the 2006–07 Ashes series MCC took the real urn to Australia. It was pertinent timing since Australia regained them in comprehensive fashion by winning all five Tests against England.

Tests have been played over three, four and five days and for a period there was no limit at all. In 1939 at Durban after ten days, one of which was rained off, time had to be called on the final Test between South Africa and England because the touring side, 654 for five in their second innings, had to catch the boat home.

Thankfully Tests are no longer timeless, though there is still debate about the optimum length of playing time. Some people, like the former Australian captain Steve Waugh, advocate Tests being reduced to four days, though the prevailing mood favours the five-day match with the proviso, which is sadly often ignored, that the pitch offers a balanced contest between bat and ball.

At its best Test cricket offers endless possibilities for

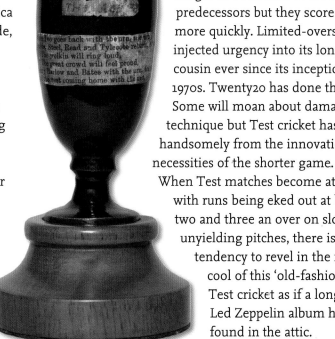

uncertainty, surprise and dramatic ebb and flow. Five days and it can still be a draw? Yes, but there are few things as tense or exciting as a match in its final minutes with the last pair of batsmen grimly hanging on to avoid defeat knowing that the Test could end the very next ball.

Modern players generally take longer to bowl their overs than their predecessors but they score their runs more quickly. Limited-overs cricket injected urgency into its longer-format cousin ever since its inception in the 1970s. Twenty20 has done the same. Some will moan about damage to technique but Test cricket has benefited handsomely from the innovations and necessities of the shorter game. When Test matches become attritional with runs being eked out at between two and three an over on slow, unyielding pitches, there is a tendency to revel in the retro cool of this 'old-fashioned' Test cricket as if a long-lost Led Zeppelin album had been found in the attic.

Viv **RICHARDS**

Viv Richards turned the batsman's walk to the crease into an art form. With a slow, unique swagger, like a lion stalking its prey, he would announce his entrance, chewing gum, maybe with a swing of the arms or a tweak of his maroon West Indies cap. It was always a cap. Viv, known also as King Viv and the Master Blaster, never bothered with a helmet.

Once the bowler released the ball the languid exterior would be replaced by vicious power, laced with an irresistible style. He had such sureness of eye that he would happily move across his stumps and whip the ball through or over mid-wicket on the leg side while the traditionalists choked on their MCC coaching manuals. Every aspect of his on-field demeanour screamed confidence and intent.

He was only the second Test player that the tiny island of Antigua in the eastern Caribbean had produced, the first being the fast bowler Andy Roberts who made his debut a few months earlier than Richards.

He announced himself to a global audience in 1976 when he made 1,710 Test runs in the calendar year against India and England. Only the Pakistani Mohammad Yousuf, 30 years later, has scored more in a 12-month period. Richards' 829 runs in England that year included a monumental 291 at The Oval.

He was an integral part of the great West Indies side that dominated world cricket through the late 1970s and 1980s. More than any of his teammates, he considered himself an ambassador for the Afro-Caribbean male. He never shrank from confrontation.

In the first World Cup final against Australia at Lord's in 1975 he showed off his feline brilliance in the field. Four years later on the same stage he scored a match-winning century against England. In 1984 at Manchester he played arguably the greatest one-day innings of all time: 189 not out from a total of 272, next top score 26, turning almost certain defeat into comfortable victory.

He took over from Clive Lloyd as captain of West Indies in 1984 and never lost a series during his seven years in charge. In 1986, on his home ground, he scored the fastest Test century of all time, off 56 balls, brutalizing England's bowling attack.

He was an heroic figure too in English county cricket with Somerset where he forged a lifelong friendship with Ian Botham. In retirement he has been honoured in the Caribbean and in Britain. Streets and stadiums in Antigua bear his name while he can now proudly call himself Sir Vivian Richards. In 2000 *Wisden* selected him as one of its five Cricketers of the Century.

> 'He was a black man proving race and skin colour count for nothing in terms of genuine sporting competition'
> — David Gower

Full name: Isaac Vivian Alexander Richards
Born: 7 March 1952, St John's, Antigua
International career span: 1974–91
Role: Right-hand top-order batsman, occasional right-arm off-spin bowler
Notable numbers: 121 Tests, 8,540 runs at 50.23, highest score 291, 24 centuries; 187 ODIs, 6,721 runs at 47.00, highest score 189 not out, 11 centuries; second most Test runs in a calendar year: 1,710 in 1976; 829 runs v. England in 1976 is highest aggregate for four Tests
Extras: Also played football for Antigua; awarded an OBE in 1994, knighted in 1999

The Oval 1882: Australia's seven-run victory that prompted the Sporting Times to mourn the death of English cricket.

Test Cricket's Timeline

1877	First Test: Australia beat England at Melbourne
1882	England lose at home to Australia and the Ashes is born
1889	South Africa's first Test
1909	Imperial Cricket Conference (now International Cricket Council) formed
1912	England, Australia and South Africa play an ill-fated triangular Test tournament
1928	West Indies' first Test
1930	New Zealand's first Test
1932	India's first Test
1970	South Africa banned
1982	Sri Lanka's first Test
1991	Neutral umpires introduced
1992	South Africa's first Test after readmission
1992	Zimbabwe's first Test
2000	Bangladesh's first Test
2009	Decision Review System introduced

The table (*opposite*) shows how batting run-rates in Test cricket peaked in the early part of the 20th century, a period known as the Golden Age when some of the great batsmen like Australia's Victor Trumper were around. From then on, though, until the Australians of the 1990s gripped the world game, runs were accumulated at between two and three an over rather than racked up at four or more as is often the case now.

Some of the most dramatic Tests are low-scoring affairs where runs are hard to come by but the key components are intent and balance. Test cricket can seem the most tedious, futile, unbearable pastime if the game is drifting, if batsmen are simply milking mediocre bowling on a slow pitch. Or if the bowling side have given up all hope of taking a wicket and are simply trying to avoid conceding runs.

In baseball the playing surface is irrelevant but in cricket, because the ball bounces before reaching the batsman, it is an integral part of the game and raises endless discussion and disagreement. Over a five-day period interesting and unpredictable things can happen to a 22-yard strip of turf that affect the course of a match.

Until the 1970s pitches were uncovered while matches were in progress. Batting on a damp or drying pitch could be a hazardous affair and only the most technically skilled batsmen could survive.

In December 1950, at Brisbane, the England batsman Len Hutton played one of the finest wet-wicket innings, scoring an unbeaten 65 out of England's losing total of 122. But what was remarkable about this Test was how the weather, and the changing pitch conditions, shaped the teams' tactics. Australia made 228 in the dry, then England declared their first innings on 68 for seven so they could bowl at Australia with the pitch at its trickiest. Australia then declared on 32 for seven leaving England to chase 193. England even rejigged their batting order – the opener Hutton came in at No.8 – but to no avail.

Spin bowlers were especially dangerous in these conditions and until the 1970s it was standard practice for most Test sides to have at least two such bowlers in their side. But the covering of pitches and the emergence of quality pace bowlers in Australia and the Caribbean changed the nature of Test cricket. There were

Surface tension: Australia celebrate victory in the first Ashes Test at Brisbane in 1950. England captain Len Hutton (far right) was unbeaten on 62 out of his side's 122 all out, a masterclass of technique on a damp pitch or a 'sticky dog' as this Brisbane pitch was known.

Interesting things can happen to a 22-yard strip of turf over five days

still spinners of quality in Asia but the mood of 1980s' cricket was relentless, sometimes artless, pace. Would the spinners ever return?

Thankfully they did, proving that Test cricket was not simply a linear progression towards a harder, faster, harsher world. There are so many variables, so many subtleties to the game that it is a constantly evolving organism. In 1991 came Shane Warne, then Muttiah Muralitharan and the Pakistani off-spinner Saqlain Mushtaq with his new delivery, the *doosra* or 'the other one'.

The expansion of the one-day game brought increased workloads for players so it became harder for pace bowlers to sustain themselves.

The International Explosion
How the game has grown over the decades

	Tests	ODIs	T20s	Test scoring-rate
1877–1909	105	-	-	2.62
1910s	29	-	-	3.01
1920s	51	-	-	2.66
1930s	89	-	-	2.71
1940s	45	-	-	2.62
1950s	164	-	-	2.30
1960s	186	-	-	2.49
1970s	198	82	-	2.69
1980s	266	516	-	2.86
1990s	347	933	-	2.86
2000s	464	1405	127	3.20
2010–11	82	288	89	3.24

The umpire's decision is final ... or not: England batsman Jonathan Trott calls for a television review after being given out lbw against Pakistan in 2010. Teams are allowed two unsuccessful reviews per innings of a Test match.

Since one-dayers were deemed to be all about run-scoring, pitches became more batsmen-friendly: another obstacle for the fast men.

Cricket seems to be in perpetual crisis. Perennial concerns are entertainment value and interest from spectators, player behaviour and standards of umpiring, the threat of limited-overs cricket and controversies such as throwing (illegal bowling actions) and match-fixing.

These issues have been addressed with varying degrees of rigour over the years. Neutral umpires were introduced in 1991, taking much of the heat out of contentious decisions that many touring sides had in the past blamed on biased home-country umpires. In 2002 the ICC introduced an elite panel of umpires who, by and large, perform to a remarkably high standard and have developed a healthy relationship of mutual respect and understanding with the players.

But in 2009 came one of the most fundamental changes to Test cricket with the introduction of the Umpire Decision Review System. For the first

Test cricket is a robust beast but it is also a sensitive soul

time players could challenge umpiring decisions they felt to be wrong. Not everyone is a fan – the Indians refused to endorse it – and technology still has its limits. But it has eliminated the howler (for example, the lbw where the batsman has hit the ball or the catch behind where he has missed it by a mile) and has also shown how most umpires' judgement, though not all, is exceptional.

The Test game's current challenge is how to preserve and nurture itself in the 21st century. The buzz of a full house at Lord's or the Melbourne Cricket Ground on the first morning of an Ashes Test is a unique sporting thrill and at that moment it seems absurd to think that Test cricket could be an institution under threat. Yet when the stands are empty in Pakistan's home away from home in Dubai one wonders what all this is for.

As the game has become increasingly commercialized administrators have become increasingly cynical in their scheduling of matches. Priorities in many countries are now to stage lengthy one-day series while squeezing in a couple of Tests if they can.

Test cricket has shown itself to be a robust beast but it is also a sensitive soul. Its followers are creatures of habit, as they have to be to immerse themselves in an event lasting five days. The Tests that still haul in the crowds are the ones that have, as the marketing men would say, an 'appointment to view'. So the main Lord's Test of the English summer or the Christmas holiday Tests at Melbourne, Sydney or Cape Town all command big attendances and a sizzling atmosphere. In India, by contrast, Tests are often scheduled at the last minute at venues where the spectator experience is uninviting.

The ICC's decision to postpone the proposed World Test Championship play-offs from 2013 to 2017 did not suggest that the five-day game is a priority. For all the discussions about night-time Test matches under lights with a pink ball, the five-day game just needs a bit of TLC from money-obsessed administrators.

Top Ten Test Batsmen
(according to ICC rankings at end of January 2012)

1 Kumar Sangakkara (Sri Lanka, above)
2 Jacques Kallis (South Africa)
3 Michael Clarke (Australia)
4 AB de Villiers (South Africa, right)
5 Alastair Cook (England)
6 Jonathan Trott (England)
7 Thilan Samaraweera (Sri Lanka)
8 Misbah-ul-Haq (Pakistan)
9 Shiv Chanderpaul (West Indies)
10 Younis Khan (Pakistan)

Top Ten Test Bowlers
(according to ICC rankings at end of January 2012)

1 Dale Steyn (South Africa)
2 Saeed Ajmal (Pakistan)
3 James Anderson (England)
4 Peter Siddle (Australia)
5 Stuart Broad (England)
6 Graeme Swann (England)
7 Ben Hilfenhaus (Australia)
8 Morne Morkel (South Africa)
9 Abdur Rehman (Pakistan)
10 Zaheer Khan (India, left)

KEVIN PIETERSEN

Before Kevin Pietersen's Test call-up for England's much awaited series against Australia in 2005, there were plenty of doubts about whether this tall, flash-and-dash batsman with a quirky technique could cut it in the five-day game, not to mention the unease among many England fans about his South African origins and the blond streak in his dark hair.

By the end of an unforgettable Ashes series that was clinched in England's favour by his heart-in-mouth 158 in the final match at The Oval, his maiden Test hundred, there were no doubts about his aptitude or attitude.

'He's a match-winner. He's one of those guys who can take the game away from you on his own' — Michael Clarke

A year later mouths gaped again as he stretched credulity with a left-handed swipe for six off the Sri Lankan legend Muttiah Muralitharan. Adjusting his stance and switching his hands on the bat as the bowler ran in, Pietersen defied convention and, some believed, the laws of the game.

As well as the outrageous switch-hit (*pictured*), he also patented a shot that came to be known as the 'flamingo' because he would end up on one leg. Moving across to the off side like Viv Richards did decades earlier, he would whip the ball, almost like Roger Federer playing a top-spin forehand, through the leg side.

He doesn't do ordinary. A maverick choice as captain to replace Michael Vaughan in 2008, he was out of the job five months later after an irretrievable fall-out with the coach Peter Moores, who also lost his job.

He came to England because he perceived that his chances in his native South Africa were restricted by the racial quota system in domestic cricket. At the time he was an off-spinner and lower-order batsman struggling to get into the Kwa-Zulu Natal side. He reinvented himself as a top-order batsman and made an immediate impact in county cricket with Nottinghamshire. England picked him in the one-day side as soon as he had qualified by residence in 2004.

His batting, innovative and infuriating in equal measure, has touched greatness without ever acquiring the consistency of a true champion. At times he has given the impression of being more interested in cultivating a celebrity status. Married to a pop star and living in an exclusive area of London, KP, as he is universally known, has an even more detached relationship with domestic cricket than his England team-mates who rarely appear for their county sides.

The captaincy debacle appeared to take something from Pietersen. His devil-may-care self-confidence was diluted and it was not until the World Twenty20 of 2010 that he rediscovered proper form. A double hundred in the Ashes later that year was his only significant contribution to England's triumphant regaining of the urn.

Full name: Kevin Peter Pietersen
Born: 27 June 1980, Pietermaritzburg, Natal
International career span: 2004–
Role: Right-hand top-order batsman; occasional off-spin bowler
Notable numbers: Reached 1,000 ODI runs in 21 matches, quicker than anyone apart from Viv Richards; scored more Test runs in his first 25 matches than any batsman apart from Don Bradman
Extras: Married to former Liberty X singer Jessica Taylor, one son; played in Indian Premier League for Bangalore Royal Challengers and Deccan Chargers; county cricket for Nottinghamshire, Hampshire and Surrey

We got there first: England captain Rachael Heyhoe Flint with the women's World Cup trophy in 1973, two years before the men's version. The women's game has grown rapidly in recent years with standards and breadth of participation increasing all the time.

ONE DAY AT A TIME

Limited-overs international cricket began by accident. The third Ashes Test between Australia and England at Melbourne in January 1971 was completely washed out. On the final scheduled day of the Test a one-day, 40-overs-a-side match was arranged to appease the disappointed spectators. Forty-six thousand of them turned up to see Australia win by five wickets and the one-day international (ODI) was born.

Four years later came the first World Cup. The women had already beaten the men to it by staging a World Cup in England in 1973. There had been discussions for some time about a men's tournament, though originally the idea was a Test-match competition. But enthusiasm was limited.

The traditionalists at Lord's were resistant and the Australians were indifferent too, despite the success of that first ODI in 1971.

The first World Cup started out as a low-key, almost experimental affair with eight teams competing over a fortnight. The matches were 60 overs per side with no fielding restrictions. The players wore white clothes and used a red ball. The climax, though, was the best possible advert for the limited-overs game. It remains arguably the greatest one-day international ever played.

On midsummer's day Lord's was blessed by perfect weather and a full house. The world's two best teams, West Indies and Australia, had their full array of talents on show: the express pace of

West Indies won shortly before 9 pm. It was a long day but a perfect one

Dennis Lillee and Jeff Thomson versus the feline flair of Clive Lloyd and Viv Richards. Lloyd made an 82-ball hundred, Richards contributed two brilliant run-outs and West Indies won by 17 runs shortly before 9 pm. It was a long day but a perfect one. There was no going back.

The 1979 tournament was also in England and run over the same format. West Indies won it again, though in slightly lower-key fashion as England threw away a good position to lose comfortably. The number of group matches was doubled for the 1983 World Cup, hosted again by England. Again West Indies were the favourites and were well set in the final, chasing only 184 to win. But the match turned when Viv Richards mistimed a hook off the medium-pacer Madan Lal and Kapil Dev took a fine catch over his shoulder at mid-wicket. West Indies collapsed and India pulled off a stunning victory that sparked a national obsession with cricket, which has shaped the whole world's relationship with the game.

The 1983 tournament was also notable for another unlikely result. Captained by Duncan Fletcher, Zimbabwe beat Australia at Nottingham. Unlike football, where organization, fitness and bloody-mindedness can mask all manner of technical inadequacies, cricket does not lend itself to shock results.

The nature of the game requires both the major disciplines – batting and bowling – to be delivered. There is no hiding, no 'parking the bus' trying to nick a point. The shorter format of Twenty20 obviously increases the possibility but World Cup giant-killing is rare.

Zimbabwe beat England in 1992 and Sri Lanka's triumph in 1996 was a surprise of a different kind. The expansion of the tournament has created a mass of one-sided matches so the odd upset tends to get lost amid the predictability. In 2003 Kenya reached the semi-finals where they lost to India. Then in 2011 the typically hapless England were beaten by both Ireland, who had beaten Pakistan in the 2007 tournament, and Bangladesh in the space of ten days.

Ireland's victory over England was spectacular. They were chasing 328, a hefty enough target anyway but, when they were 111 for five, their slim prospects seemed to have been snuffed out. But an astonishing have-a-go hundred from their beefy all-rounder Kevin O'Brien turned the game on its head. He made 113 from 63 balls before being run out in a nail-biting finish.

Champions in waiting: West Indies, captained by Clive Lloyd, during the inaugural World Cup in 1975.

World Cup winners

1975	(Lord's)	West Indies beat Australia by 17 runs
1979	(Lord's)	West Indies beat England by 92 runs
1983	(Lord's)	India beat West Indies by 43 runs
1987	(Kolkata)	Australia beat England by seven runs
1992	(Melbourne)	Pakistan beat England by 22 runs
1996	(Lahore)	Sri Lanka beat Australia by seven wickets
1999	(Lord's)	Australia beat Pakistan by eight wickets
2003	(Johannesburg)	Australia beat India by 125 runs
2007	(Bridgetown)	Australia beat Sri Lanka by 53 runs (D/L)
2011	(Mumbai)	India beat Sri Lanka by six wickets

Harbouring ambition: the nine captains pose in Sydney before the 1992 World Cup, which was won by Pakistan.

The first three World Cups retained all the traditional trappings. The clothes were white, the ball red and matches, at 60 overs per side, were about as long as they could be for a single day.

But elsewhere the game had already changed out of all recognition. Kerry Packer's rebel World Series Cricket revolution in Australia had introduced floodlights and coloured clothing. When the Australian board finally resolved its differences with Packer the legacy was substantial. In November 1979 Australia played West Indies at Sydney in the first official one-day international under floodlights.

It was billed as a World Series and was a triangular tournament also involving England. This was the template for the next two decades of one-day cricket in Australia: three-way series that involved an endless round-robin stage before the top two teams played off in a best-of-three final series. It was made-for-TV heaven and the cash rolled into the Australian board's coffers.

The appetite for one-day cricket seemed to have no bounds. In the Gulf state of Sharjah a new stadium was built and between 1984 and 2003 it hosted 198 one-day internationals, appealing to the large ex-patriate communities from India and Pakistan as well as TV audiences in Asia.

The World Cup finally moved out of England

In 1999 the ICC cashed in by selling TV rights to Murdoch for $550m

in 1987 when India and Pakistan were joint hosts but the players were still clad in white. The overs, though, had been reduced to 50 per side which, despite England bucking the trend for years, had become the standard one-day format. Surprisingly given the location, the final was an Anglo-Aussie affair. The Australians prevailed, assisted by the England captain Mike Gatting's rush of blood when he tried to reverse-sweep the first ball from his opposite number Allan Border.

In 1992 the World Cup changed drastically. Coloured clothes were worn and the group stage of the competition was a single-league format that included South Africa for the first time. In their semi-final against England, South Africa found themselves needing 21 to win off the last ball after a rain delay and the subsequent readjustment of the target. It was a farce and exposed the dire need for a fairer method of settling rain-affected one-day games. Two British statisticians Frank Duckworth and Tony Lewis devised a complex mathematical formula that analysed a batting team's 'resources' (i.e.: wickets and overs left) at any point of a match. The Duckworth-Lewis method is now as much a part of an one-day international as coloured clothing.

Through the 1990s the one-day game was growing exponentially. In 1999 the world governing body, the ICC, cashed in when it sold the TV rights to its next five global events to Rupert Murdoch's Global Cricket Corporation for $550m. In addition to the World Cup the ICC introduced the Champions Trophy, another 50-over tournament for the world's top sides.

The 1996 World Cup was a joyful triumph for Sri Lanka and was a watershed moment for the non-Test-playing nations with the expansion from nine teams to 12. But it also marked a major step-up in the commercial exploitation of the tournament. It went on longer than ever before and was staged in so many venues across India and Pakistan that travel became a major challenge. On the field there was a shift in how batting sides set about their innings. First seen in Australia but now standard in one-day internationals were the fielding restrictions in the first 15 overs of an innings that allowed only two fielders more than 30 yards from the batsman. Top-order batsmen who could hit through or over the in-field became a must-have accessory for one-day teams.

The format of the World Cup kept changing and getting longer, though it made little difference to the Australians who won three successive tournaments from 1999 to 2007. The 2007 tournament, held for the first time in the Caribbean, was disappointing for a number of reasons. Again the schedule, dictated by television, was too long and the crowds were poor, in part because of inflexible ticketing arrangements and restrictions that diluted the unique flavour of West Indian cricket watching.

The one-day game is always evolving. By the end of the 1980s no international side had scored more than 360 from a 50-over innings. But then at Johannesburg in 2006 the record was smashed twice in the same match, Australia's 434 for four overhauled by South Africa. Fielding has improved out of all recognition and bowlers are in a perpetually changing cat-and-mouse game with batsmen, seeking new, fail-safe ways to restrict scoring and exert pressure.

The framework of the ODI has been tinkered with too. The recent introduction of powerplays, where both sides get a chance to select a block of overs when fielding restrictions will apply, was designed to invigorate a format that, due to over-use, had become formulaic.

A one-sided one-dayer can be boring but a tight one is close to cricket at its epic best. And the emotional outpouring in Mumbai when India won the 2011 World Cup was a memorable chapter in the history of the one-day game.

Top Ten ODI Batsmen
(according to ICC rankings at end of January 2012)

1 Hashim Amla (South Africa, right)
2 AB de Villiers (South Africa)
3 Virat Kohli (India)
4 Jonathan Trott (England)
5 Mahendra Singh Dhoni (India)
6 Shane Watson (Australia)
7 Kumar Sangakkara (SL)
8 Mike Hussey (Australia)
9 Michael Clarke (Australia)
10 Umar Akmal (Pakistan)

Top Ten ODI Bowlers
(according to ICC rankings at end of January 2012)

1 Saeed Ajmal (Pakistan)
2 Mohammad Hafeez (Pakistan)
3 Lonwabo Tsotsobe (South Africa)
4 Daniel Vettori (New Zealand, left)
5 Graeme Swann (England, top)
6 Mitchell Johnson (Australia)
7 Morne Morkel (South Africa)
8 Shakib Al Hasan (Bangladesh)
9 Doug Bollinger (Australia)
10 Lasith Malinga (Sri Lanka)

JACQUES KALLIS

Most players have a career graph that resembles a heart monitor with highs and lows. But the plotting of Jacques Kallis's progression is a broadly straight line that seems to go on forever.

He is the only consistently world-class all-rounder of his generation: a powerful, classical batsman, a bowler capable of pace, swing and bounce and a brilliant slip fielder.

His only major dip in batting form came in 2008 when the retirement of Shaun Pollock forced him into bowling more than he was used to or wanted to. He still scored a Test century and took more wickets than he had for six years.

But at an age when most players are winding down, Kallis, into his mid-30s, seemed to be cranking it up again. In two years from the end of 2009 when he faced England at home he averaged 73 in Test cricket and scored the first double-centuries of his career. He also started scoring his runs more quickly as if the prospect of cricketing mortality was freeing up a mind that has often been accused of selfishness.

He started slowly in 1995 with a single double-figure score in his first five Tests. But then in his seventh he made a match-saving last-day century at Melbourne, driving handsomely and impervious to the traditional Aussie chatter.

His match-saving 87 against Sri Lanka at Kandy in 2000 exemplified his technique and temperament. He batted for four hours on a turning pitch whose bounce was uneven against Muttiah Muralitharan on one of his most productive grounds. Kallis's innings helped set up a seven-run victory for South Africa. By contrast, he holds the record for the fastest Test fifty, off only 24 balls against Zimbabwe in 2005.

His barrel-chested, multitasking abilities have made him a rock on which the South African team has depended for over 15 years in the long and short forms of the game. In 2003 he bowled his side to victory against England at Leeds with six wickets. He is a doer rather than a thinker: out of almost 500 international matches he has captained only 15.

He has played in English county cricket and the Indian Premier League, though his first IPL experience, having been hired by Bangalore Royal Challengers for $900,000 in 2008, was forgettable. The following year when the IPL relocated to South Africa he made three times as many runs at a strike-rate of over 100.

> ## 'People don't understand how hard he works. He has always had a hunger to perform' – Graham Ford

When he dismissed Sachin Tendulkar in 2001 at Bloemfontein he became the eighth player to score 3,000 Test runs and take 100 wickets. But he has since bettered those all-round numbers to stand alongside Garry Sobers. He is one of only four men with 5,000 runs and 200 wickets. But only he and Sobers can boast 8,000-plus runs and more than 200 wickets.

Full name: Jacques Henry Kallis
Born: 16 October 1975, Cape Town
International career span: 1995–
Role: Right-hand middle-order batsman, right-arm fast-medium bowler
Notable numbers: 150 Tests, 12,260 runs at 57.02, 41 hundreds, 55 fifties – fourth-leading run-scorer in history; 274 wickets at 32.51; 180 catches; 319 ODIs, 11,481 runs at 45.55; 267 wickets (to 9 Feb 2012)
Extras: Has played county cricket for Glamorgan and Middlesex; ICC cricketer of the year and ICC Test player of the year 2005

Innovation: Sri Lankan batsman Tillakaratne Dilshan plays the Dilscoop, a shot that goes over the wicketkeeper's head.

TWENTY20 VISION

There had been other attempts at shortened, innovative formats before, like Cricket Max in New Zealand, the brainchild of the great Kiwi batsman Martin Crowe. In Cricket Max extra runs were scored for hitting the ball in certain areas, Max Zones, and ultimately that was the game's problem. It was tricked up. It was not the game people were familiar with. Twenty20 was a shocking aberration to many but at least it was the same game people were used to.

The launch of Twenty20 in the English summer of 2003 was accompanied by a host of marketing gimmicks. Some, like mascots and music, were borrowed from other sports but others were way out of left-field like Worcestershire's boundary-side jacuzzi where spectators could splash around while the action took place on the field.

Just as the fully professional English domestic game, with its commercial necessities, had invented limited-overs cricket in the 1960s to bring the crowds in, so Twenty20 was born out of desperation as a way of luring crowds back to county cricket. Lengthy and expensive market research by the England and Wales Cricket Board had told them that plenty of people were well-disposed towards cricket but felt the game took too long and did not take place when they could watch it. So Twenty20 was devised.

The widespread scepticism of the new format was blown away by the sight of packed grounds and enthused players. It was not to everybody's taste but it was certainly a success. In 2004, the second year of the competition, Lord's was sold out to a 28,000 capacity for the London derby between Middlesex and Surrey. The ground had not been full for a county match (apart from cup finals) since the 1950s.

The game sprung some surprises. While the emphasis, of course, is on big hitting and scoring every ball it is not simply a sloggers' charter. Batsmen like Sri Lanka's Tillakaratne Dilshan, whose deft flick-shot over the shoulder on bended knee became known as the 'Dilscoop', are as much a part of the game as the power-hitters like the West Indian left-hander Chris Gayle who created a storm when he said ahead of a Test tour of England that he 'wouldn't be so sad' if Tests died out.

And whereas the nagging medium-pacers held sway for many years in 50-over cricket the best Twenty20 bowlers are smart-thinking spinners with good changes of angle and pace or those with extreme pace. With only four overs to get through in a match, a quick bowler can give it everything without worrying if he will have to bowl 20-odd overs in a day as in a Test match. So just as the one-day game infused Test cricket with new urgency, so the 20-over format has brought innovation and new thinking.

There was initial indifference to Twenty20 in Australia and India until the first international tournament, the World Twenty20 held in South Africa in 2007. As a concept the tournament had

Just the start: Surrey's Adam Hollioake lifts the Twenty20 Cup in England in 2003, the world's first 20-over competition.

an energy and vitality that its 50-over cousin had ceased to possess. But the big thing was that India won and just like their World Cup win of 1983, that changed everything. Suddenly India was in love with Twenty20 and within months there was an unofficial tournament called the Indian Cricket League. But by early 2008 came the officially sanctioned Indian Premier League (IPL), the brainchild of the Indian administrator and businessman Lalit Modi whose impact on the game has been as profound as Kerry Packer's a generation earlier.

The IPL combined Bollywood glamour, cricketing celebrity and American-style razzmatazz to produce an event the like of which the game had never witnessed.

The eight teams were all franchises owned by some of the biggest players in Indian business and the biggest names in the country's vast film industry. The players came from all over the world, auctioned off to the highest bidder. Cheerleaders were flown in from American football.

Lalit Modi's impact on the game is as profound as Kerry Packer's

World Twenty20 Winners

2007 (Johannesburg) India beat Pakistan by five runs

2009 (Lord's) Pakistan beat Sri Lanka by eight wickets

2010 (Bridgetown) England beat Australia by seven wickets

Winning smiles: Chennai Super Kings celebrate after winning the 2011 IPL against Royal Challengers Bangalore.

Modi is unlike any other cricket administrator. Educated in America, he had an acute entrepreneurial spirit. He was not interested in committees or working parties, he just wanted to get things done and get the extravaganza on the road. His sporting influences came from football on both sides of the Atlantic. From American football he brought the glitz and the centralized, franchised control of the NFL. His ambition was to generate the sort of global following enjoyed by football's Premier League in England.

The IPL was actually born out of a plan for a Twenty20 Champions League bringing together domestic T20 champions from around the world. This tournament is now an established part of the calendar but has been dwarfed by the IPL.

The IPL's television rights for a ten-year period were sold for $1bn, while in the first player auction Mahendra Singh Dhoni was hired by

Chennai Super Kings for $1.5m. In 2012 the Indian all-rounder Ravindra Jadeja became the most expensive player in the IPL's brief history when he was acquired, also by Chennai, for $2m.

England's players missed out on the first IPL tournament because of international commitments. Because it is played in April and

Indian Premier League Winners

2008 (Mumbai) Rajasthan Royals beat Chennai Super Kings by three wickets

2009 (Johannesburg) Deccan Chargers beat Royal Challengers Bangalore by six runs

2010 (Mumbai) Chennai Super Kings beat Mumbai Indians by 22 runs

2011 (Chennai) Chennai Super Kings beat Royal Challengers Bangalore by 58 runs

The IPL's influence has spread with imitation leagues springing up

May it continues to be an issue for England, but once the players had seen the success of the initial IPL season they knew they wanted to be part of it. So they negotiated a small window of availability with the ECB and for the second IPL in 2009, Andrew Flintoff and Kevin Pietersen were bought by Chennai and Royal Challengers Bangalore, respectively, for $1.5m each.

But money does not equal success. The first tournament in 2008 was won by Rajasthan Royals, captained and coached by Shane Warne, who had spent the least of any franchise on players.

There was something of a divide between the franchises who, perhaps driven by celebrity owners, wanted to fill their teams with big-name stars and those who wanted to craft a winning outfit. The first IPL match, on 18 April 2008, was between two of the glitziest teams, Bangalore and Kolkata Knight Riders, who both finished in the bottom three of the league table.

After a laser show and firework display, Kolkata took the field in an all-black uniform with gold helmets and pads. For the IPL and their grand aspirations it could not have been a better start. The New Zealander Brendon McCullum made the highest-ever Twenty20 score, 158 not out off 73 balls with 13 sixes.

The legacy of the Mumbai terrorist attacks in late 2008 caused the IPL to move house in 2009 to South Africa. It was an ambitious move fraught with difficulty but one which was pulled off with remarkable skill and there has been talk of playing games outside India on a more regular basis.

Deccan Chargers, from Hyderabad, were the champions in 2009 led by the Australian Adam Gilchrist who, at 37, showed, as Warne had done, that Twenty20 need not necessarily be a young man's game. The next two tournaments were both

Global star: Adam Gilchrist, who captained Deccan Chargers to the IPL in 2009, hits out for Kings XI Punjab in 2011.

won by Chennai with Dhoni at the helm, the man with the Midas touch.

The 2011 season included two new franchises but evidence of reduced interest with attendances and television audiences down on previous years. However the IPL's influence spreads far and wide with imitation leagues springing up across the globe. For now Twenty20 is where the cash is.

Champions League Twenty20 Winners

2009 (Hyderabad) New South Wales (Aus) beat Trinidad & Tobago (WI) by 41 runs

2010 (Johannesburg) Chennai Super Kings (Ind) beat Warriors (SA) by eight wickets

2011 (Chennai) Mumbai Indians (Ind) beat Royal Challengers Bangalore (Ind) by 31 runs

ADAM GILCHRIST

Adam Gilchrist was the accelerator on the Australian juggernaut that ploughed relentlessly through world cricket in the late 1990s and 2000s.

Gilchrist had moved to Western Australia because his first-team possibilities were restricted in his native New South Wales. He would have to wait a long time too for a chance in Australia's Test side. He had played 76 one-day internationals before he finally ousted Ian Healy from behind the stumps.

The quality and speed of his batting brought an extra dimension to Australia's already awesome assembly of talent. The depth of their line-up meant that he never regularly batted higher than No.7 in Test matches, a luxury that caused slavering envy in every other Test-playing country and reframed the requirements for all future wicketkeeper/batsmen. In the one-day game he opened the innings and formed a partnership with Matthew Hayden that had spectators licking their lips and bowlers crossing their fingers.

In only his second Test he produced one of his greatest innings. With Australia 126 for five, chasing 369 to win against Pakistan at Hobart, he scored 149 not out off only 163 balls and put on 238 for the sixth wicket with Justin Langer. 'He could be playing in his own backyard,' said the captain, Steve Waugh.

There were plenty of other memorable performances. In 2002 at Johannesburg against South Africa he scored the fastest Test double hundred, though the record was broken by New Zealander Nathan Astle three weeks later. At one point he aimed at – and almost hit – a target beyond the boundary offering a substantial cash bounty if anyone did hit it.

In late 2006, when his powers seemed to be on the wane, he took England apart in the Ashes on his home ground at Perth, scoring a hundred off 57 balls, one short of equalling Viv Richards' all-time Test record. A few months later he set the tone for Australia's third successive World Cup triumph with 149 off 104 balls against Sri Lanka at Bridgetown.

'A player who should be remembered as even better than his statistics suggest' – Ian Healy

His wicketkeeping was adequate rather than artistic but he did not drop many and formed a devastating partnership with Shane Warne. Indeed his 'Bowled, Warney' gee-up, overheard ball after ball via the stump microphone, became a defining refrain of this era of Australian dominance.

Gilchrist surprised everyone, including his disbelieving colleagues, when, despite being given not out by umpire Rudi Koertzen, he knew he had edged an attempted sweep that was caught off his pad, gave himself out and 'walked' in the semi-final of the 2003 World Cup.

He was a major draw for the Indian Premier League when it launched in 2008 and led Deccan Chargers to victory in the 2009 final.

Full name: Adam Craig Gilchrist
Born: 14 November 1971, Bellingen, New South Wales
International career span: 1999–2008
Role: Left-handed batsman (No.7 in Tests/opener in one-dayers), wicketkeeper
Notable numbers: 5,570 runs in 96 Tests is the most by a Test keeper; 416 Test dismissals as keeper is second all-time behind South Africa's Mark Boucher; scoring rate was 81 runs per 100 balls in Tests, 96 per 100 balls in ODIs
Extras: Voted world's scariest batsmen by bowlers in a 2005 magazine poll; played Twenty20 for Middlesex in 2010; involved with a number of charities

ENGLAND

Leg theory: Australian captain Bill Woodfull drops his bat after a ball from Harold Larwood during the Adelaide Test in January 1933 when the Bodyline controversy blew up. Previous page: Andrew Strauss catches Adam Gilchrist at Nottingham in the 2005 Ashes.

FEAR AND LOATHING

One simple word coined, it is believed, by a cash-strapped journalist has come to describe one of the most tempestuous, controversial and enduringly intriguing series in the game's history.

When, in 1933, a Sydney-based reporter sent a telegram from Adelaide to his newspaper he decided to keep the cost down by changing the phrase 'in the line of the body' to Bodyline.

Bodyline was a tactic devised by the England captain, Douglas Jardine, to combat the relentless run-scoring of Australia's Don Bradman, the world's greatest batsman who, in 1930, had scored a phenomenal 974 runs in seven Test innings in England at an average of 139, including a triple hundred and two doubles. It remains a record for the highest number of runs in a series.

Jardine was a haughty, steely son of Empire, born in India and educated at one of Britain's leading boarding schools, Winchester College.

Rather than wear an England cap he chose to sport the multicoloured Harlequin cap from his Oxford University days.

He had a competitive instinct that was out of kilter, some might say ahead of its time, with the more genteel attitudes of the era. He also had a contemptuous dislike of Australians, a feeling that was to become entirely mutual. He was not prepared simply to go blithely over the top into

'There are two teams out there. One is playing cricket. The other is not'

the hail of a Bradman onslaught. Instead, he became obsessed with calculating a means to stop Australia's unstoppable run-machine.

Selecting a battery of fast bowlers, he set out a game plan which he and his sympathizers would refer to as 'leg theory' but opponents would angrily decry as Bodyline.

With the Nottinghamshire fast bowler Harold Larwood as its spearhead, the tactic was to direct the ball towards the batsman's body, rather than the traditional off-stump line, and force him to play into the leg side where the majority of fielders were placed, including a number of close catchers. At the time there was no restriction on the number of fielders that could be placed behind square on the leg side, a law that was amended as a result of Bodyline.

The tactic was considered by many to be unfair because the batsman had no way of scoring runs without playing the ball in the air towards the fielders. But more pertinently the batsmen, with only rudimentary protection, were in huge physical danger. Flimsy pads and rubber-spiked gloves were the only barriers between the 1930s' batsman and pain.

Bradman missed the first Test, which England won, through illness. Australia levelled the series at Melbourne and then the Bodyline controversy exploded in all its fury in the third Test at Adelaide, which *Wisden Cricketers' Almanack* said 'will go down in history as probably the most unpleasant ever played'. Almost 80 years on that is still a legitimate claim.

Bill Woodfull, the Australian captain, had been hit over the heart during the second Test and by the start of the third public anger towards Jardine and his team was building towards boiling point.

Woodfull was hit over the heart again and the wicketkeeper Bert Oldfield on the head, an incident that sparked uproar in the crowd ('pandemonium reigned', said *Wisden*) but also an exchange between Woodfull and Pelham Warner, the England manager, that would come

Heroes or villains: England's Ashes winners with Harold Larwood centre stage.

to embody the whole episode. Woodfull told Warner: 'There are two teams out there. One of them is trying to play cricket. The other is not.'

The comment was leaked to the press – the identity of the mole was a source of intrigue for decades to come – and a diplomatic row ensued with cables flying back and forth between Australia and England. The Australian board of control accused MCC, who ran the English game, of being 'unsportsmanlike', an accusation for which MCC, who publicly supported Jardine's tactics, demanded a retraction.

The retraction came and the series continued. England, still using Bodyline, went on to win the last two Tests for a 4-1 victory. Bradman was tamed to the extent he averaged *only* 56 in the series, compared with his peerless career average of 99.94.

Jardine continued to use Bodyline in England in the summer of 1933 but it was outlawed the year after. He captained England in India in 1933–34 but never played for his country again.

Larwood was asked to apologize for bowling Bodyline by MCC but refused and emigrated to Australia in 1950, where he lived until his death in 1995.

A 1929 cartoon of Douglas Jardine.

LAKER AND LEN

In 2004 *The Wisden Cricketer* magazine polled 25 experts to select England's greatest post-war XI. Six of the chosen players had appeared in the final Test of the 1953 Ashes, a series-clinching victory in the Queen's coronation year. For much of England's cricketing history they have had delusions of grandeur, but the 1950s was a decade when they could legitimately claim to be the best in the world.

It was the first time England had held the Ashes since the Bodyline series 20 years earlier but they took advantage of Australia's post-Bradman era, not losing a Test series from 1950 until 1959.

The side was captained by the Yorkshireman Len Hutton, the first professional cricketer to lead England. His finest hour was the Ashes tour of 1954–55 when England came back from a heavy defeat in the first Test at Brisbane to win the series. It was a victory based in large part on the raw pace of the Northamptonshire bowler Frank 'Typhoon' Tyson. He played only 17 Tests in all but his 28 wickets in five Tests against Australia defined his career.

Through the 1950s the batting flair came from Denis Compton, Peter May, who would succeed Hutton as a hugely successful captain, and later Colin Cowdrey while the unsung hero Ken Barrington, whose career Test batting average is a mightily impressive 58, provided the ballast.

The bowling attack was impressively balanced. There was pace from fiery Fred Trueman and relentless accuracy from Alec Bedser. The complementary Surrey spin twins Jim Laker and

World class: the England team that beat Australia at The Oval to win the 1953 Ashes. Back row, left to right: Trevor Bailey, Peter May, Tom Graveney, Jim Laker, Tony Lock, Johnny Wardle, Fred Trueman; front row, left to right: Bill Edrich, Alec Bedser, Len Hutton, Denis Compton, Godfrey Evans.

Tony Lock offered flight and guile. At Manchester in 1956 the Yorkshire-born Laker achieved a feat unmatched in history when he took 19 of the 20 Australian wickets to fall in a Test that sealed the Ashes for England. It was a controversial match with the pitch, which started to break up from tea on the first day, a constant topic of discussion.

England, who won the toss, had the best of the conditions, batting first and making 459.

Australia were dismissed for 84 in the first innings, undone by Laker's sharply turned off-breaks and a solitary wicket by his county teammate, the

Denis Compton batting at The Oval.

left-armer Lock. It was when Australia started their second innings, following on, that a row broke out over the nature of the pitch with the Australians accusing England of preparing the wicket to suit their spinners.

The weather also turned nasty midway through the Test and for a while it seemed that rain would deny England a victory. But in those days pitches were uncovered during the match so rain could change the entire nature of the playing surface. And a pitch was never more spiteful for batsmen than while it dried after rain.

Batting was easier for a while for the Australians on the final day but in due course the ball turned more than at any time in the match. According to *Wisden* 'the tension mounted as Laker captured his eighth and ninth wickets'. At the other end Lock was trying his best to take

Laker sat at the bar unrecognized by any of the other customers

wickets too, to complete the victory, but he kept passing the bat. Then when Laker appealed for lbw against the wicketkeeper Len Maddocks he had all ten wickets in the innings, the first bowler to achieve the feat in Test cricket.

The Manchester crowd cheered but Laker, not a man for histrionics, simply took his sweater from the umpire, draped it over his shoulder and led his team from the field. On his drive home he stopped for a beer and a sandwich in a pub. On the tiny television in the corner, footage of Laker's heroics flickered away but he sat at the bar unrecognized by any of the other customers. Those were the days.

Crowd pleasers: Denis Compton and Bill Edrich and other players make their way through the Oval crowd after clinching the Ashes in 1953.

FRED TRUEMAN

The former British Prime Minister Harold Wilson described Fred Trueman as 'the greatest living Yorkshireman'. When asked for a suggested title of his own autobiography Trueman said: 'T'Definitive Volume on t'Finest Bloody Fast Bowler That Ever Drew Breath'.

'Trueman was heroic, epic, nostalgic, dramatic, comic and earthy' – John Arlott

In 1964 he became the first man to take 300 Test wickets but his fame and significance reached well beyond the cricket field. In a country reawakening and readjusting after the war years, he became a national celebrity known as Fiery Fred or even simply Fred. He was a working-class icon in a sport still bound by old-school traditions.

Thickset, with his slick mop of coal-black hair, his angled run to the wicket was smooth and would end in a classical, side-on gather at the stumps before he unleashed a fizzing out-swinger or maybe a brutish bouncer. He combined pace and accuracy to devastating effect and was not averse to offering the batsman verbal encouragement or instruction, treading ever so slightly on the game's still genteel codes of behaviour.

He had grown up in south Yorkshire and worked briefly at a coal mine (rather than down it). He played up to the stereotype of the voluble, opinionated Yorkshireman. Trueman anecdotes abound – some of them even true – and he was happy to cultivate this larger-than-life image through his playing career and beyond when he became an outspoken BBC radio summarizer, known for his bewildered take on the modern game: 'I don't know what's goin' off out there.'

His England debut in 1952 was spectacular. Playing on his home ground at Headingley, he took three wickets to reduce India's second innings to nought for four.

Trueman's greatest performance came also at Headingley in 1961 when ran he through the Australians to end a run of eight Ashes Tests without a victory stretching back five years. 'This will be remembered as Trueman's Match,' proclaimed *Wisden*. In the first innings he took five wickets for 16 to instigate a collapse from 187 for two to 237 all out. He repeated the feat in the second innings, taking six wickets for five runs in 7.5 overs. This time he came in off a shorter run and bowled off-cutters, skilfully moving the ball into the right-handed batsmen off the pitch rather than through the air. Australia collapsed from 99 for two to 120 all out, leaving England a modest 59 to win.

Three years later he broke the 300-wicket barrier, also against Australia, in front of a rapturous crowd at The Oval. Asked if anyone was ever likely to beat his record, he said in typical fashion: 'If they do, they'll be bloody knackered.' It has been broken of course but, just like Roger Bannister's sub-four-minute mile, the significance of Trueman's milestone remains undiluted.

Full name: Frederick Sewards Trueman
Born: 6 February 1931, Stainton, South Yorkshire
Died: 1 July 2006, Keighley, West Yorkshire
International career span: 1952–65
Role: Right-arm fast, swing bowler; right-hand batsman
Notable numbers: 307 wickets in 67 Tests at an average of 21 and strike-rate of 49; the first man to take 300 Test wickets; third-leading England wicket-taker behind Bob Willis (325) and Ian Botham (383)
Extras: BBC radio commentator; TV presenter; after-dinner speaker; his daughter Rebecca married the son of film star Raquel Welch

HEROES OR ZEROES

A Test series victory in Australia in 1970–71, against a fine side and questionable umpiring, was a great achievement for England, captained by the tough, smart Yorkshireman, Ray Illingworth.

Later in the decade players emerged with great talent, class and personality. Test cricket was a constant summer presence on one of the handful of television channels available at the time so individuals like Ian Botham, David Gower, the Mikes – Brearley and Gatting – and Bob Willis became etched in the public consciousness.

Brearley, the professorial captain of Middlesex, was once described by the Australian bowler Rodney Hogg as having 'a degree in people' and to an extent he did. After finishing his cricket career he became a psychoanalyst.

He took over the England captaincy from Tony Greig, who lost his position after it emerged he had been secretly recruiting for Kerry Packer's rebel World Series Cricket circus.

Brearley never captained England against West Indies who, stung by a mid-1970s' thrashing in Australia, were emerging as one of the greatest of all international sides. Brearley (*right*) was fortunate too that Packer depleted some of the sides against which he skippered, but his outstanding record (18 wins in 31 Tests) and his ability to get the best out of stars like Botham afford him revered status in the English game.

Botham made his debut in the 1977 Ashes victory over Australia, a series notable too for Geoff Boycott's hundredth first-class hundred, achieved with delicious timing by the Yorkshire opener on his home ground at Leeds. Boycott remains a figure who polarizes opinion. His dogged batting, though prolific, once caused him to be dropped for slow scoring and his sacking as captain of Yorkshire sparked a cricketing civil war in the county. He controversially took himself out of international cricket from 1974–77 and also went on the first rebel tour of South Africa in 1981–82, a decision that ended his England career.

The summer after Botham's debut, a 21-year-old left-handed batsman with a fuzz of blond, curly hair went out to bat against Pakistan at Edgbaston. He nonchalantly pulled his first ball in Test cricket, from the medium-pacer Liaqat Ali, for four and a star was born.

Dream start: Ian Botham running into bowl in his debut Test at Nottingham against Australia in 1977. He took five wickets.

Local hero: Geoff Boycott is engulfed by fans after making his 100th first-class century on his home ground at Leeds v. Australia in 1977.

No English batsman since Compton gave such pleasure from batting

David Gower (*right*) made 58 in that innings. By the time he played his last Test in 1992 he had made 8,231 runs and at one point he was England's leading run-scorer of all time.

In 1985, as captain, he flayed the Australians with apparent ease, scoring hundreds in three successive Tests. He was also part of the side that retained the Ashes in Australia the following year.

No English batsman since Denis Compton in the 1950s had given such pure pleasure from his batting, playing with a delicacy and flair that inspired a loyal, affectionate following.

When he was omitted from England's tour to India in 1992–93, there was such public outrage that members of MCC called for a vote of no confidence in the selectors. It was a futile gesture.

Gower could be frustrating. He gave the misleading impression of being laid-back and almost careless, which was not a good look when results were going against him. The player himself would admit he could have scored more heavily, given the depth of his talent.

He had two periods as captain but both ended in ignominious defeat: 5-0 by West Indies in 1985–86, the second of two so-called 'blackwashes', followed by home defeat to India, and then in 1989 when England surrendered the Ashes at home and would not see the urn again for 16 years.

His outlook on life was broad. He was dedicated to cricket but not obsessed with it and his relaxed attitude to training did not chime with the more professional regime ushered in by captain Graham Gooch and coach Micky Stewart.

The 1980s was a decade of Ashes highs and Caribbean lows with many other reverses too: the world was leaving England behind.

TONY GREIG

Tall of stature and forceful of personality, Tony Greig left South Africa to make a career for himself in England. He proved good enough to captain his adopted country.

However, his legacy stretches far beyond his performances for England. Having met the Australian media mogul Kerry Packer during the Centenary Test between England and Australia at Melbourne in early 1977, he was to become a key figure and recruiter of players in Packer's ambitious, highly controversial breakaway World Series Cricket that tore the international game apart in the late 1970s.

For that Greig was never forgiven by many England supporters who felt betrayed by his action, much of which had been going on in secret. He played his last Test in 1977 and subsequently emigrated to Australia where he is a distinctive, and much impersonated, member of the Channel 9 television cricket coverage.

Whatever one's view of Greig the man, there is no arguing with the impact or importance of Packer's revolution. All the trappings of the modern game like coloured clothing and floodlit matches stemmed from his brash pioneering.

Greig was a fine player, though, and England were a good side under his leadership. Five of his eight Test hundreds came overseas: two in 1974 in West Indies, two in India and one against Dennis Lillee and Jeff Thomson on the brutalizing Ashes tour of 1974–75. He was also a versatile bowler, able to switch between seam and spin.

He was not one to shrink from confrontation. In the West Indies in 1974 he tried to run out Alvin Kallicharran as the batsman left his crease at the end of a day's play. The incident caused a furious response from the home crowd and the batsman was reinstated after England withdrew the appeal.

In Australia Greig wanted his bowlers to direct bouncers at Lillee, the Australian fast man. When his teammates refused Greig took on the

'If they're down, they grovel, and I intend … to make them grovel'

challenge himself. Lillee was so incensed at the tactic that when he got back to the dressing room after being dismissed in one innings he said: 'They might have started this but we're going to bloody finish it.' England lost the series 4-1.

Before the 1976 home series against West Indies Greig gave a TV interview in which he said that he didn't think the West Indies side were 'as good as everyone thinks they are' before adding 'if they're down, they grovel, and I intend … to make them grovel'.

West Indies, inspired by these inflammatory words from a white South African, won the series 3-0 and embarked on a period of unprecedented world dominance.

England's next series, though, was Greig's finest hour in an England cap. He led the side to a series win in India, where they had not won a series since the 1930s. In the second Test Greig made a match-winning hundred with a temperature on a difficult pitch. He regarded it as his finest innings.

Full name: Anthony William Greig
Born: 6 October 1946, Queenstown, South Africa
International career span: 1972–77
Role: Right-hand middle-order batsman and right-arm bowler of medium-pace and off-spin
Notable numbers: 58 Tests; 3,599 runs at 40.43; eight hundreds and 20 fifties; 141 wickets at 32.20
Extras: Played county cricket for Sussex; television commentator: one of the faces and voices of Australia's Channel 9 coverage for decades; his brother Ian also played for England in the 1980s

The miracle is on: Bob Willis gets John Dyson caught behind on the final day of the third Ashes Test at Leeds. Australia 68 for six.

BOTHAM'S ASHES

By the third evening of the third Test in the 1981 Ashes, English spirits had plumbed such depths that even sanguine bookmakers were in outlandish mood. England were 1-0 down in the series and, following on 227 runs behind, had already lost one of their second-innings wickets. The Ladbrokes odds of an England victory flashed up on Headingley's electronic scoreboard: 500-1.

After a bibulous rest day (as was the custom back then) spent at Ian Botham's north Yorkshire home England's players checked out of their Leeds hotel on the Monday morning in anticipation of impending defeat. When they were 135 for seven, still 92 behind, in the afternoon their foresight seemed sound enough.

That was when Botham was joined by the late Graham Dilley, a young fast bowler with vanilla-blond locks escaping from the back of his batting helmet. Botham had been captain in the first two Tests of the series, resigning after making a pair (out for nought in both innings). Insensitively, the selectors informed the media that he would have been sacked anyway.

When asked after his resignation at Lord's who should replace him, Botham had only one name on his lips: Mike Brearley, the man whose retirement from the top job had prompted Botham's promotion. So the grey-haired Brearley captained England at Headingley and Botham, not coincidentally, had taken his first five-wicket haul

Botham said simply to Dilley: 'Let's give it some humpty'

Humpty: England tail-ender Graham Dilley hooks Geoff Lawson during his match-turning partnership with Ian Botham at Leeds.

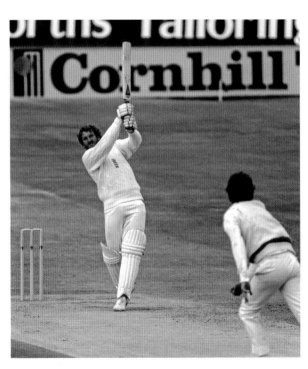

'Into the confectionery stall and out again': Ian Botham launches Terry Alderman for six in his 149 not out at Leeds.

and scored a fifty for the first time since before he was captain.

As Botham and Dilley met in mid-pitch to discuss tactics, Botham said simply, 'Let's give it some humpty', so desperate was the situation. And they did, adding 117 runs in 80 minutes. The left-handed Dilley, who made 56, drove with bullish panache through the off side; Botham threw his physicality and personality at the bowling.

Bareheaded, he swatted, swiped and scythed the Australian bowlers apart. Not every shot came from the middle of the bat but each was played with conviction. The probing swing bowler Terry Alderman was hit back over his head for six. 'Don't bother looking for that ... it's gone straight into the confectionery stall and out again,' said TV commentator Richie Benaud memorably.

Australia, from a position of such certain victory, were now in some disarray, unsure about how best to stem this unlikely tide. The cracks in

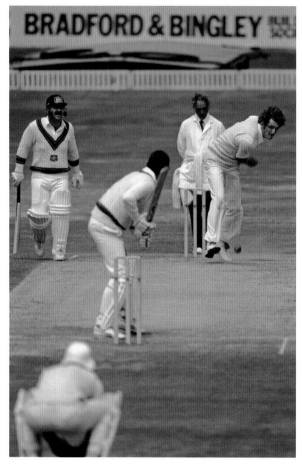

Steaming in: Bob Willis bowling during his match-winning eight for 43 performance at Leeds.

their camp, that would properly be acknowledged only years later, were starting to show.

By the end of the innings, early on the fifth morning, Botham was 149 not out and England led by 129. Already a miracle had been witnessed but the Australians were still expected to win. When they were 56 for one their victory looked assured but Bob Willis, England's leonine fast bowler, changed ends to bowl with the wind.

Charging in off his long run, mop of auburn hair bouncing with every ungainly stride, he bowled like a man possessed. He took eight wickets for 43, the last nine Australian wickets falling for 55 runs. While his teammates greeted each dismissal with wild excitement, he remained impassive, as if in a trance. On taking the winning wicket he simply raised his arms, bowed his head

and sprinted for the sanctuary of the dressing room as hordes of disbelieving, jubilant children swarmed on to the outfield.

It was the first time in the 20th century that a team had won a Test after following on and only the second time in history. With the royal wedding of Prince Charles and Diana Spencer eight days away, patriotic fervour had gripped a nation.

The next Test at Birmingham, a low-scoring affair, climaxed with Australia requiring another modest total, 151, to win. And once again they appeared well set. On a turning pitch Brearley was preparing to use his two off-spinners, John Emburey and Peter Willey, in harness but changed

The series captivated a nation beset by recession, unemployment and riots

his mind and threw the ball to Botham. It was only the second occasion that Test cricket had been played on a Sunday (the first being the first Test of the series at Trent Bridge) in England and the sun-drenched Birmingham crowd created a football-style atmosphere as their hero charged in. In 28 deliveries Botham took five Australian wickets for a single run. He had done it again and the series had officially become Botham's Ashes. 'He didn't want to bowl, you know,' revealed Brearley afterwards.

A grey Saturday afternoon at Manchester was the setting for Botham's third tour de force in the fifth Test. Despite having a first-innings lead of 101 England were making a hash of their second innings. They had taken 69 overs to make 104 for five when Botham joined Chris Tavaré. Even though Botham started slowly, making 28 off his first 53 balls, he overtook the stonewalling Tavaré.

When Australia took the new ball, Botham unleashed a violent attack, hooking Lillee and pulling Alderman for sixes. He reached his hundred off 86 balls, a relatively commonplace scoring-rate in the modern game but an explosive rarity in that era. When he was out he had made 118 and put on 149 for the sixth wicket with Tavaré. Botham's brilliance had snuffed out any prospect of an Australian comeback and the lower-order batsmen also scored runs with abandon.

Australia were set 506 to win and, although both Graham Yallop and Allan Border made centuries, they lost by 103 runs. England had retained the Ashes and Botham was man of the match for a third time in a series that had captivated an entire nation beset by recession, unemployment and race riots in London and Liverpool.

The series would come to define Botham's career and would cast a lengthy shadow over English cricket for a generation to come as a demanding public yearned impossibly for heroes and performances to match those of the unforgettable 1981 Ashes.

Hold on to your hats: Bob Taylor and Ian Botham run the gauntlet after the extraordinary Leeds victory.

England v. Australia 1981

(† denotes team winning toss; * not out)

1st Test, Nottingham, 18–21 June England 185 (MW Gatting 52; TM Alderman 4-68) and 125 (IT Botham 33; DK Lillee 5-46, Alderman 5-62); †Australia 179 (AR Border 63) and 122-6 (J Dyson 38; GR Dilley 4-24). Australia won by four wickets.

2nd Test, Lord's, 2–7 July England 311 (P Willey 82, Gatting 59; GF Lawson 7-81) and 265-8 dec (G Boycott 60, DI Gower 89); †Australia 345 (Border 64) and 90-4 (GM Wood 62*). Drawn.

3rd Test, Leeds, 16–21 July †Australia 401-9 dec (Dyson 102, KJ Hughes 89, GN Yallop 58; Botham 6-95) and 111 (Dyson 34; RGD Willis 8-43); England 174 (Botham 50; Lillee 4-49) and 356 (Botham 149*, Dilley 56; Alderman 6-135). England won by 18 runs.

4th Test, Birmingham, 30 July–2 August †England 189 (JM Brearley 48; Alderman 5-42) and 219 (Gatting 39; RJ Bright 5-68); Australia 258 (MF Kent 46; JE Emburey 4-43) and 121 (Border 40; Botham 5-11). England won by 29 runs.

5th Test, Manchester, 13–17 August †England 231 (CJ Tavaré 69, PJW Allott 52*; Lillee 4-55, Alderman 4-88) and 404 (Tavaré 78, Botham 118, APE Knott 59, Emburey 57; Alderman 5-109); Australia 130 (Kent 52; Willis 4-63) and 402 (Yallop 114, Border 123*). England won by 103 runs.

6th Test, The Oval, 27 August–1 September Australia 352 (Wood 66, Kent 54, Border 106*; Willis 4-91, Botham 6-125) and 344-9 dec (Border 84, DM Wellham 103, RW Marsh 52; M Hendrick 4-82, Botham 4-128); †England 314 (Boycott 137, Gatting 53; Lillee 7-89) and 261-7 (Gatting 56, Brearley 51, Knott 70*; Lillee 4-70). Drawn.

England won the series 3–1

In the zone: England's players celebrate a wicket at Leeds but Bob Willis remains unmoved.

IAN BOTHAM

It is hard to overstate the impact of Ian Botham on English cricket or, indeed, on English society. Two decades since he last played and more since his performance peak, 'Beefy' remains the most famous cricket personality in the country.

In part that is because he is a key component of Sky Sports' television coverage, passing comment with the same unblinking self-confidence that defined his playing career. There is also his contribution over a quarter of a century to the cause of leukaemia research for which he was knighted in 2007.

He will forever be associated with the 1981 Ashes, a *Boy's Own* tale of unparalleled improbability and sporting heroism. Having resigned the England captaincy after two Tests with his form in tatters, he produced three successive match-winning performances to turn the series on its head.

His captaincy tenure was brief and unsuccessful, failing to win any of his 12 Tests in charge though ten of them were against the world-champion West Indies. But for the three years prior to becoming captain – his first three as an international cricketer – he was supreme, particularly as a bowler, swinging the ball both ways at pace.

His first Test wicket, at Nottingham in 1977, was the great Australian batsman Greg Chappell and he took five wickets in the innings. His capacity for show-stealing would never leave him.

He rarely rediscovered the late 1970s' peak of performance as a back injury and a colourful lifestyle took its toll. From the start of the 1980s he was front- and back-page news in an era before footballers' lifestyles became a source of regular tabloid interest.

In 1986 he was banned by the English cricket authorities for three months for admitting to once having smoked cannabis. On his return,

in the final Test of the summer against New Zealand, he took a wicket with his first ball. Graham Gooch took the catch in the slips and asked Botham: 'Who writes your scripts?'

That winter he would play a leading role in England's last Ashes victory in Australia for 24 years, confirming yet again his ability to raise his game against England's oldest foe.

'The word for me that sums him up best is bravado' – David Gower

In the first Test at Brisbane Botham made his 14th and last Test century, his first for three years. It was brilliantly destructive and set the tone for the series. In the fourth Test at Melbourne he took five wickets when only half-fit, having missed the previous Test through injury. He did not even bowl well but the hold he had over the Australians was unbreakable.

He played for five more years and reached a World Cup final in 1992 but the 1986–87 Ashes was his last great contribution on the international stage.

Full name: Ian Terence Botham
Born: 24 November 1955, Heswall, Cheshire
International career span: 1977–92
Role: Right-hand middle-order batsman, right-arm fast-medium swing bowler
Notable numbers: 102 Tests; 5,200 runs at 33.54; 383 wickets at 28.40; England's leading Test wicket-taker; one of only three men to have scored a century and taken ten wickets in a Test; first man to score 5,000 Test runs and take 300 wickets
Extras: Charity walks; knighted in 2007; played football for Scunthorpe; son Liam played county cricket and pro rugby

LORD'S

Known globally as 'the home of cricket', Lord's is the venue every cricketer wants to play at and every cricket-lover wants to visit.

Founded by the 19th-century entrepreneur Thomas Lord, the ground was originally situated a mile or so away from its current north London home in Marylebone. Hence, in 1787, Marylebone Cricket Club (MCC) was established before the current venue of Lord's was set up in 1814.

MCC, with its distinctive red and yellow colours, is an exclusive private club, with around 18,000 members worldwide, and remains the guardian of the Laws of Cricket and until the 1960s effectively ran the game in England.

In 1877 MCC invited Middlesex to play their home-county matches at Lord's, as they still do today. Every overseas touring side to England expects to play a Test at Lord's but there have been a host of other traditional fixtures there down the years. The schools match between Eton and Harrow, which was first played at the old Lord's in 1805, is the oldest continuing match at the ground. Then there is the university match between Oxford and Cambridge and even the

Lord's notable numbers (up to 9 Feb 2012)

Capacity: 28,000
No. of Tests: 123 (1884–2011)
Highest team score: 729-6 dec, Australia v. England 1930
Lowest team score: 42, India v. England 1974
Highest individual score: 333, Graham Gooch for England v. India 1990
Most Test runs: 2,015, Graham Gooch (England), 1975–94
Best individual bowling: 8-34, Ian Botham for England v. Pakistan 1978
Most Test wickets: 69, Ian Botham (England), 1978–92
No. of ODIs: 52 (1971–2011)
Highest ODI team score: 334-4, Eng v. Ind 1975
Highest ODI individual score: 138*, Viv Richards for West Indies v. England 1979

But for all the history and tradition Lord's has innovated and modernized

final of the National Village Cup. In 1987 a five-day unofficial Test between MCC and Rest of the World commemorated the club's bicentenary. And in 2012 the ground was to be used for the archery competition of the London Olympics.

The grand Victorian pavilion is one of sport's iconic buildings. It is through the famous Long Room that the players emerge to reach the field. The Long Room contains valuable cricketing memorabilia and portraits of great players, including Don Bradman and WG Grace. The museum behind the pavilion houses the Ashes,

the tiny, terracotta urn that symbolizes the ancient rivalry between England and Australia.

But for all the history and tradition at Lord's it has also developed a reputation for innovation and modernization with some stunning new architecture like the tented roofs of the Mound Stand, Grand Stand and the futuristic media centre.

While all players love to play at Lord's, not all succeed. Brian Lara, Ricky Ponting and Sachin Tendulkar are three of the greatest batsmen in history. Yet in 23 Test innings between them at Lord's, they made only one fifty between them.

The great showdown: Mike Atherton and South Africa's Allan Donald stare each other down at Nottingham in 1998.

HICK-UPS AND COCK-UPS

Rarely has the burden of expectation weighed so heavily as it did on the shoulders of Graeme Ashley Hick (*right*). This quiet, athletic Zimbabwean-born batsman was the subject of many England supporters' wildest dreams, a willow-wielding saviour who would transfer the Bradmanesque feats of his county cricket apprenticeship into the Test arena.

Yet four matches into his chilli-hot baptism against the still-imperious West Indies in 1991 he was dropped. It was a fate to which he would become frustratingly accustomed during a ten-year Test career that yielded only six of his 136 first-class centuries.

It was his misfortune that, after a lengthy residential qualification period, he should begin his England career against some of the finest pace bowling around. He was a big target for the quicks and, it emerged, diffident under pressure. Damned by the New Zealand spinner, and late coach, John Bracewell as a 'flat-track bully', Hick's struggles, and those of the similarly fêted Mark Ramprakash, were symptomatic of an unsettled period for the English game.

It was a time of inconsistent team selection and unreasonable expectations, of dashed hopes and routine

Ashes defeats. But there was also a World Cup final appearance, the occasional thrilling Ashes victory and a grippingly hard-fought series win over South Africa in 1998.

Donald v. Atherton was 'irresistible force met immovable object'

The wreckage of the decade proved fertile ground for the supporters' gallows humour. On the tour of Australia in 1994–95 the blindly loyal England followers were christened the 'Barmy Army' by the admiring and bewildered Australian media. The name stuck and is now a successful travel business. It remains the label by which England's travelling cricket support is known, even if they are neither barmy nor an army.

Heroes emerged, though. Mike Atherton (*right*), a fresh-faced Cambridge University graduate, was appointed captain at the age of 25 in the midst of the 1993 Ashes defeat. He would ultimately fall on his sword in Antigua after a five-year tenure typified in equal measure by collective failure and his own brave, rearguard actions as an opening batsman.

In the victory over South Africa in 1998 he was involved in one of Test cricket's most highly charged passages of play. England had held on thrillingly for an unlikely draw in the third Test but were still 1-0 down going into the fourth Test of five at Trent Bridge. With England needing 247 to win, Atherton faced down the full fury of Allan Donald, the fastest white bowler in the world. 'An

Hat-trick hero: Darren Gough dismisses Ian Healy, the first wicket of his Sydney hat-trick 1999.

irresistible force met an immovable object,' as Tim de Lisle wrote in *Wisden*. Atherton was given not out when he had clearly gloved a catch to the wicketkeeper Mark Boucher. Donald tried to stare the batsman out. Atherton responded in kind. When Nasser Hussain was dropped by Boucher, Donald unleashed a blood-curdling roar of frustration. Atherton finished on 98 not out while Alec Stewart, the captain in his first series, hit the winning runs.

England won the series – their first victory in a five-Test rubber since 1986–87 – in a see-saw final Test at Headingley with Darren Gough taking the winning wicket.

Gough was a bright light in the darkness of the 1990s. Not for nothing was he known as 'Dazzler'. He made his name with six wickets and a swashbuckling half-century in the Sydney Test of 1994–95.

Work in progress: England's first overseas coach Duncan Fletcher and captain Nasser Hussain, with whom he rebuilt England's reputation.

On the next tour of Australia four years later he took a hat-trick. The Australians took to him too, relieved at last to see a Pom with fire in his belly. He was also injured on that 1994–95 tour which summed up a career that could have yielded even more impressive figures than the 229 Test and 235 one-day international wickets that, combined, put him second only to Ian Botham on the list of England's all-time leading bowlers.

Both Gough (*right*) and Stewart were around long enough to contribute to England's rebirth crafted at the turn of the millennium by Hussain, the angry young man turned obdurate taskmaster, and Duncan Fletcher, the inscrutable Zimbabwean coach. Fletcher had a knack for shrewd selections, most notably Michael

Vaughan and Marcus Trescothick, who were both picked without a track record of consistent runs in county cricket.

The career of Stewart, supremely fit and always immaculately turned out, stretched from the late 1980s through to 2003 when he retired as England's most capped Test player. He had also lost more Tests than any other England player, a statement on the era in which he played rather than his own ability. Variously he opened the batting, kept wicket and captained the side. Stewart never did all in the same Test but normally had two of the three jobs on his plate at any time.

Fittingly for such a chest-out patriot, Stewart scored a century in his 100th Test on the Queen Mother's 100th birthday in August 2000 in a series that turned out to be England's first victory over West Indies since the 1960s. As Hussain held the Wisden Trophy aloft after the clinching

Fletcher had a knack for shrewd selections, notably Vaughan and Trescothick

win at The Oval, he could reflect that the jubilant scenes were markedly different from a year earlier when he was booed by the disenchanted crowds after defeat to New Zealand.

The improvement in England's fortunes continued in the winter of 2000–01 when they achieved hard-fought and thoroughly unexpected victories in Pakistan and Sri Lanka. Gough was man of the series as he had been in the summer against West Indies.

The Ashes would elude them for a while longer but light was appearing at the end of the tunnel. Off the field too things were changing with the top England players employed directly by the England and Wales Cricket Board rather than their clubs and the 18-team County Championship split into two divisions with promotion and relegation. English cricket was at last getting ruthless.

Mad dogs and Englishmen: the Barmy Army in full voice.

England in the 1990s

Aug 1989	Australia regain the Ashes. They will not relinquish them until 2005
Jul 1990	Graham Gooch makes 333 v. India at Lord's
Mar 1992	England lose to Pakistan in the World Cup final
Aug 1993	Mike Atherton replaces Gooch as England captain
Mar 1994	England are bowled out for 46 by West Indies in Trinidad
Apr 1994	Alec Stewart scores a century in both innings as England become the first side to win a Test in Barbados for 59 years
Aug 1994	Devon Malcolm takes nine wickets for 57 to defeat South Africa at The Oval
Nov 1995	Atherton bats for almost 11 hours to make 185 not out and defy South Africa
Dec 1996	England draw 0-0 in their first-ever series against Zimbabwe. Coach David Lloyd famously says; 'We flippin' murdered 'em.'
Aug 1998	Muttiah Muralitharan takes 16 wickets in Sri Lanka's first Test win in England at The Oval
Aug 1999	England lose 2-1 to New Zealand, having earlier in the summer gone out in the group stage of their home World Cup

Proud and patriotic: Alec Stewart celebrates a century in his 100th Test on the Queen Mother's 100th birthday.

GRAHAM GOOCH

With the droopy moustache and the lolloping gait, Graham Gooch often exuded an air of despondency. This was partly a sign of the times in which he played when he was often shoring up a fragile, maddeningly inconsistent England batting line-up.

'He reconstructed and reinspired the England team and did a similar job on himself' – Simon Barnes

That at least was the story of the latter part of his lengthy career. He made nought in both innings of his Test debut in 1975 when his bat was something of a dashing blade. Over time he made himself into an impressively dependable batsman whose appetite for run accumulation grew rather than diminished as he got older. He is the most prolific run-scorer in history when his runs across all the various top-flight formats are combined.

He took England to the World Cup final in 1987, the first tournament to be held outside England, with a masterful century in which he opted to sweep or pull India's spin bowlers.

For Essex he chewed up county bowling attacks year after year. But it was only after a horrific Ashes series in 1989, when he averaged 20, that he seemed to crack Test cricket.

Crack it, he undoubtedly did, though. For a period at the start of the 1990s he was the best batsman in the world. His 333 against India at Lord's in 1990 made him famous but his match-winning 154 not out (opening the batting) out of 252 at Headingley against a mighty West Indies is remembered as one of the great Test innings.

But he is an ambivalent figure in English cricket. He was banned for three years for leading a rebel tour to South Africa in 1981–82. He was made England captain in 1988 when his leadership was described by the soon-to-be chairman of selectors Ted Dexter as like being slapped in the face with a wet fish.

He resigned the captaincy in 1993 midway through a losing Ashes series after a period notable for a fall-out with and later non-selection of David Gower, a batsman whose individualistic flair clashed with Gooch's desire for an uber-professional regime. Gooch and the England manager Micky Stewart were less than amused by Gower's prank of flying a Tiger Moth plane over the ground where England were playing an upcountry warm-up match on the 1990–91 tour of Australia. The personal relationship between these two great England batsmen was never properly repaired.

Gooch was later a selector but that also ended in a gloomy departure in 1999, during a series against New Zealand when England fell to the bottom of the Test rankings.

More recently he has been England's batting coach and held in high regard by the current crop for his work ethic and expertise. In recognition of his value to the side he was given a full-time role in early 2012.

Full name: Graham Alan Gooch
Born: 23 July 1953, Leytonstone, east London
International career span: 1975–95
Role: Right-hand opening batsman, occasional right-arm medium-pace bowler
Notable numbers: 8,900 Test runs at 42.58 in 118 Tests; England's leading Test run-scorer; scored 333 v. India at Lord's, the third highest Test score by an England batsman; all-time leading run-scorer in all forms of the game (67,057)
Extras: Selector, coach (Essex and England), occasional commentator, promotes hair-replacement therapy; lifelong supporter of West Ham United football club; awarded OBE

Great sport, great sportsmanship: Andrew Flintoff consoles Brett Lee after England win the second Test by two runs at Birmingham.

THE GREATEST SERIES

England had not beaten Australia in a Test series since 1987, at home since 1985. That they did in 2005 was a cause of national celebration and relief. That they did in what came quickly to be regarded as the greatest series of all time catapulted cricket and England's protagonists into the national consciousness in a way not seen since 1981.

Freddie Flintoff, Kevin Pietersen and Michael Vaughan became household names while cricket agnostics of all ages, genders and backgrounds became unhealthily obsessed with the form of Ashley Giles or the state of Simon Jones's knee.

As England, under the shrewd captaincy of Vaughan and the meticulous orchestration of coach Duncan Fletcher, showed a consistent improvement in the lead-up to the series, the hype became unbearable and pessimism born of painful experience dictated that the home side would end up with egg on their faces.

Sure enough, after Australia had contrived to lose one-day matches to Somerset and Bangladesh and also been beaten by England in a Twenty20 match, they won the first Test at Lord's by 239 runs. Normal service had been resumed, or so it seemed.

England's players reacted in different ways to the defeat. Flintoff disappeared to the south of France while Vaughan worked on his batting technique in Leeds with Fletcher. What followed when the teams reconvened at Birmingham was beyond prediction.

Who knows what would have happened if Glenn McGrath, Australia's leading quick bowler who had taken his 500th Test wicket at Lord's, had spotted the errant cricket ball at his feet, the result of a stray practice shot by England's Ian Bell? But he didn't. He trod on it, turned his ankle and was out of the Test. He did play again in the series but was below full capacity.

Despite this apparent catastrophe Ricky Ponting, the Australian captain, put England in to bat, convinced of the groundsman's prematch suggestion that the Edgbaston pitch was damp.

Whatever the conditions, England were hot, batting with an untypical, almost Australian fearlessness. Scoring 300 runs in a day of Test cricket used to be respectable but Australia had based their generation of dominance on batting big and fast. England made 407 all out on a remarkable day of Test cricket that reinstated the pre-series belief for their long-suffering supporters and told Ponting the series would not be as easy as he might have thought after Lord's.

The Test ebbed and flowed. England took a 99-run first-innings lead but then collapsed until Flintoff rescued them. His straight six off Brett Lee, Australia's quickest bowler, that went on to the roof of the pavilion elicited two unforgettable words as the ball was in mid-flight from the TV commentator Mark Nicholas: 'Hello … massive!'

Starting the fourth morning, Australia were 175 for eight in their second innings, chasing 282 for an unlikely victory. Edgbaston was packed again for what might theoretically have been only two balls of play. But Shane Warne had other ideas. England were well accustomed to Warne's destructive brilliance with the ball but less attuned to his stubbornness with the bat. He chipped away at the runs required while Lee bravely fended off

Game on: England level the series at Birmingham as Michael Kasprowicz is caught behind off Steve Harmison.

a flurry of Flintoff bouncers. Eventually, with 62 needed, Warne was out, treading on his stumps as he tried to turn the ball down the leg side. But still Australia fought on and England supporters started to contemplate the horrific prospect of a defeat that would leave their team 2-0 down with confidence and dreams shattered once more.

The last batsman, Michael Kasprowicz, spooned a ball to third man where Simon Jones, the Glamorgan fast bowler, spilled the catch as he ran in from the boundary. Edgbaston gasped.

With only four runs required, Lee smashed a full toss from Steve Harmison through the off side and anxious TV viewers thought that was the winning stroke, only to see a boundary fielder keep the batsmen down to a single run.

Two balls later the match ended: Kasprowicz fended a Harmison bouncer off his glove down the leg side where England's Australian-raised wicketkeeper Geraint Jones dived forward to take a vital, career-defining catch.

Decision maker: umpire Billy Bowden.

As the ball was in mid-flight, Mark Nicholas said: 'Hello … massive!'

Dropping the Ashes: Shane Warne puts down Kevin Pietersen on the final day of the series at The Oval. Pietersen went on to make 158.

The New Zealand umpire Billy Bowden raised his famous crooked finger and in the TV commentary box the veteran Richie Benaud was measured as always amid the mayhem: 'Kasprowicz … Jones … Bowden.' England had won by only two runs.

While all England was delirious, Flintoff went to console Lee. The picture of the two opponents on their haunches, Flintoff's left hand on Lee's shoulder, their right hands interlocked, became the series' defining image.

By time the third Test started at Manchester four days later DVDs of what was being called The Greatest Test were already on sale.

Play your natural game, KP was told. And so he did, taking on Lee

No one anticipated another nail-biter. England were the dominant force now as local interest in the series surged. As England closed in on victory, around 10,000 people were turned away from Old Trafford on the final morning of the Test. On TV, almost eight million watched as Ponting, with an epic seven-hour 156, was the lone hand of defiance for Australia.

The next highest score was 39 and when Ponting was the ninth man out, four overs from the end, he trudged from the field, head bowed, like a soldier on Remembrance Sunday.

Australia hung on for the draw, though, a result that caused an elated eruption on their dressing-room balcony. On the field Vaughan, the England captain, called his players into a huddle and told them to observe how much this escape meant to the previously indomitable Australians.

England were so much the better side in the fourth Test at Trent Bridge that another close finish seemed improbable. Wrong again. Chasing only 129 to take the lead in the series for the first time, England's batsmen got the jitters in the face of Warne's supreme competitiveness. He dismissed Marcus Trescothick with his first ball and spread the sort of panic through the dressing room England had been suffering ever since his Ashes debut in 1993. England found two unlikely batting heroes, Ashley Giles and Matthew Hoggard, whose eighth-wicket stand of 13 was, like Geraint Jones's catch at Edgbaston, set to frame their careers.

Because Australia held the Ashes, they needed only to draw the series to retain the urn so, with one Test remaining, they still had a chance.

The end of the fifth Test at The Oval was eccentrically anticlimactic, a classic cricketing oddity, but there had been plenty more drama on the way. David Graveney, England's chairman of selectors, even had to repair to the car park to stay calm. Five days of tension culminated with Warne, fielding at first slip, dropping Kevin Pietersen, who had just come in, with England on 68 for 3 in their second innings and leading by only 74.

By lunch on the final day England led by 133 with only five wickets left. Pietersen, playing in only his fifth Test, asked captain Vaughan over lunch how he should approach the afternoon session. Play your natural game, he was told. And so he did, taking on Lee, bowling at 95mph, in an innings of unimaginable bravado. He made 158 and secured the draw for England.

As he left the field late in the afternoon, he turned, arms aloft, sweat dripping from his controversial 'skunk' haircut, to acknowledge the ovation from The Oval's full house.

Nottingham nail-biter: England celebrate going 2-1 up.

England v. Australia 2005

(† denotes team winning toss; * not out)

1st Test, Lord's, July 21–24 †Australia 190 (JL Langer 40; SJ Harmison 5-43) and 347 (DR Martyn 65, MJ Clarke 91, SM Katich 67); England 155 (KP Pietersen 57, GD McGrath 5-53) and 180 (Pietersen 64*; McGrath 4-29, SK Warne 4-64). Australia won by 239 runs.

2nd Test, Birmingham, August 4–7 England 407 (ME Trescothick 90, Pietersen 71, A Flintoff 68; Warne 4-116) and 182 (Flintoff 73; B Lee 4-82, Warne 6-46); †Australia 308 (Langer 82, RT Ponting 61) and 279 (Lee 43*; Flintoff 4-79). England won by two runs.

3rd Test, Manchester, August 11–15 †England 444 (Trescothick 63, MP Vaughan 166, IR Bell 59; Lee 4-100, Warne 4-99) and 280-6 dec (AJ Strauss 106, Bell 65; McGrath 5-115); Australia 302 (Warne 90; SP Jones 6-53) and 371-9 (Ponting 156; Flintoff 4-71). Drawn.

4th Test, Nottingham, August 25–28 †England 477 (Trescothick 65, Vaughan 58, Flintoff 102, GO Jones 85; Warne 4-102) and 129-7 (Warne 4-31); Australia 218 (Lee 47; SP Jones 5-44) and 387 (Langer 61, Clarke 56, Katich 59). England won by three wickets.

5th Test, The Oval, September 8–12 †England 373 (Strauss 129, Flintoff 72; Warne 6-122) and 335 (Pietersen 158; Warne 6-124); Australia 367 (Langer 105, ML Hayden 138; MJ Hoggard 4-97, Flintoff 5-78) and 4-0. Drawn.

England won the series 2-1

It was the sort of ostentation that had prevented many England followers from taking the South African-born batsman to their hearts but in these circumstances no one was complaining.

Andrew Flintoff

Only in times of crisis was Andrew Flintoff referred to by his given name. The rest of the time he was simply Freddie or Fred, nicknamed in his teens by a Lancashire coach after the cartoon character Fred Flintstone.

With an earthy charm and a rugby player's build, he was the natural successor to Ian Botham for the British public as a swashbuckling cricketer who could hit the ball hard, bowl it fast and catch the flying edges in the slips.

'He was the ultimate impact cricketer. He put his body on the line'
– Andrew Strauss

Growing up in Preston, north Lancashire, and playing with his family at the St Anne's club, he was spotted early by his county and went on to captain England Under-19. He made his Test debut as a 21-year-old against South Africa in 1998 but he was continually under scrutiny for his weight. In 2000 he was man of the match in a one-day international against Zimbabwe and greeted the post-match interviewer with the deadpan comment: 'All right for a fat lad.'

Progress up the international ladder was slower than media and selectors hoped but by 2003, when he made a cavalier maiden Test hundred against South Africa at Lord's, he had become an integral member of coach Duncan Fletcher's improving England side.

From May 2003 to September 2005, he scored more than half of his Test runs at an average of 43 and took 110 of his 226 Test wickets at 27 runs per wicket. During his career-best innings of 167 at Birmingham against West Indies in 2004 one six-hit remarkably picked out his father Colin in the stands but Flintoff senior dropped the ball.

The epic 2005 Ashes series brought him fame across the cricketing world – even Australians took to him. Though he did play notable innings, it was his bowling that was for a while world-class. He was quick, strong and created awkward bounce. He could also reverse-swing the old ball and was a handful for Australia's left-handers in particular, dismissing Adam Gilchrist and Matthew Hayden four times each.

The footage of Flintoff staggering – tired and emotional to put it politely – from the team hotel on to the open-top bus that would take the team on a celebratory parade of London after that win was part of the summer's iconography.

His career never touched those heights again. A knee injury was followed by a disastrous tour of Australia in 2006–07, when he was controversially named captain in the absence of the injured Michael Vaughan. Then at the 2007 World Cup he was disciplined for attempting to pilot a pedalo into the Caribbean in the early hours following England's defeat to New Zealand.

Injury became a continual obstacle that ultimately defeated him but not before he had written another chapter in Ashes history in 2009, bowling England to their first Test win over Australia at Lord's since 1934. After more knee operations he retired a year later.

Full name: Andrew Flintoff
Born: 6 December 1977, Preston, Lancashire
Role: Right-hand middle-order batsman; right-arm pace bowler
Notable numbers: 3,845 runs in 79 Tests at 31.77; 226 wickets at 32.78, five Test hundreds and 26 half-centuries; also 141 one-day internationals
Extras: Married to Rachael, three children; was a schoolboy chess champion; co-owner of a racehorse called Flintoff that ran in the 2010 Aintree Grand National; awarded the MBE in 2006; loves darts and has assisted with Sky Sports commentary at the World Championship

Team togetherness: Andrew Strauss addresses his players during the Lord's Test of 2009, England's first win over Australia there since 1934.

RISE TO THE TOP

So much for a happy New Year. In late afternoon on the last day of 2008 a story broke on the website of the *Daily Telegraph* that changed the course of English cricket.

The report claimed that Kevin Pietersen, the team's most high-profile player and captain for only four months, had fallen out with the coach Peter Moores. Within a week Pietersen resigned and Moores was removed from his position.

At the time it seemed a catastrophic meltdown for the national team but the subsequent appointments of Moores' assistant Andy Flower as coach and Andrew Strauss as captain set England on the road to their first global trophy, the 2010 World Twenty20, first Ashes victory in Australia for 24 years and the No.1 Test ranking.

The prospect of those achievements, though, seemed a lifetime away when England were bowled out for 51 by West Indies in Jamaica, the first Test in charge for Flower and Strauss. Despite some close calls they failed to win a Test and lost the rubber 1-0. But England would lose none of their subsequent nine Test series.

That forgettable West Indies tour was notable for the emergence of Graeme Swann, the effervescent off-spinner who had made a fleeting international appearance as a 20-year-old ten years earlier. Selected as the backup spinner to Monty Panesar for the tour in India in late 2008, Swann usurped the left-armer in the Caribbean and had a profound effect on England's fortunes in the next two years.

Panesar played his part, though, in an epic, last-wicket stand with Jimmy Anderson at Cardiff to save England from defeat in the first Test of the 2009 Ashes. On a slow pitch the unremarkable match reached an extraordinary conclusion with Panesar and Anderson, England's last pair, hanging on for 11 overs to save a game that looked lost when England were 102 for five at lunch on the final day, still 137 runs behind Australia.

Who knows how differently the series might have turned out but for that last-wicket stand? As it was, England moved on to Lord's, where they had not beaten Australia in a Test since 1934, relieved and hopeful. Australia, no longer with the match-winning greatness of Shane Warne and Glenn McGrath, were at last vulnerable.

Andrew Flintoff (*right*), having announced his impending retirement from Test cricket the day before the match, completed the historic victory with five second-innings wickets but the tone was set by an opening partnership of 196 between Strauss and Alastair Cook. Together they broke the fragile morale of Mitchell Johnson, the left-arm quick who was leading Australia's bowling attack in his debut Ashes. He left Lord's bewildered and belittled by the unforgiving home crowds. Yet such was his mercurial talent that two Tests later at Leeds, he produced a match-winning display that demolished England by an innings and levelled the series with one match to play.

England had to win to regain the Ashes and the pitch at The Oval was uncommonly dry, indicating assistance for the spinners and the likelihood of a positive result within the five days. Remarkably Australia omitted their spinner Nathan Hauritz and paid the price. Though the series lacked

Straight bat: Monty Panesar defends against Peter Siddle during England's last-gasp draw against Australia at Cardiff in 2009.

the consistent quality of the 2005 Ashes it still provided a gripping, turbulent drama. Statistically, England's 2-1 victory was eccentric. They scored fewer runs and lost more wickets than Australia and the centuries count was 8-2 in the visitors' favour. Strauss summed it up neatly: 'When we were bad we were very bad, but when we were good we were just good enough.'

Regaining the Ashes was a cause of national celebration, though there were no open-top bus parades as there had been in 2005. Flower and Strauss knew that they faced a tougher test that winter: a four-Test series in South Africa who had taken Australia's spot as the world's top Test side.

A 1-1 draw in South Africa was a major coup for this re-emerging England side though they needed more tail-end heroics, twice having to thank the broad bat and steely nerves of their No.11, the Durham bowler Graham Onions.

'When we were bad we were very bad, when we were good we were just good enough' – Strauss

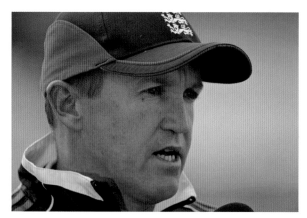

Power behind the throne: the coach Andy Flower formed a winning partnership with captain Andrew Strauss.

The two Tests in Bangladesh that followed were less of a challenge and they provided an opportunity for Strauss to take a break with the Ashes looming later in 2010. The captain received criticism for the decision but hindsight shows it to be an example of the attention to detail and forward-planning that epitomized the new improved England set-up Flower was building.

While expectations were raised by these improvements in the Test arena, England's limited-overs performances were at best unpredictable and often wretched, as the 6-1 one-day series drubbing by Australia after the 2009 Ashes showed. Consequently, there was precious little anticipation of a strong showing in the World Twenty20 that took place in the Caribbean in early May 2010.

Yet England won the tournament on the back of a surprising return to form from Kevin Pietersen (*right*), who had hobbled out of the 2009 Ashes with an achilles tendon injury and made a single half-century on his return in the Test series in South Africa. He top-scored against Pakistan, South Africa and Sri Lanka in the semi-final and was named man of the tournament. He even had time to miss a game to fly home for the birth of his son Dylan. To beat Australia in the final was the perfect conclusion for England, especially with the Ashes only six months away.

With the football World Cup competing for the public's attention, the 2010 summer series against

Before the Ashes England went to Germany for a military-style boot camp

Bangladesh and Pakistan were played out in the context of Ashes preparation, at least until the final Test of the summer at Lord's when newspaper revelations broke about the bowling of deliberate no-balls as part of a spot-fixing scam. This scandal overshadowed not only England's match and series victory but world cricket as a whole for the next 15 months, until the three Pakistan players involved were convicted in a criminal court and jailed on corruption charges.

Before England ventured to Australia, where they had not won a series since 1986–87, the squad were taken to Germany for a military-style boot camp of bonding and brutality. Organized by their security manager, an Australian ex-policeman called Reg Dickason, the trip was a shock to the system in every sense for the players who were not aware even of the destination until arriving at Heathrow airport. They spent five days ('tough but rewarding', according to Strauss) on team-building exercises and visited the memorial site at Dachau, the Nazi concentration camp.

The significance of such activities can be over-interpreted but it bore all the hallmarks of Flower's attitude to hard work, physical conditioning and togetherness. The way they performed over the next few months in Australia certainly legitimized all the pre-tour preparation.

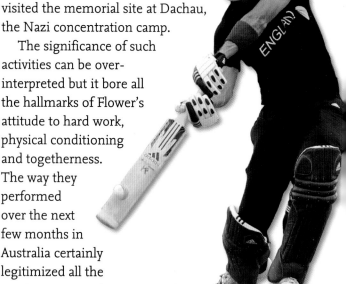

Bradmanesque: Alastair Cook ripped up the record books in the 2010-11 Ashes, scoring 766 runs in the series.

The departure of Strauss to the third ball of the series at Brisbane dredged up England's worst mid-1990s' nightmares. But by the end of the drawn Test the momentum was with England, as Alastair Cook, whose form had been wretched the previous summer until a career-stabilizing hundred at The Oval, and Jonathan Trott shattered records in an unbroken second-wicket stand of 329. Their second innings closed on 517 for one and Cook's 235 not out beat Don Bradman's 226 as the highest at the ground.

After 13 balls of the second Test at Adelaide, Australia were two for three and never recovered. Swann capitalized on a Pietersen double-hundred and dismissed Australia with five second-innings wickets before the city of churches suffered the forecast biblical deluge. That the rain had not denied England their deserved victory allowed their faithful followers to think that this at last might be their year.

Despite a drubbing at Perth, where the wayward Mitchell Johnson's radar was properly aligned for the only time in the series, England completed crushing victories in the traditional holiday Tests at Melbourne and Sydney.

Having seen their side bowled out for only 98 on Boxing Day, a large chunk of the 84,000 crowd had departed the MCG long before the close of a momentous first day by which time England had a lead of 59 and all first-innings wickets standing.

Jimmy Anderson, who had endured a torrid time on his previous Ashes tour four years earlier, was unplayable, confirming his status as England's attack leader.

More surprising was the way that fringe bowlers slotted into the side with immediate impact. The 6ft 8in Chris Tremlett, a wild-card pick by the selectors, replaced Stuart Broad, who injured his side during the Adelaide Test, and took eight wickets at Perth.

ANDREW STRAUSS

Twice Andrew Strauss had filled in as England captain. Third time was definitely lucky, although luck had little to do with a full-time tenure that began in January 2009 and brought two Ashes series victories, including England's first in Australia for 24 years, followed by England becoming the No.1 Test side in the world.

Born in South Africa but educated at Radley, one of England's leading private schools, Strauss has never exuded the sporting X-factor possessed of some of his teammates. Even at school he was outshone by peers who would go on to have fine careers in county cricket.

'He is a magnificent leader who commands universal respect' – Graeme Swann

At Durham University he was an archetypal student: laid-back and disorganized. He imagined that he would end up working in the City like some of his friends.

But Duncan Fletcher, the England coach from 1999 to 2007, liked the character and temperament of the Middlesex batsman. After initially breaking into England's one-day side, Strauss got his chance in the Test team against New Zealand in 2004 because of an injury to Michael Vaughan. On his home ground at Lord's he made 112 and 83.

In 2006 he took over the captaincy when Andrew Flintoff, himself a long-term stand-in for the injured Vaughan, broke down against Sri Lanka. Strauss's calm authority was evident in a comfortable series victory over Pakistan but the job was controversially handed back to Flintoff for the disastrous 2006–07 Ashes tour, which ended in a 5-0 defeat for England. By late 2007 Strauss was out of the team.

Opponents had begun to stifle his relatively limited range of shots: he liked to score square of the wicket rather than straight down the ground. He was dropped for a tour of Sri Lanka but recalled for the next trip to New Zealand. There was little sign of recovery until his final opportunity of the three-Test series when he played what can only be described as a career-saving innings of 177 at Napier. After ten hundreds in his first 30 Tests he had gone 15 games without one.

His form was still sketchy when Vaughan gave up the captaincy during the 2008 home series against South Africa. But the job was available when Kevin Pietersen resigned the following January. Strauss was the only candidate and his credibility had been enhanced by two centuries in the same Test at Chennai, the second of Pietersen's three matches as captain.

His batting form as captain has not been spectacular but he makes telling contributions such as the 161 at Lord's in the 2009 Ashes. And his leadership qualities are unquestioned. His determined, understated alliance with the teak-tough Zimbabwean coach Andy Flower – the 'Andocracy' as they have been called – was the cornerstone of England's exceptional rise to the top of Test cricket in 2011.

Full name: Andrew John Strauss
Born: 2 March 1977, Johannesburg, South Africa
International career span: 2004–
Role: Left-handed opening batsman
Notable numbers: 21 wins out of 42 Tests (after Pakistan series in Jan 2012) as England captain is second only to Michael Vaughan and the win percentage (50.00) is third behind Vaughan (50.98) and Mike Brearley (58.06) of those who have captained in 20 Tests or more; 6,340 runs in 89 Tests at 41.98; 19 hundreds, highest score 177
Extras: Married to Australian actress Ruth MacDonald, two sons; awarded the MBE in 2005 and the OBE in 2011

The end is nigh: Mitchell Johnson is bowled first ball by Chris Tremlett at Sydney and England are three wickets from Ashes victory in 2011.

He took five more at Melbourne while Tim Bresnan, a well-built Yorkshire all-rounder who was selected ahead of the penetrative but expensive Steven Finn, bowled with all the accuracy and nous of a ten-year veteran.

The final Test at Sydney provided another crushing victory for England, the third by an innings. Cook took his aggregate for the series to 766, the second highest by an England batsman in an Ashes series. Only Bradman had scored more at a better average in a series between England and Australia.

Australia, battered and bewildered by now, had shuffled their pack again, picking two debutants. One of them was a left-arm spinner called Michael Beer, who was the latest to be given the impossible task of filling the boots of Warne. He was also the last man out, his stumps splattered by Tremlett. 'If it is possible to finish third in a two-horse race, Australia did so,' wrote the eminent Australian journalist Gideon Haigh.

England had developed the sort of belief that Australians used to have

All that remained was for England's players to perform the 'sprinkler' dance that had achieved cult status after its appearance on Swann's online video diaries. The stands of the Sydney Cricket Ground were populated almost exclusively by jubilant England supporters, many of them members of the Barmy Army, which had been conceived in the mid-1990s amid the hopeless despair of England's ritual Ashes floggings. How times had changed.

Having rewritten the accepted narrative of Ashes contests, England had the opportunity to climb the summit. To do so by the end of the 2011 summer they needed to beat the current No.1, India, by two clear Tests in a four-match series.

With Sachin Tendulkar on 99 international hundreds and England's Ashes-winning former coach Duncan Fletcher now in charge of India, it was a contest rich in context. The hope was for a classic exhibition of the five-day game between two top-class sides.

But once Zaheer Khan, India's leading bowler, pulled up with a hamstring injury on the first day of the series, it became apparent that India were under-prepared for a series in which every aspect of their cricket was rigorously examined by a disciplined and ruthless England side.

Even when they were on the ropes England found ways to escape and counterpunch. At the start of the second Test at Trent Bridge they were 88 for six but a bold stand from Stuart Broad and Graeme Swann restored credibility and helped them to 221 all out. India were building a tidy lead at 267 for four when Broad, on his home ground, took a hat-trick to add to his top-scoring 64. England had contained India's first-innings lead to 67 and won the Test by 319 runs.

They had developed the sort of impervious belief that they could win from any situation – a belief that had previously been the preserve of the great Australian sides of the 1990s and early 2000s. India meanwhile were failing a major test of character. Only Rahul Dravid, who had not played in the World Cup earlier in the year and appeared fitter and fresher than many of his colleagues, held their batting together.

England's bowlers, led by Jimmy Anderson (*right*), had pace and power. They sensed weakness against the short ball and exploited the deficiency with brutal efficiency. India managed 300 only once in the series.

After three Tests England had already usurped India at the top of the

Dance when you're winning: England's players perform the 'sprinkler' after retaining the Ashes at Melbourne, 2010.

world rankings and there was no let-up in the final Test. The last afternoon of the series, in front of a packed, Indian-centric crowd at The Oval, was a battle between Tendulkar, trying to reach his historic milestone, and England trying to complete a clean sweep. Tendulkar had scored 91 with a series of let-offs: two dropped catches, a missed stumping and two lbw appeals that TV replays indicated were out. Swann was infuriated by Sachin's five lives. 'If you don't get it today, you'll never get it,' he was heard to say. Eventually, Tendulkar was trapped by Bresnan to a marginal lbw decision and Swann finished off the innings as the spin-friendly conditions indicated he should.

It was England's sixth victory by an innings since the start of the Ashes the previous November. They were officially the best Test side in the world and playing as well as any England side in history. There was chuntering about the feebleness of India's performance but, simply, England never allowed them to play.

It had been a remarkable year for English cricket and one that needed to be savoured rather than questioned.

GRAEME SWANN

The younger of two brothers who have both played the game professionally, Graeme Swann seemed to have missed the boat of international cricket.

Yet a recall to England's one-day side in 2007, seven years after his only previous international appearance, led to a Test debut a year later. Within three years he would be ranked as the top spinner in Test cricket and the No.1 one-day bowler in the world while being an integral part of England's rise to the top of the Test tree.

'I'm a person that you need a break from after a while' – Graeme Swann

His sharp wit and constant ebullience led to inevitable confrontations in his early years. But those same personality traits, allied to a degree of maturity and a consistent level of performance, became much admired, sought-after qualities.

He was an Under-19 World Cup winner with England in 1998 and great things were expected as he tried to progress his career on the spin-friendly pitches of his native Northamptonshire. Yet he grew stale and frustrated and it was only after a move to the higher-profile Nottinghamshire in 2005 that his career took off.

He took two wickets in his first over of Test cricket at Chennai against India in December 2008 and started a remarkable trend of striking in the first over of a spell.

Early in 2009 he took Monty Panesar's place as England's first-choice spinner and never looked back. For years England followers had seen their spinner used as a means of containment or to give the quick bowlers a rest unless conditions were in his favour. Even then the spinner would often be so attuned to a defensive mindset that he was incapable of playing the match-winning role required of him.

Swann bucked this accepted wisdom. He had always been a big spinner of the ball but he also had the super-confident, aggressive attitude of a fast bowler and the brainpower to outsmart batsmen.

In 2009, his first full year of Test cricket, he took 54 wickets in 11 matches and had moved ahead of the great Muttiah Muralitharan in the world rankings. He took the wicket that regained the Ashes for England in 2009 at The Oval and was then man of the match in the first two Tests of their tour to South Africa, not generally regarded as a safe haven for spin bowlers of any kind, least of all orthodox finger spinners.

Swann's technique might be orthodox, old-fashioned even, but his confrontational attitude is contemporary. He was brave enough to taunt Sachin Tendulkar about the quest for his hundredth international century in England's final Test of 2011 against India at The Oval as they pursued a 4-0 clean sweep. Swann's contribution to the series had been minimal up to that point. But in dry conditions, tailor-made for him, he was expected to finish off the Test. And he did, taking six wickets in the innings and nine in the match.

Full name: Graeme Peter Swann
Born: 24 March 1979, Northampton
International career span: 2000–
Role: Right-arm off-spin bowler; right-hand lower middle-order batsman
Notable numbers: By Feb 2012 he was England's third-leading Test spinner of all time with 166 wickets in 39 Tests; his strike-rate (balls per wicket) of 57.7 is the best of England spinners with 120 wickets or more; was leading Test wicket-taker in 2010 with 64 in 14 matches
Extras: Lead singer in his own band (Dr Comfort and the Lurid Revelations); fan of Newcastle United football club

THE OVAL

In 1880 The Oval hosted the first Test in England and two years later it was the venue where the Ashes legend was born. After England collapsed to 77 all out, chasing only 85 to win, the *Sporting Times* published its famous obituary for English cricket.

The ground has continued to be a part of Ashes folklore with series-deciding matches in 1953, 2005 and 2009 as well as Don Bradman's final Test in 1948 when he was greeted by an ovation from the crowd and three cheers from the England players only to make a duck.

Traditionally hosting the final Test of the English domestic season, The Oval is London's second major venue, providing an urban, more egalitarian counterpoint to its upmarket cousin on the other side of the River Thames.

The raucous, carnival atmosphere provided by West Indies supporters in the 1970s and 1980s prompted the team's captain Clive Lloyd to liken playing at The Oval to a home game for his team.

In addition The Oval has hosted FA Cup finals (1872–92), football and rugby union internationals and baseball.

The Oval's notable numbers (to 9 Feb 2012)

Capacity: 23,500
No. of Tests: 94 (1880–2011)
Highest team score: 903-7 dec, Eng v. Aus 1938
Lowest team score: 44, Aus v. Eng, 1896
Highest individual score: 364, Len Hutton for England v. Australia 1938
Most Test runs: 1,521, Len Hutton (England), 1937–54
Best individual bowling: 9-57, Devon Malcolm for England v. South Africa 1994
Most Test wickets: 52, Ian Botham (England), 1978–91
No. of ODIs: 48 (1973–2011)
Highest ODI team score: 347-4, New Zealand v. USA 2004
Highest ODI individual score 145*, Nathan Astle for New Zealand v. USA 2004

Clive Lloyd said playing at The Oval was a home game for West Indies

In 2004 the ground hosted the final of the 50-over ICC Champions Trophy between England and West Indies.

Owned by the Duchy of Cornwall, the private estate of the Prince of Wales, it is the county ground of Surrey whose chocolate brown caps bear the distinctive Prince of Wales feathers as their crest. Surrey have won 18 County Championship titles, bettered only by Yorkshire, and between 1952 and 1958 they won seven successive titles. The county has provided some of England's greatest players and The Oval bears

witness to this with stands named after Peter May, a former England captain, Sir Alec Bedser, the supreme seam bowler, and the spinner Tony Lock. One set of gates is named after Sir Jack Hobbs, arguably England's finest batsman, the other after Alec Stewart, England's most capped player whose father Micky captained Surrey to the county championship in 1971.

While Lord's is known for its grandeur, The Oval's iconography comprises the nearby gasholder and a reputation for hard, bouncy pitches that produce exhilarating cricket.

AUSTRALIA

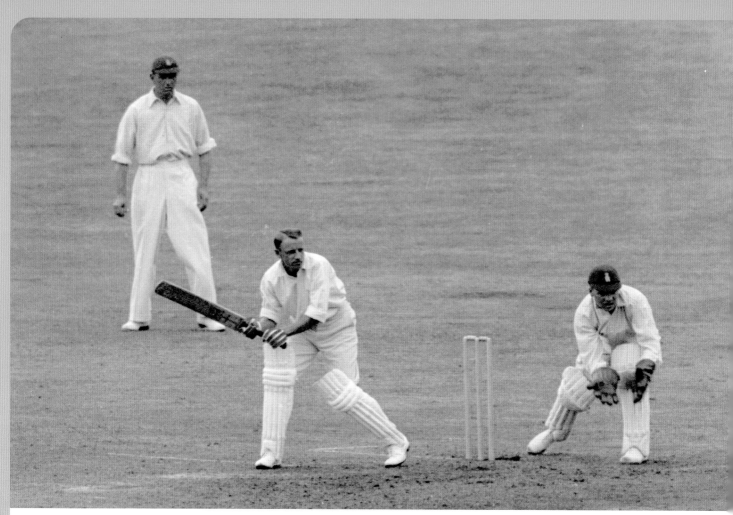

Record breaker: Don Bradman batting against England at Leeds in 1930, the match in which he scored a world-record 334.
Previous page: Shane Warne dismisses England's Sajid Mahmood at Melbourne in the 2006–07 Ashes that Australia won 5-0.

THE BRADMAN ERA

When *Wisden Cricketers' Almanack* canvassed the opinions of a hundred experts to nominate five cricketers of the 20th century for its millennium edition only one player received a unanimous vote.

Comparing eras in sport is a fun but futile business. But when it comes to Sir Don Bradman there is simply no argument. No batsman in the history of the game has come close to his Test batting average of 99.94. And there is a perfectly legitimate argument that 'The Don', as he became known, is the greatest of all sportsmen because his comparative excellence is so measurable.

He played only 52 Test matches – his career straddling World War II – so some of his records

have been overtaken but his numbers are still beyond belief. Most batsmen would be delighted if they could convert half of their fifties into hundreds. Bradman, however, reached 50 in a Test innings 42 times and went on to score a century on 29 occasions. That phenomenal output remained unsurpassed until 1983 when the Indian Sunil Gavaskar scored his 30th hundred in his 99th Test.

Bradman grew up in rural New South Wales and honed his batting technique by hitting a golf ball against a cylindrical water tank with a cricket stump. He would do this for hours on end and transferred these exceptional powers of concentration, determination and hand-eye coordination into the elite cricket arena. He lived his life with similar focus and his puritanical streak caused ongoing tension with some of his more gregarious, fun-loving team-mates. He was also an accomplished pianist.

He had a seemingly insatiable appetite for batting and was a ruthless accumulator of runs, hardly ever hitting the ball in the air. His attitude had more in common with the modern professional game than the more gentlemanly interwar period in which he played most of his cricket. There were more stylish batsmen but none who rattled the scoreboard so relentlessly.

Bradman remained a significant figure in the game until his death

Idol: Bradman walking out to bat in the Leeds Test of 1938. He made 103, after successive triple-hundreds there.

Bradman came to stand for all the aspirations of the average Australian as the young country grew and developed in the early part of the 20th century. He was a country boy made good, respected and admired around the world. He would remain a significant figure in the game until his death in 2001, aged 92, when thousands of mourners lined the streets of Adelaide to pay their respects.

Ashes cricket was the centrepiece of the Anglo-Australian sporting world of the time and Bradman was the leading light.

His greatness was such that England, and their controversial captain Douglas Jardine, devised a whole mode of bowling simply to stop Bradman. England won the infamous Bodyline series of 1932–33 4-1 but Bradman still averaged 56, a successful series for mere mortals but relative failure for him.

Bradman's legend grew quickly. He made an impact in secondary-school cricket and scored a century on his first-class debut for New South Wales in 1927. A year later he was in the Australian side but was dropped after a single Test that Australia lost to England by 675 runs.

He was back in the side for the third match of the series, though, and scored a hundred. He would never be omitted again.

The following season Bradman served notice of his unbeatable capacity for run-scoring when he posted a world-record 452 not out for New South Wales against Queensland at Sydney.

When he toured England in 1930 some judges expected him to struggle on English pitches. They had to review their predictions after the opening match of the tour when he made 236 at Worcester. There followed a feast of run-scoring the like of which has never been seen.

Hats off: England players give Bradman three cheers before his final innings at The Oval in 1948. He made a duck.

In the five Test matches his scores were 8, 131, 254, 1, 334, 14, 232: a total of 974 runs at an astonishing average of 139. But on the tour as a whole, adding in the matches against English counties, he scored almost 3,000 runs at 98.

His feats were front-page news in England and his innings became events in themselves. Only Sachin Tendulkar comes close in terms of this cult of celebrity. Spectators would go to extraordinary lengths just to see Bradman bat and were left sorely disappointed should he happen to be out cheaply or even be rested or unfit for a particular match. Indeed, Bradman's wife Jessie once said that Tendulkar was the modern player whose style most closely resembled her husband's batting.

The British television presenter Michael Parkinson told of how his father, a Yorkshire miner, walked 30 miles to see Bradman bat in the Headingley Test of 1930. It was worth the effort. Bradman, having scored 254 in the previous Test at Lord's, had a hundred before lunch on the first day and by close of play had amassed a colossal 309. He was out for 334, a world-record Test score.

Icon: a bust of The Don at the Bradman Museum in Bowral, the New South Wales town where he grew up.

His final Test innings at The Oval became the most famous duck in history

After the Bodyline blip he was back for second and third helpings of the English bowlers in 1934 and 1938, averaging 94 and 108, respectively.

In 1948 Bradman announced his retirement. He led Australia not only to a 4-0 Ashes victory but to an unbeaten tour of England that would result in his side being known for evermore as 'The Invincibles'.

For Bradman himself the Test series ended in the most extraordinary and excruciating fashion, his final brief innings becoming the most famous duck in history. He arrived at The Oval needing only four runs for once out to leave the game with a Test career batting average of 100. When he came out to bat in the first innings he was given a standing ovation from the crowd. The England captain, Norman Yardley, shook his hand and called for his team to give three cheers. Bradman survived one ball from the leg-spinner Eric Hollies before being bowled by his googly. There was no second innings. Thus was established the game's most discussed statistic: Bradman's batting average of 99.94.

Bradman's brilliance overshadowed some other outstanding performers during a period in which Australia consistently held the upper hand in Ashes contests with England, the Bodyline series aside.

Bill Ponsford, the opener, was one of the most prolific batsmen of his time and it was his world record that Bradman broke for New South Wales. There was Stan McCabe, whose unbeaten 187 at Sydney during Bodyline was one of the bravest innings ever seen. The bowling was led by two great, but very different, leg-spinners, Clarrie Grimmett and Bill 'Tiger' O'Reilly.

The New Zealand-born Grimmett was a match-winner on the 1930 tour with a round-arm style. O'Reilly was taller and bowled quicker, using bounce to discomfort the batsman.

O'Reilly became a perceptive writer on the game and in his autobiography he had this to say about his relationship with Bradman: 'On the field Bradman and I had the greatest respect for each other. Off the field we did not have much in common. You could say we did not like each other, but it would be closer to the truth to say we chose to have little to do with each other. Don Bradman was a teetotaller, ambitious, conservative and meticulous. I was outspoken and gregarious, an equally ambitious young man of Irish descent.'

Legend: Bradman at 80, acknowledging the Sydney crowd at a Test in 1988 to commemorate Australia's bicentenary.

The Don and his numbers

Full name: Donald George Bradman
Born: 27 August 1908, Cootamundra, New South Wales
Died: 25 February 2001, Adelaide
International career span: 1928–48
Role: Right-hand batsman
Career record:

Tests	Runs	HS	Avge	100s	50s
52	6996	334	99.94	29	13
F-c	**Runs**	**HS**	**Avge**	**100s**	**50s**
234	28067	452*	95.14	117	69

Note: F-c = first-class matches   HS = highest score

KEITH MILLER

A fighter pilot in World War II, Keith Miller was a charismatic, flamboyant all-rounder who brought a smile to the years of post-war austerity in Australia and Britain.

He played the game with a tremendous sense of fun and is credited with one of the great cricket quotes in response to a question about feeling pressure on the field: 'Pressure is a Messerschmitt up your arse.' He was part of Australia's 1948 'Invincibles' tour of England when Australia won the Tests 4-0 and were unbeaten in all of their 31 first-class matches. In one match they scored a record 721 in a day against Essex at Southend and Miller let himself be bowled first ball because he found such a one-sided contest so tedious.

Being the golden boy he was nicknamed 'Nugget' and was adored by men and women alike. His friendly duels with Denis Compton, England's dashing batsman, symbolised the attitudes of the times that cricket was not the only thing in life. Miller and Compton were good friends who enjoyed life off the field too.

Miller liked a drink and a bet on the horses and came to move in the highest echelons of society. He was a friend of the Queen's sister Princess Margaret and was a regular at the Royal Ascot race meeting when he was in England.

Having made 181 on his first-class debut for Victoria, he first made his mark at international level in the Victory Tests in 1945, scoring two centuries. He also scored a magnificent 185 for a Dominions XI against England at Lord's in only three hours when the next top score was 40. One of his sixes landed in a commentary box on the top tier of the pavilion.

As a bowler he formed a formidable new-ball partnership with Ray Lindwall and had an array of variations or yorkers, bouncers and even leg-breaks. In only his second Test, at Brisbane in 1946, he took advantage of some damp conditions

'Keith Miller is the most unpredictable cricketer I have played against. I am never quite sure what he is going to do next and I don't think he knows himself until he is about to do it' – Len Hutton

to bowl England out and achieve what would remain his best Test figures of seven for 60.

At Lord's in 1956, aged 36 and on his final tour of England, he had to lead the Australian attack because both Lindwall and Alan Davidson were injured. He bowled 70 overs in the match and took five wickets in each innings to secure Australia's only win of the series and their first in England for eight years.

Having scored 109 at Lord's in 1953 it meant that at the time Miller was one of only three people to have both scored a century and taken five wickets in a Test innings at Lord's.

Full name: Keith Ross Miller
Born: 28 November 1919, Sunshine, Melbourne
Died: 11 October 2004, Mornington Peninsula, Melbourne
International career span: 1946–56
Role: Right-hand middle-order batsman; right-arm fast bowler
Notable numbers: 55 Tests, 2,958 runs at 36.97, seven hundreds; 170 wickets at 22.97, best bowling seven for 60
Extras: Awarded the MBE in 1956 and the Order of Australia posthumously in 2005; in retirement was a journalist and columnist, employed by the *Daily Express* in London for 20 years

THE MCG

The Melbourne Cricket Ground, or simply the G as Melburnians call it, is a colosseum of sporting theatre. It hosts the traditional Boxing Day Test when it is packed to its lofty rafters with anything between 80,000 and 90,000 spectators.

Then there is Aussie rules football. The G hosts a number of the main Melbourne teams and the AFL Grand Final, a guaranteed sell-out and the biggest event in the Australian sporting calendar. It has hosted soccer internationals, rugby of both codes, papal visits and the 1956 Olympic Games.

And for all of the claims of Lord's to be the home of cricket, the MCG was the venue for the first-ever Test played in March 1877 between Australia and England. The Australian Charles Bannerman became Test cricket's first run-scorer and the first century-maker and both teams spent the first evening at the opera. England lost by 45 runs, their pursuit of 154 for victory possibly hampered by a beery lunch.

The capacity of the MCG has been as much as 125,000 until modernizations in the 1980s and 1990s reduced it to a mere 100,000. That figure

MCG's notable numbers (to 9 Feb 2012)

Capacity: 100,000
No. of Tests: 104 (1877-2012)
Highest team score: 604, Aus v. Eng, 1937
Lowest team score: 36, South Africa v. Australia, 1932
Highest individual score: 307, Bob Cowper for Australia v. England, 1966
Most Test runs: 1,671, Don Bradman (Australia), 1928-48
Best individual bowling: 9-86, Sarfraz Nawaz for Pakistan v. Australia, 1979
Most Test wickets: 82, Dennis Lillee (Australia), 1972-83
No. of ODIs: 133 (1971-2012)
Highest ODI team score: 344-8, ICC World XI v. Asia XI 2005
Highest ODI individual score: 173, Mark Waugh for Australia v. West Indies 2001

England lost the first Test in 1877 possibly hampered by a beery lunch

does include some standing room which is used at the discretion of individual event organizers. So for most events it is more like 97,000.

The Great Southern Stand sweeps round half the stadium and contains about half the MCG's spectators. It also houses the infamous Bay 13, a section of the crowd known for giving boundary fielders a torrid time.

The record attendance for a day's cricket was 90,800 for Australia against West Indies in 1961 though the first day of the 2006 Ashes Test ran it close with 89,155 people witnessing the local boy

Shane Warne take his 700th Test wicket on a day of classically fickle Melbourne weather when the summer temperature was 10°C.

Other memorable matches include the 1992 World Cup final between England and Pakistan and one of the closest Test finishes when England beat Australia by three runs in 1982.

The G was also the venue for the two highest team totals in first-class history, the only two scores over 1,000 both made by Victoria. In 1923 they racked up 1,059 against Tasmania and three years later 1,107 against New South Wales.

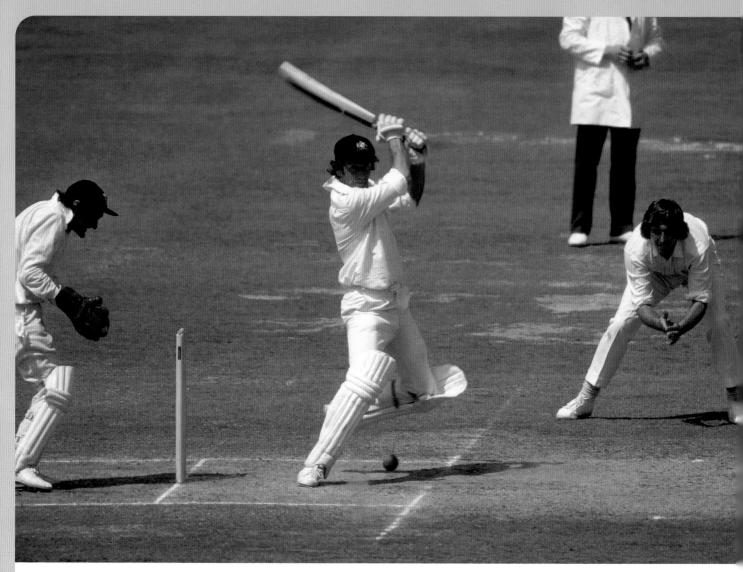

Forceful: Australian captain Ian Chappell batting during the Lord's Test against England in 1975.

THUNDER DOWN UNDER

Often a new captain takes the reins at the end of a losing series in the hope that he can arrest the slide and orchestrate a change in fortunes. So it was that Ian Chappell took over from Bill Lawry for the final Test of the 1970–71 Ashes. England had won the series to hold the urn for the first time in 15 years. The previous year Australia had been trounced 4-0 in South Africa.

Chappell infused the team with all his own energy and aggression, turning them into the best side in the world for much of the 1970s. He was part of a cricketing dynasty to match England's Grace family of the Victorian era.

Chappell's grandfather was Victor Richardson, a former captain of Australia who played in the Bodyline series of 1932–33. Ian's younger brother Greg, a teammate though not so much a mate, was one of Australia's finest-ever batsmen and the youngest Trevor also wore the baggy green cap, though his was an inglorious legacy.

'There's no prize for running second, pal,' said Ian Chappell

England retained the Ashes in 1972 at home after a 2-2 draw but the emergence of Dennis Lillee, who took 31 wickets, was a real plus point for Australia. In the second Test at Lord's they won – after a run of 12 Tests without a win via an astonishing debut performance from a West Australian swing bowler, Bob Massie (*below*). Utilizing humid, overcast conditions and also benefiting from the hostility of Lillee at the other end, Massie swung the ball prodigiously. He took eight wickets in each innings yet played only five more Tests in his career.

Lord's was clearly Massie's Match but Greg Chappell made a vital century and added a century stand with Ian that stabilized Australia's first innings. Both brothers made centuries in the final Test of the series at The Oval, which Australia won to level the series. The previous Test at Leeds had been hugely controversial. On a pitch described by the commentator and former Australian captain Richie Benaud as 'a disgrace to the name of Test cricket', Derek Underwood, the England spinner, took ten wickets in the match to secure the Ashes.

Spot the difference: the Chappell brothers, Greg (left) and Ian, walk out to bat at Southampton against Hampshire in 1975.

The Chappell brothers might not have been soulmates but they certainly formed an effective bond at the crease. They batted 37 times together in Tests, putting on six century stands and averaging 52 runs each time they paired up, mostly with Ian coming at No.3 and Greg at four.

They could not have been more different. Ian wore his shirt unbuttoned, was aggressive and attacking as batsman and captain. 'There's no prize for running second, pal,' he said when he took over the captaincy. Greg had his hair cut neatly, often wore his shirt buttoned to his wrists and batted with a modest style that marked him out as Australia's best batsman of his generation.

Ian was a champion of workers' rights and fought against the Australian board about the poor wages players were paid. This was a conflict that led to the establishment of Kerry Packer's rebel World Series Cricket series in the late 1970s and caused Australia, and many other countries, to lose their best players to the new venture. Ian went on to become a respected and outspoken commentator and newspaper columnist while Greg became a cerebral and not always popular coach. He famously fell out with the captain Sourav Ganguly when he was coach of India in 2007.

After the farce of the Leeds Ashes Test in 1972 Australia lost only one Test in the next two years, beating Pakistan at home, West Indies away and New Zealand home and away before welcoming

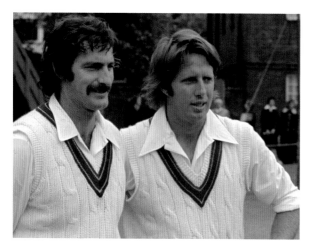

Don't be fooled by the smiles: pacemen Dennis Lillee (left) and Jeff Thomson in less threatening mode at Lord's in 1975.

'I just shuffle up and go whang' was how Thomson described his unique style that involved his bowling arm being stretched straight behind his back before catapulting the ball over his shoulder towards the batsman. Greg Chappell tells a story about captaining Thomson at state level when at the start of a season his first few balls were no-balls. Chappell could not understand what was going wrong so approached Thommo who nonchalantly asked his skipper if he knew how long his run-up was supposed to be.

Australia would better the England scoreline when they took on Clive Lloyd's West Indies side in 1975–76, just a few months after the Windies had beaten them at Lord's in the inaugural one-day World Cup final.

On the first morning of the series West Indies were 125 for six, a tempestuous session that set the

England back in 1974–75. This series and the one that followed a year later against West Indies represents the high-water mark for this Australia era of the Chappells, Dennis Lillee and the great wicketkeeper Rod Marsh.

England were left battered, bruised and broken, often in the most literal sense. The opening batsman Geoff Boycott withdrew a month before the squad left for Australia because 'he couldn't do justice to himself'. Three batsmen suffered broken bones and the captain Mike Denness was so traumatized that he dropped himself from the team for the fourth Test. England even summoned the 41-year-old Colin Cowdrey to bolster their beleaguered batting line-up. It didn't work. Cowdrey's top score was 41 and Australia regained the Ashes with a 4-1 thrashing.

Australia caught the old enemy totally unawares both with the recovery to full fitness of Lillee and with the discovery of Jeff Thomson, from New South Wales, who bowled as fast, if not faster, than any bowler has ever done. In 1978 he took part in a contest to measure bowling speeds and was clocked at 92mph (147.9km/h), ahead of Michael Holding and Imran Khan.

One of the defining images of that 1974–75 Ashes is of the England batsman David Lloyd doubling up after being hit in the groin by a ball from Thomson that reared up from a good length.

Bumble rumbled: England's David Lloyd caught by Thomson off Lillee at Sydney during Australia's 4-1 Ashes win in 1974-75.

Ian Chappell: 'I don't think West Indies realized how good they were'

tone for the series. West Indies' array of young, talented but naïve batsmen just tried to take on the Aussie bowlers and came unstuck. 'I don't think they realized how good they were,' said Ian Chappell who had passed on the captaincy to Greg by this stage. The West Indies batsmen became known as 'the Hapless Hookers'. 'It took us a while to learn that the grounds were bigger,' said the captain, Clive Lloyd.

Greg scored two centuries in that first Test at Brisbane. In the series as a whole he made 702 runs at 117. Ian made a very respectable 449 at 44.

For West Indies it was a series that crystallized their belief that fast bowlers rather than spinners were the way forward, a tactical decision that would shape the cricket world for the next decade and more.

For Australia this was the end of a brief but brilliant era. The defections to Packer's breakaway circus would weaken their team substantially until the conflict with officialdom was resolved.

In February 1981 Trevor Chappell, the youngest of the three brothers, would make his mark in the game's history. With New Zealand needing six to win off the last ball of a one-day international at Melbourne, his brother Greg, the Australian captain, instructed him to bowl underarm along the ground. Marsh was disapproving behind the stumps and brother Ian equally unhappy in the Channel 9 television commentary box. The former Australia captain Richie Benaud, summing up for Channel 9, described it as 'one of the worst things I've ever seen on a cricket field'.

In January 1984 three legends, Greg Chappell, Marsh and Lillee, retired at the same time, leaving Australia bereft of world-beating talent. They would recover, of course, and then some but it would take a while.

Pretty in pink: West Indies, in the coral pink uniforms, take on Australia at Sydney in 1979 during World Series Cricket.

World Series Cricket

When the Australian Cricket Board refused to sell the broadcasting rights for Test cricket to the media mogul Kerry Packer, who owned the commercial Nine Network, Packer decided to set up his own rival cricket venture, called World Series Cricket (WSC).

He recruited the best players from Australia and around the world and paid them serious money, dwarfing the meagre salaries they received from their governing bodies who maintained an antiquated view of employer-employee relations.

The International Cricket Council initially tried to ban Packer recruits from all forms of official cricket, a decision that was overturned in the London High Court in 1977.

WSC kicked off in December 1977 with a series of 'Supertests' involving Australia, West Indies and a World XI. The matches were under floodlights and the players wore coloured clothing. Cricket had never seen anything like it.

With the main cricket venues out of bounds to Packer, the games took place at Australian rules football venues on some spicy pitches that led to a number of injuries.

The players involved remember WSC as some of the fiercest, most intense, high-quality cricket they ever played, even though the crowds were poor.

After two seasons of WSC Packer finally got his wish and secured the television rights to cricket in Australia, which Channel 9 still holds. The game and the way it was staged, for better or worse, had changed forever.

Dennis Lillee

There was no more stylish exponent of the fast bowler's art than Dennis Lillee. His run to the wicket and side-on bowling action were full of grace and fluidity, a perfect example of how it was supposed to be done.

But allied to the style and beneath the trademark drooping 1970s' moustache was an abundance of snarling menace. 'Lill-ee, Lill-ee,' the vast, baying crowds across Australia would chant gleefully as his approach to the stumps picked up pace.

Lillee was the spearhead of a great Australian side who played hard on the field, drank hard off it. They weren't shy of a verbal joust with opponents but happy to share a cold beer at the end of play.

He was ferociously fast in the early part of his career. When South Africa's tour of Australia in 1971–72 was cancelled a series against a World XI was scheduled. In the second match at Perth Lillee announced himself. Despite nursing a virus and feeling 'shocking', he took eight for 29 to dismiss the World XI for 59. He followed that with 31 wickets at an average of 17 in the 1972 Ashes series in England.

'Few bowlers had finer physique or technique, or such a gloriously flowing action' – John Arlott

But a stress fracture of the back kept him sidelined for over a year and threatened his career. It was only through his sheer desire and dedication that he was able to make a comeback.

When England toured Australia in 1974–75 they had assumed that Lillee was done for. Instead they were greeted by a rehabilitated Lillee plus an unknown tearaway called Jeff Thomson. The pair formed one of most frightening and effective bowling combinations in history to demolish England 4-1.

As his fitness and confidence returned, Lillee bowled 'with a hostility that bordered on savagery', according to *Wisden*. He did not take more than four wickets in an innings during the series but finished with 25 wickets at 23 apiece while Thomson took 33. He was fast and accurate too in the Centenary Test of 1977 at Melbourne, taking 11 wickets in the thrilling match that Australia won by 45 runs.

Whatever compromises Lillee had to make on pace over time, he more than made up for in guile. He knew how to get batsmen out. In the Melbourne Boxing Day Test of 1981, he achieved his best Test figures of seven for 83 against West Indies and passed the 309 of West Indian spinner Lance Gibbs to become the world's leading Test wicket-taker in the process, a title he still held when he retired in 1984.

In 1979 he came out to bat against England with an aluminium bat. After Lillee had played one shot with it his captain, Greg Chappell, ordered him to change it. He responded by throwing the bat back towards the pavilion. The laws of the game were amended to specify that bats had to be made of wood.

Full name: Dennis Keith Lillee
Born: 18 July 1949, Perth
International career span: 1971–84
Role: Right-arm fast opening bowler; right-hand lower-order batsman
Notable numbers: 70 Tests, 355 wickets at 23.92, best bowling seven for 83, 23 five-wicket innings; one ten-wicket match; world's leading Test wicket-taker 1981–86; remained Australia's leading wicket-taker until 2000
Extras: Set up a renowned pace-bowling academy in Chennai; continued to play competitive cricket until he was 50; statue of him situated outside the MCG

Sweeping statement: Australia captain Allan Border batting at Lord's during the 1989 Ashes, a series Australia won 4-0.

BAGGY GREEN GIANTS

It is possible to mark the moment exactly. On 3 May 1995 Australia defeated West Indies at Sabina Park in Jamaica to clinch a 2-1 series win.

West Indies had not lost any of their previous 29 Test series stretching back to 1980. Australia had not won a series in the Caribbean since the early 1970s. For Australia this victory meant the world, literally. They had finally slain the giant and they would dominate the cricketing planet for the next decade and beyond.

From the start of the series in the Caribbean to the start of the 2005 Ashes (which England won for the first time in 18 years) they played 118 Tests, winning 78 and losing only 22. They drew a tiny number too, only 18, which was an example

of the relentlessly attacking, positive cricket that they played, inspired by their smart captain, Mark Taylor. Their batsmen sought to exert pressure from the off, rather than build it slowly and patiently as Test cricket's traditions dictated. And then it was over to Glenn McGrath and Shane Warne to take the wickets.

McGrath's career was in its infancy at this point but he had to learn fast because Australia's two leading pace bowlers of the time – Craig McDermott and Damien Fleming – both missed the series through injury.

It was a brutal and controversial series dominated surprisingly by the bowlers and the batting of Steve Waugh who, despite a

The Ashes became a ritual display of Antipodean excellence

reputation for struggling against short-pitched bowling, made 429 runs in the four Tests at 107. The decisive final-Test victory in Jamaica was founded on an epic partnership of 231 between the Waugh brothers. Steve made 200, putting to bed the notion that he couldn't play short-pitched bowling, while his more flamboyant twin Mark made a highly disciplined 126. The stand broke West Indies, reducing their fast bowler, Winston Benjamin, to tears.

In the first Test in Barbados Steve Waugh had claimed a catch off Brian Lara that TV replays later showed to have hit the ground. Waugh claimed he was certain it was a clean catch but the incident led to him being booed every time he came in to bat, verbal confrontations with senior West Indies players and threatening phone calls in the middle of the night. The night before his decisive innings at Sabina Park he was woken by a hotel security guard rummaging through his belongings.

The Asian subcontinent remained a bridge too far for Australia but in every other territory they were too hot to handle.

The Ashes, which had been regained in 1989 under the hard-boiled leadership of Allan Border (*right*), became a ritual display of Antipodean excellence. Every two years England would try to convince themselves they had a chance. Time and again they came up short.

In 1997 England even won the first Test of the series, the first time they had led in the Ashes for ten years. But in the second Test at Lord's Glenn McGrath

Metronomic miser: Glenn McGrath, scourge of the Poms (and of Mike Atherton in particular) bowling at The Oval in 2001.

was unplayable. The match was actually drawn because so much time was lost to rain but McGrath, in his first full Ashes series, was devastating once play got under way on the second day.

He took eight wickets for 38 runs to dismiss England for 77. This was McGrath in his element. The pitch was uneven, the murky weather favouring the bowlers, and he probed away unremittingly from the pavilion end. Bowling from that end at Lord's means the famous slope (eight feet from the Grandstand side to the Tavern) has the potential to take the ball

Lording it: Glenn McGrath leads the Australian team from the field at Lord's in 1997, having taken eight for 38.

into the right-handed batsman. Alec Stewart left a McGrath delivery alone only to see the ball nip back and clatter his stumps.

McGrath would return to Lord's every four years with a smile while batsmen frowned and tensed at the other end. He would even have a spell playing county cricket there for Middlesex.

He had taken up cricket only in his teens when he was spotted playing for his club in upcountry New South Wales. He was persuaded to move to Sydney to pursue his ambitions, where he lived off baked beans in a caravan.

He was a fast bowler to begin with but refined his method to become one of the most consistently accurate seam bowlers the game has seen. A gentle, straight run to the crease led to a ball dropped on the same awkward spot: just outside off stump, full enough for the batsman to think about playing forward to but not full enough to drive. He extracted bounce because

of his height and he had just enough pace for most of his career to hurry batsmen.

McGrath took a wicket every nine overs through his Test career and was especially productive against England whose batsmen turned into jibbering wrecks at the mere sight of him marking out his run-up. He took 157 of his 563 Test wickets in Ashes contests, 19 of them Mike Atherton.

The next Ashes series in 1998–99 marked the end of Taylor's captaincy

Top of the world: Australia, captained by Steve Waugh, with the World Cup trophy after beating Pakistan at Lord's in 1999.

Not for the first or last time Waugh made fools of his doubters

reign. A few months earlier against Pakistan in Peshawar he had equalled Don Bradman's highest Test score by an Australian. Having made 334 not out, Taylor declared. It was simply a tactical judgement though it was tempting to interpret that Taylor did not wish to eclipse The Don's score.

Taylor was succeeded by Steve Waugh (*left*) who was already one-day captain. Taylor had been such an impressive and popular leader that there were concerns that Waugh's drive and intensity would not lend themselves to being the skipper. Not for the first or last time in his career Waugh made fools of his doubters.

Despite losing his first series as Test captain – an astonishing four-match rubber in the Caribbean lit up by Brian Lara – Waugh would end the millennium with a World Cup trophy and his side in the midst of a record-breaking run of Test wins.

West Indies set the record of 11 successive victories in 1984 and fittingly they were the opponents at Brisbane in late 2000 when Australia equalled it. The Test was another triumph for McGrath who bowled 33 overs and conceded only 27 runs while taking ten wickets.

Australia won five more Tests before their run came to a spectacular end in India in early 2001. They had won the first Test of the series at Mumbai and were heading for victory in the second at Kolkata's Eden Gardens when India produced an astonishing recovery to become only the third side in history to win a Test after a following on.

STEVE WAUGH

Once damned by Ian Chappell as 'not even the best all-rounder in his own family', Steve Waugh's own desire for self-improvement became a symbol for the Australian team's relentless, ruthless drive for excellence.

A less stylish batsman than his younger twin Mark, he made his debut in Australia's 1986–87 Ashes defeat as a medium-pace bowler and gung-ho middle-order batsman. Over time the bowling would become occasional while the batting was modified to avoid risk and increase his scoring percentages.

He took 42 innings to make a Test hundred but once he did, scoring 177 not out at Leeds in the first Test of the 1989 Ashes, he did not stop for 15 years. He scored 350 runs in that series before England could get him out and would be a thorn in their side for his entire career.

He coined the phrase 'mental disintegration', a euphemism for the verbal taunts (sledging) and gamesmanship that became a theme of Australia's dominance through the 1990s and early 2000s. He led Australia in 15 of their 16 record-breaking Test wins between 1999 and 2001.

When he took over from Mark Taylor as Test captain in 1999 he elevated Australia's baggy green cap from simply a piece of headwear to the status of holy relic. And Waugh's faded, threadbare cap itself had the look of a relic by the time he retired in 2004. In the past new caps had been dished out at the start of each series or tour but in the Waugh years players clung to a single baggy green come hell or high water, or hours sweating in the hot sun.

Some opponents tired of Waugh's devotion, seeing self-righteousness, where supporters simply revelled in the success. Before the 2001 tour to England Waugh took his players to Gallipoli in Turkey, where 9,000 Australian soldiers died during World War I.

'He gave grit a good name when everyone seemed obsessed with flair' – Rahul Dravid

On that tour Waugh tore a calf muscle in the third Test and it was presumed he would miss the rest of the series. Yet he returned three weeks later to play in the final Test at The Oval and scored 157 not out. He was always at his most effective when the odds were stacked against him and his side needed a contribution.

At Sydney in the final Test of the next Ashes in January 2003 he equalled Allan Border's record of Test appearances: 156. With the final ball of the second day he smashed a boundary through the off side to reach his 29th Test hundred and his home ground rose as one.

He played on for another year, finally calling it a day against India at Sydney. He just missed out on a fairy-tale hundred, caught on the boundary when he had made 80. 'It shows that after 168 Tests you can still lose the plot under pressure,' he said.

Full name: Stephen Rodger Waugh
Born: 2 June 1965, Canterbury, New South Wales
International career span: 1986–2004
Role: Right-hand middle-order batsman, right-arm medium-pace bowler
Notable numbers: 168 Tests (second most behind Sachin Tendulkar), 10,927 runs at 51.06, 32 hundreds, 50 fifties; 7,569 ODI runs in 325 matches
Extras: Set up a children's charity in India; awarded the Order of Australia in 2003; in 2011, as a member of MCC's world cricket committee, he called for lie detector tests as a match-fixing deterrent; nicknamed 'Tugga'

Melbourne milestone: Shane Warne congratulated by teammates after taking his 700th Test wicket: Andrew Strauss.

REVENGE MISSION

While England were wallowing in the gleeful glory of the 2005 Ashes, Ricky Ponting and his Australian side were plotting revenge for the Poms' visit in late 2006. England and their supporters deluded themselves that the 2005 victory, their first in the Ashes for 18 years, was the start of something big. Injury and complacency actually meant it was the high-water mark for a team that seemed to have much going for it.

Australia might have been an ageing team in 2005 but they were not finished. The backlash started immediately with the reclaiming of the Tasmanian bowling coach Troy Cooley, who had been so instrumental to England's 2005 win.

End of an era: three retirees – Warne, Glenn McGrath and Justin Langer – before the fifth and final Test at Sydney.

At the MCG the great showman engineered the neatest curtain call

Deadly double act: McGrath and Warne leave the international stage for the final time after the 5-0 win is sealed at Sydney.

Their first post-Ashes opponents were an ICC World XI. It seemed like a good idea on paper, pitting this great Australian side against the best of the rest. But the Test and three one-dayers were one-sided affairs that were not to be repeated and reaffirmed that the only international cricket that really matters is a contest between two countries. Australia were well-prepared and motivated while the World XI were neither of those things.

Australia did not lose another Test for more than two years and matched the 16-game winning streak of the Steve Waugh era.

The 2005 defeat in England was avenged in the most comprehensive, glorious way possible: a 5-0 whitewash that crowned the peerless careers of Warne and McGrath. Both these legends of the game retired from international cricket after the final Test at Sydney along with Justin Langer, whose opening partnership with Matthew Hayden had set the tone for many an Aussie victory.

Langer it was who was facing Steve Harmison for the first ball of the series at Brisbane. He may well have been expecting the sort of rib-tickler that he received at Lord's 16 months earlier. Instead, he watched as the ball veered so wide it went straight to Andrew Flintoff, England's ill-fated captain, at second slip. The direction of the Ashes had been set.

England should have stemmed the tide in the second Test at Adelaide, having racked up 551 for six declared. But on the final day, as England were theoretically batting out time for a draw, Warne drew on his mystical powers and reopened all the old English wounds.

From 69 for one they collapsed to 129 all out and Australia knocked off the runs as the Adelaide Oval filled with excited, disbelieving fans who heard something remarkable was happening.

The Ashes were regained at Perth before Warne announced his intention to retire at the end of the series. On a freezing cold Boxing Day on his home ground at the MCG, Warne took his 700th Test wicket when he bowled Andrew Strauss and 89,000 people clicked their camera phones to record the moment. The great showman had engineered the neatest curtain call.

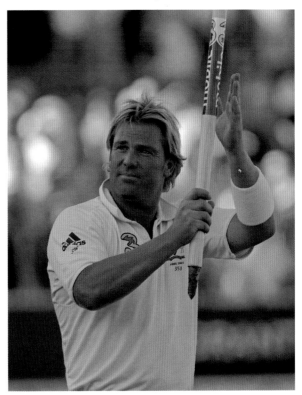

Stumped again: Warne takes the Adelaide applause after initiating England's final-day meltdown that put Australia 2-0 up.

SHANE WARNE

The look on Mike Gatting's face spoke volumes. The sharp intake of breath through his grey-bearded chops was one of shock and some pain, as if someone had just stood on his foot. As he walked from the field, dismissed by what the English tabloids instantly labelled 'the ball of the century', his discomfort turned to bewilderment. It was Manchester, 1993: Shane Warne's first delivery in an Ashes Test.

'We will never see anything closer to perfection' – Mike Atherton

Australia had not had a great leg-spinner since the 1930s and the rest of the world barely knew what one looked like any more in a game dominated by fast bowlers. Warne changed all that. He was a spinner with a fast bowler's mind-set. Always attacking, always probing, always thinking. He became almost without argument the greatest practitioner of spin bowling in history.

He was – and still is – always centre stage on and off the field whether it's skittling the Poms, duelling with Tendulkar or talking his way out of a sex scandal. He received a doping ban in 2003 and in 1998 admitted, along with Mark Waugh, receiving money from a bookmaker for information.

He has a shrewd cricket brain and but for his unpredictable lifestyle would surely have captained Australia (he did 11 one-dayers as a stand-in).

Initially, his sporting ambitions lay in Australian rules football with his beloved St Kilda club but he turned his attentions to cricket. He left the Australian cricket academy by mutual consent, an early sign that he would not be tamed by convention. He lived on cheese sandwiches, chips and what he would jokingly refer to as a fruit platter: ham and pineapple pizzas.

Warne was not intimately acquainted with modern training methods but he was physically resilient, coming back from shoulder and finger injuries, and mentally always one step ahead of his opponents. He toyed with England for a decade and more and labelled the South African batsman Daryll Cullinan his 'bunny'.

With chunky fingers and an iron wrist, he fizzed the ball this way and that, mastering an armoury of variations that diddled most batsmen who faced him. Only in India, the home of spin bowling, was he blunted with any consistency.

His leadership ambitions were fulfilled in English county cricket with Hampshire, whom he helped transform into trophy contenders, and Rajasthan Royals in the Indian Premier League. Without the assistance of a coach he led the unfancied Royals to the inaugural IPL title.

He retired on a high, having become the first man to take 700 Test wickets and secured a 5-0 Ashes whitewash. In late 2011 he came out of retirement to play for the Melbourne Stars in Australia's revamped Twenty20 competition, the Big Bash League.

Full name: Shane Keith Warne
Born: 13 September 1969, Ferntree Gully, Victoria
International career span: 1992–2007
Role: Right-arm leg-spin bowler, right-hand lower-order bat
Notable numbers: 145 Tests, 708 wickets (second all-time to Muttiah Muralitharan), 37 five-wicket innings and ten ten-wicket matches; holds record for most Test runs (3,154) without a century – highest score 99
Extras: One of five Wisden Cricketers of the Century; TV commentator; professional poker player; divorced from first wife Simone (three children) and now engaged to the English actress and model Elizabeth Hurley

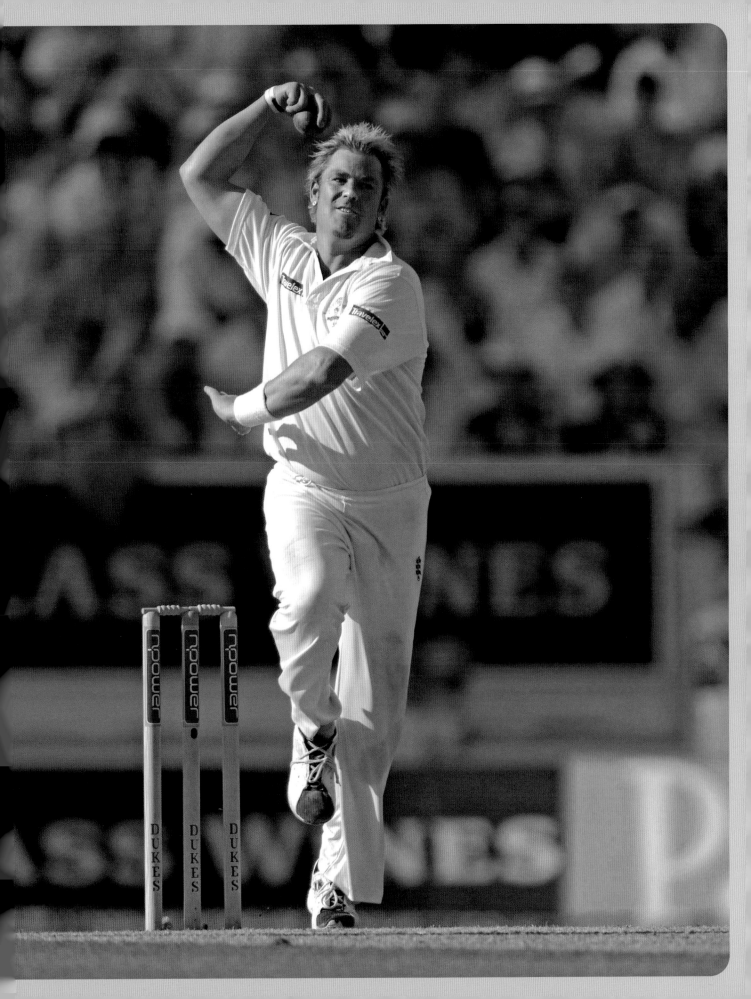

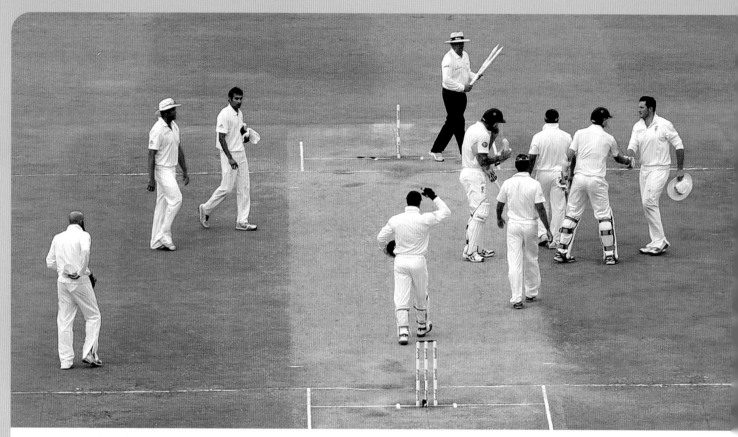

Cummins and goings: South Africa captain, Graeme Smith (far right), congratulates Australia's tail-enders after the 18-year-old debutant Pat Cummins had hit the winning runs at Johannesburg to complete a two-wicket win and level the two-match series.

GENERATION NEXT

Officially the crown slipped in mid-2009 when South Africa took over from Australia as the No.1 Test side in the world. But the tipping point had come in late 2008 when Australia lost a home Test series to South Africa for the first time.

The cracks had been evident at the start of 2008 when the traditional New Year Test at Sydney, with India the opponents, turned nasty. An allegation of racism was levelled by the mixed-race Australian all-rounder Andrew Symonds at Harbhajan Singh, the Indian spinner.

India threatened to call off the tour while the Australians denied the accusations. Then there seemed to be a watershed moment when the late Peter Roebuck, the *Sydney Morning Herald* columnist, called for Ricky Ponting to be sacked as captain. It was not that Australia were not performing – they won the series – but a sense that they were losing control of the aggression

that had been central to their decade or so of dominance. Australia clearly still had talented players but they were becoming unpredictable. In the past they always won the big moments in a match, like that point in an arm-wrestle where suddenly one contestant can down his opponent and a seemingly even tussle is over in an instant.

Now those big moments were being won by Australia's opponents. At Perth in December 2008 South Africa were set a huge 414 to win and got them for the loss of four wickets. In the next Test at Melbourne South Africa were 184 for seven, replying to Australia's first innings of 394, but finished with 459 thanks to a ninth-wicket stand of 180 between the young left-hander JP Duminy and the No.10 batsman Dale Steyn. South Africa won the Test easily and with it the series.

Shane Warne was, inevitably, proving irreplaceable and the selectors rifled through an

Hitting out: Andrew Symonds, here batting against England at Melbourne, was at the centre of a race row at Sydney in 2008.

selectors changed and a performance manager with a rugby union background was introduced. And in late 2011 a non-Australian was appointed national coach for the first time: the South African Mickey Arthur who had guided his own country to the No.1 Test spot via the 2008 victory in Australia.

Arthur's first summer in charge was a rollercoaster. At Cape Town they skittled South Africa for 96, only to sink themselves to a jaw-dropping 47 all out and lose the Test. They won the next one in a nail-biting finish as they chased down 310. Pat Cummins, an 18-year-old fast bowler making his debut, took seven wickets in the match and hit the winning runs.

New Zealand were crushed at Brisbane only for more wretched batting at Hobart to hand the Kiwis their first Test win on Australian soil for a generation.

But the visit of India and their *galacticos* was a stunning triumph with Australia inflicting on India their second 4-0 thrashing within a matter of months. Ben Hilfenhaus and Peter Siddle, pace bowlers tarnished by Ashes failures, re-emerged with 50 wickets between them while Ponting and the new captain, Michael Clarke, both averaged over 100 with the bat. Just like the good old days.

endless assortment of spin bowlers searching for the next blond bombshell. In the five years following Warne's retirement in January 2007 Australia picked 11 different specialist spinners.

In the 2009 Ashes they outscored England – eight of their batsmen scored hundreds to England's two – yet they lost the series 2-1. They would have less cause to quibble about the result in the return Ashes series of 2010–11 when they lost three Tests by an innings. In March 2011 they lost a World Cup match for the first time since 1999, a run of 34 matches without defeat.

The 2010–11 Ashes defeat prompted the sort of reappraisal of the whole way Australian cricket is run that had been the preserve of the English for the previous 15 years. The captaincy changed, the

The selectors rifled through an endless assortment of spinners

Changing Times

Australia v. Pakistan, Lord's, July 2010	Australia v. New Zealand, Hobart, December 2011
Shane Watson	David Warner
Simon Katich	Phil Hughes
Ricky Ponting (capt)	Usman Khawaja
Michael Clarke	Ricky Ponting
Mike Hussey	Michael Clarke (capt)
Marcus North	Mike Hussey
Tim Paine (wk)	Brad Haddin (wk)
Steve Smith	Peter Siddle
Mitchell Johnson	James Pattinson
Ben Hilfenhaus	Mitchell Starc
Doug Bollinger	Nathan Lyon

RICKY PONTING

Ricky Ponting was the youngster of Australia's golden generation, a super-talented teenager who was given his first sponsored bat deal aged 12 and made his Test debut at 20 in 1995. Consequently, he was the last man standing after Warne, McGrath, Gilchrist and others had all taken their leave at much the same time.

He is Australia's leading Test run-scorer but has captained his side to defeat in three Ashes series. As a batsman he will be remembered with due reverence, a combination of power and panache who overcame personal demons, admitting to an alcohol problem, to become one of the greats. In terms of run-scoring records (*see below*), he is pretty much second only to Sachin Tendulkar in most categories.

He captained by example rather than tactical nous and struggled to come to terms with being in charge of a side that no longer possessed a stash of get-out-of-jail-free cards.

But rather than walk away from the job as life became tougher he stuck at it, determined, it seemed, to lead Australia back to the top. The crushing Ashes defeat in 2010–11, and his own declining form with the bat, made that impossible and he was replaced by Michael Clarke.

Once he was freed of the captaincy, though, the runs returned in the 4-0 whitewash of India: a double-hundred, a century and three fifties. In early 2012 he was dropped from the one-day side and announced his retirement from that format.

In the latter stages of his career a vulnerability against the swinging ball became increasingly apparent but in his pomp he was so quick on his feet and so strong in his wrists that bowlers had no margin for error. Too full and the ball would be punched through the covers, a fraction too short and Ponting would lash the ball through the leg side with his signature pull-shot.

His front-foot aggression was as effective in the one-day arena and his unbeaten 140 at

'Ponting may trail Tendulkar on batting aesthetics but not on perseverance' – Ian Chappell

Johannesburg against India in 2003 was the ultimate captain's innings and, at the time, the highest in a World Cup final. It sealed the second of Australia's three successive titles.

In the field he was hawk-eyed and agile, equally adept in the slips for a Test match or patrolling the covers in a one-dayer.

He is, as Michael Parkinson wrote in *Wisden*, a typical Australian working-class hero. He will fight to the bitter end, as his epic 156 to save the Manchester Test of 2005 showed. He is driven to prove a point, routinely crafting an innings of substance when his powers are being questioned.

And he has always been physically tough: fielding at silly point just yards from the batsman during the 2009 Ashes, he was hit in the mouth by a cover drive from Matt Prior who asked him if he was all right. Ponting's response was unrepeatable. He just spat out a bit of blood and carried on.

Full name: Ricky Thomas Ponting
Born: 19 December 1974, Launceston, Tasmania
International career span: 1995–
Role: Top-order right-handed batsman
Notable numbers: As of Feb 2012, third-highest Test run-scorer of all time (13,200); equal second most Test hundreds (41); second highest ODI run-scorer in history (13,689); second most ODI hundreds (30); second highest World Cup run-scorer (2,278)
Extras: His uncle Greg Campbell played four Tests for Australia from 1989–90; nicknamed 'Punter' because he likes to bet on greyhound racing (also owns greyhounds)

The scoreboard shows:

BOWLER	RUNS			BATSMEN	
EDRICH		AUST. 1ST INNS.	405	CHAPPELL	5 15
AMISS		ENGLAND 1ST INNS.	295		
FLETCHER		AUST. 2ND INNS.			
LLOYD		Nº OF OVER	10		
COWDREY		OVERS LST HR			
UNDERWOOD				BATSMEN	
TITMUS				REDPATH	16
GREIG				G.CHAPPELL	18
ARNOLD	20			FOR	40
WILLIS	19			SUNDRIES	

1975 ROYAL EASTER SHOW 21ST MARCH TO 1ST APRIL

UNAUTHORIZED ➤ ENTRY TO PLAYING AREA IS PROHIBITED

BENSON and HEDGES CRICKET AWARDS

THE SCG

With its historic green-roofed Members' Pavilion and Ladies Stand, the Sydney Cricket Ground is redolent of a bygone age. While the rest of the ground has modernized these two stands retain their traditional characteristics and inspire memories of Bradman scoring his timeless runs and O'Reilly spinning batsmen out with his leg spin.

To many Sydney is the spiritual home of Australian cricket in that the state side New South Wales is the most successful domestic team and has traditionally provided more players for the national side than any other state. But this supremacy is viewed disparagingly by Australians from elsewhere in the country who joke that when a player wins his NSW blue cap he receives an Aussie baggy green at the same time.

Opposite the SCG's Members' Pavilion is what used to be known as 'The Hill', a swathe of grassy bank populated by the most vocal supporters often fuelled by booze, dishing out home truths and tactical wisdom to opposition players. The Hill, like its Melbourne equivalent Bay 13, is gone now, replaced by the Victor Trumper stand.

The Hill was populated by the most vocal supporters often fuelled by booze

Originally the SCG was a batsman's pitch and was where Don Bradman made a world-record 452 not out for NSW in 1930. But in more recent times it became a spinner's paradise with even part-time twirlers cashing in. In 1989 Allan Border, an occasional left-arm spinner, took seven for 46 against West Indies and four more in the second innings.

According to Michael Clarke, the Australian captain and New South Welshman, conditions have changed again. 'The last couple of years it's quickened up a bit and there's been enough there for the bowlers, swing and seam,' he said.

Clarke captained Australia against India in January 2012 in the 100th Test to be played at the SCG. He marked the occasion by scoring 329 not out, the highest Test score on the ground, as Australia went 2-0 up in the series.

Before the Test a panel of experts selected all-time XIs from Australia and the rest of the world based on performances at the SCG. Current players picked were Ricky Ponting from Australia, and Sachin Tendulkar and VVS Laxman from India.

INDIA

FROM RANJI TO TIGER

India first played Test cricket in 1932 but did not win a match until 1952 when they beat England by an innings at Madras.

Their most famous cricketers in the early part of the 20th century were ones who played for England rather than the country of their birth. KS Ranjitsinhji, known simply as Ranji, was an English-educated Indian prince and one of the great batsmen. He was famous for the elegant leg glance, a shot that defied the convention of the age that dictated that gentlemen should attempt to score runs on the off side only. Ranji's nephew Duleepsinhji played 12 Tests for England between 1929 and 1931.

Getting a decent team on the field was often a problem for India in those early years. Rich patrons of the game often expected to be a part of the action. Their 1936 tour to England was captained by the Maharajah of Vizianagram, known as 'Vizzy' to his chums, who had bankrolled the first trip in 1932.

He had used his wealth and influence to take the great English batsmen Jack Hobbs and Herbert Sutcliffe to play matches in India and Ceylon (Sri Lanka). Vizzy was a poor player but insisted on selecting himself. He batted at No.9 and didn't bowl. He finished the three-Test series with 33 runs at an average of eight and was heavily criticized when he returned to India.

By the post-war period India had become a more formidable outfit with significant figures making up their middle order: the captain Vijay Hazare, Vinoo Mankad and Lala Amarnath (*right*), the scorer of India's first Test century who had two sons who also played Test cricket.

Pataudi took a view that India should play to their strengths

Prince of batsmen: Ranjitsinhji, of royal stock, was acclaimed for his elegance and the innovation of the leg glance.

Mankad was the key bowler in their maiden victory over England but he was also a controversial figure. On India's first tour to Australia in 1947–48 Mankad ran out Bill Brown, as the batsman backed up from the bowler's end, before he delivered the ball. In one of the warm-up matches he had warned Brown about leaving his crease too eagerly but in the Test at Sydney he gave no warning.

The dismissal gave rise to a new cricketing term: 'Mankading' to describe the act of a bowler running out a batsman in this way.

Lord of all he surveys: Tiger Pataudi, later to be a successful captain of India. . Previous page: Sachin Tendulkar is carried on the shoulders of his teammates after India's victory over Sri Lanka at Mumbai in the 2011 World Cup final.

It was considered by many to be against the spirit of the game but it was not until recently against the laws of the game.

Having waited 20 years and 25 Tests for a victory, India secured a second only eight months after their first. They beat Pakistan by an innings and 70 runs at Delhi in the first Test match between the two countries following the partition of India in 1947.

Having taken a 2-1 lead in the five-Test series against Pakistan, India would draw 14 of their next 16 Tests. This was indicative of a safety-first mindset where avoidance of defeat was the first, and sometimes only, priority, particularly against their newly established neighbours Pakistan. But this attitude changed when the Nawab of Pataudi, or Tiger Pataudi as he was known, became captain in 1962 aged 21 and only months after a car accident in which he had lost the sight of his right eye. Pataudi thought that India should play to their strengths rather than follow the conventional thinking that a bowling attack had to contain a balance between fast and slow bowlers. India had a number of quality spin bowlers so Pataudi's attitude was to pick them all. With three in his line-up, including Bishan Bedi and Erapalli Prasanna, he led India to their first Test win overseas against New Zealand in 1967.

The artist: slow left-armer Bishan Bedi, here preparing to bowl against England at Chennai in 1977, was the classical bowler among India's collection of spinners. His rhythmic and graceful action delighted the purists.

LIFE IN THE SLOW LANE

While West Indies struck fear into batsmen the world over with their battalion of fast bowlers, India bamboozled their opponents with an exotic array of spinners.

These days most teams would select one spinner, maybe two if conditions were especially favourable, but India in the 1970s would pick three or even four at a time.

And it was hugely successful, especially at home where pitches were slow, dry and often dusty. In a 12-year period between 1967 and 1978, India played 68 Tests and at least three of these four spinners played in 55.

And they improved their win percentage on the previous dozen years by more than 50 per cent. In the space of five months in 1971 India beat

The thinker: off-spinner Erapalli Prasanna, bowling for India v. MCC at Lord's 1974, would outsmart batsmen.

Over the course of the five-match series in West Indies the three spinners took 48 of the 68 wickets taken by bowlers.

The tactical template of the era was for the medium-pacers Abid Ali and Eknath Solkar to bowl a few token overs to take the shine off the new ball and then let the slow men spin their web.

Both Prasanna and Bedi were masters of deception. They had such command of the flight of the ball that it was changes of pace and direction as much as spin that so often did for the batsmen. Venkataraghavan, or Venkat as he was known, made use of his height. In retirement he became an international umpire.

One man not selected for that tour was the last member of the great spin quartet, the wrist-spinner Bhagwath Chandrasekhar, who like Prasanna came from Bangalore. Aged five he contracted polio and spent three months in hospital. He was left with a withered right arm but rather than hindering his progress he actually found that his bowling action had a certain whip to it that made the ball bite and spit off the surface. He even once bowled a bouncer at the West Indian quick bowler Charlie Griffith.

Although he was a wrist-spinner his stock ball was not the standard leg-break that turns from the leg side to the off. He specialized in top-spinners that would speed on with added bounce to the batsman and the googly, the wrist-spinner's famous mystery ball delivered out of the back of the hand and spinning from off to leg.

West Indies for the first time, at Port of Spain in Trinidad, and then completed a first victory in England, winning by four wickets at The Oval.

The series in the Caribbean was notable for the performances of a young opening batsman, Sunil Gavaskar, who announced himself with 774 runs in his debut series. India's sole victory was a team effort by the spin trio of Erapalli Prasanna, Srinivas Venkataraghavan (*right*), both off-spinners, and the great left-armer Bishan Bedi.

India would bamboozle batsmen with an array of exotic spinners

Against the odds: Bhagwath Chandrasekhar, bowling against Kent in 1971, overcame childhood polio to be a world-beater.

Engineer played for Lancashire and was part of their brilliant one-day side of the 1970s. He made his home in Manchester and while remaining a patriotic Indian is a familiar face in English cricket.

India's next trip to England in 1974 was a less happy affair and included a humiliating innings defeat at Lord's where they were bowled out for 42, which remains their lowest-ever Test score and the equal fifth-lowest by any side.

India's win at The Oval in 1971 sparked scenes of jubilation in Mumbai

Ajit Wadekar, the captain who had also led the side to the 1971 triumph, was now discredited. Bedi (*below*) took over as captain and led the side on a highly controversial tour of the Caribbean in 1976 that contained another Test win in Trinidad but finished in bitter and brutal circumstances on an uneven pitch in Jamaica.

Two Indian batsmen retired hurt in the first innings, one edging a ball into his mouth, the other hit above the left ear, and another broke and dislocated a finger in the process of being caught. So Bedi, keen to protect himself and Chandrasekhar, declared the innings with only six wickets down. In the second innings India had made only 97 for five when Bedi called his players in. It was assumed he had declared again but in fact the innings was completed with the scorecard showing five batsmen, including Bedi and Chandra who had been injured while fielding, absent hurt.

Having failed to defeat an Australian side that was missing their best players who had defected to Packer, India lost in Pakistan. The two countries had not played each other for 18 years and

It was Chandrasekhar, with six wickets for 38, who bowled his side to their first victory in England at The Oval in 1971. That result delivered a series win too and sparked scenes of unfettered jubilation on the streets of Mumbai.

The spinners would not have had such an effect without an able wicketkeeper to snaffle the catches and steal the stumpings. Farokh Engineer was a flamboyant cricketer whose attacking batting was as much part of his make-up as his glovework. In the Oval Test of 1971 he made a half-century and then a crucial 28 not out to steer India home for their landmark victory.

Straight bat: a young Sunil Gavaskar batting at Eastbourne on India's 1974 tour of England.

Big leap forward: Kapil Dev, India's first great fast bowler, in his delivery stride at The Oval in 1979 against England.

India's leading Test wicket-takers

(spinners in bold; stats correct to 9 Feb 2012)

Career	Tests	Wkts	Best	Avge	SR
Anil Kumble					
1990–2008	132	619	10-74	29.65	65.9
Kapil Dev					
1978–94	131	434	9-83	29.64	63.9
Harbhajan Singh					
1998–2011	98	406	8-84	32.22	68.1
Zaheer Khan					
2000–12	83	288	7-87	31.78	58.0
Bishan Bedi					
1966–79	67	266	7-98	28.71	80.3
B Chandrasekhar					
1964–79	58	242	8-79	29.74	65.9
Javagal Srinath					
1991–2002	67	236	8-86	30.49	64.0
Erapalli Prasanna					
1962–78	49	189	8-76	30.38	75.9
Vinoo Mankad					
1946–59	44	162	8-52	32.32	90.6
S Venkataraghavan					
1965–83	57	156	8-72	36.11	95.3

Best=best bowling figures in an innings. Avge=bowling average, i.e.: runs conceded per wicket. SR=strike-rate, i.e.: balls bowled per wicket.

the Indians were received with the warmest of welcomes. But they were unable to match an emerging Pakistan side and the era of the great spinners was coming to an end. A major plus point though was the appearance of a 19-year-old fast-bowling all-rounder named Kapil Dev. Plenty more would be heard from him in years to come.

Their tour to England in 1979 was also unsuccessful though notable for a remarkable double-hundred at The Oval by Gavaskar. They were set an improbable 438 to level the series in the final Test and a draw seemed the only possible outcome. However, Gavaskar and his opening partner Chetan Chauhan put on 213 for the first wicket. With 20 overs remaining India had lost only one wicket and needed 110 more to win. But when Gavaskar was out for 221, dismissed by Ian Botham, wickets fell and in a thrilling finish the match was drawn with India on 429 for eight.

SUNIL GAVASKAR

Sunil Gavaskar was the first batsman to make 10,000 Test runs and the first to make 30 centuries, passing Don Bradman's seemingly impregnable record of 29.

A fearless opening batsman with an impeccable technique and exceptional powers of concentration 'Sunny' came from a cricket-mad family (his uncle also played for India) and claimed that he learned to read numbers from looking at scoreboards.

Standing only 5ft 5in, Gavaskar was the natural heir to the dynasty of Bombay batsmanship established decades earlier by the likes of Vijay Merchant and Vijay Hazare. The baton has since been handed to Sachin Tendulkar who carries many of Gavaskar's neat, stylistic traits, including wearing the same distinctive moulded pads. Indeed, Tendulkar's original pads were hand-me-downs from Gavaskar as was the Little Master moniker so often attached to Tendulkar.

His debut series as a 21-year-old in the Caribbean in 1971 was a phenomenal success. He missed the first Test with a finger injury that, according to *Wisden*, 'he aggravated by nail-biting'. He then scored 774 runs at 154, including three hundreds and a double-century. Only once in eight innings did he score fewer than 64. His debut Test in Trinidad was India's first victory over West Indies at the 25th attempt.

It was immediately apparent that India had found a rock on which their batting line-up would be built over the next decade as they became a major international force.

It took him a while to come to terms with limited-overs cricket, though. At the inaugural World Cup in 1975 he batted through an entire 60-over innings at Lord's against England to score 36 not out. India, chasing 335 to win, finished bizarrely on 132 for three. Spectators even broke a police cordon to come on to the field and remonstrate with Gavaskar. There seemed no obvious explanation for the tactic, described afterwards by the Indian team manager, GS Ramchand, as 'the most disgraceful and selfish performance I have ever seen'. Later Gavaskar explained that he got himself into a rut and could not bring himself to slog his way out of trouble.

He made a single one-day century and made four single-figure scores in six innings during India's momentous 1983 World Cup campaign.

'He instilled pride in a generation brought up on self-esteem' – Harsha Bhogle

But these are minor scars on a career path defined by courage and mastery of his craft. His record against West Indies and their battery of quick bowlers continued to be exceptional. He averaged 55 in the 1976 series in the Caribbean and contributed a century at Port of Spain where India became only the second side in history to chase down a fourth-innings target of 400 or more.

It was against West Indies that Gavaskar produced a record-filled performance at Madras in 1983. His 236 not out was the highest Test score by an Indian and it also took him past Bradman's record of 29 hundreds.

Full name: Sunil Manohar Gavaskar
Born: 19 July 1949, Mumbai, India
International career span: 1971–87
Role: Right-hand opening batsman
Notable numbers: 125 Tests, 10,122 runs at 51.12; first man to score 10,000 Test runs; first man to score 30 Test hundreds; averaged 65 against West Indies with 13 hundreds
Extras: Newspaper columnist; broadcaster; sometime Indian cricket board official and chairman of ICC's cricket committee; his son Rohan has played one-day internationals for India

WANKHEDE STADIUM

Mumbai's Wankhede Stadium is the third major venue to be built in the city generally regarded as India's cricketing capital.

It was the scene of the 2011 World Cup final, won by India in front of 45,000 passionate supporters (*above*). The expressions of joy, relief and national pride that exploded within the

stadium spilled over on to the nearby Marine Drive, the 3-km promenade where fashionable Mumbaikars are used to taking in the views and the breeze off the Arabian Sea.

The Wankhede was born from a dispute between the Bombay Cricket Association and the Cricket Club of India, which hosted Test matches

After the World Cup win national pride and joy spilled on to the streets

at the nearby Brabourne Stadium. The original Test venue in the city was the Indian Gymkhana that hosted India's inaugural home Test against England in 1933–34.

In common with other seaside grounds, the Wankhede offers swing bowlers assistance when the ball is new, though it is traditionally a batsman's pitch. However in 2004 the pitch took spin from the off and Michael Clarke, only an occasional left-arm bowler for Australia, took six wickets for nine runs in the second innings.

The ground has not been a fortress for India in Tests. They won nine of the 22 up to the end of 2011 but only two of the last seven.

Magic of the cup: captain Kapil Dev holds up the World Cup trophy after India's shock victory over the reigning champions West Indies at Lord's in 1983. Man-of-the-match Mohinder Amarnath, who took three for 12 with his medium pace, cradles the champagne.

GAME CHANGER

In retrospect it all looks like part of a grand plan. Television and one-day cricket: a marriage made in marketing executive heaven. But in truth it was a series of coincidences, a happenstance of timing that would change the game in India and in time across the whole cricketing world.

Before 1983 India had been no lover of the limited-overs game. 'We didn't take the game seriously,' said Ajit Wadekar, who captained India in their first one-day international in 1974.

'We had no idea of field placings or tactics.' In the first World Cup in 1975 Sunil Gavaskar had batted right through a 60-over innings against England for 36 not out. That attitude was about to change in dramatic fashion.

Nor was television a huge part of most Indians' lives. That too was about to change. In 1982 colour TV had arrived along with the notion of nationwide telecasts just in time for the Asian Games that were held in Delhi.

'The 1983 final inspired a lot of young kids to take to the game' – Rahul Dravid

Less than a year later something remarkable occurred. India, 66-1 outsiders at the start of the tournament, had become World Cup winners, overcoming the great West Indies side, and back home the people had seen it happen. They hadn't had to make do with crackly radio commentary or wait a day to read about it. They had seen it. And they would not forget. Rahul Dravid, who would become one of India's great batsmen, was ten at the time: 'I remember watching that final in Bangalore. That win inspired a lot of young kids to take to the game.'

One-day cricket was about to take off in India. In the early 1990s came deregulation, privatization and satellite television. And cricket went super-commercial.

The final of the 1983 World Cup was India's 48th one-day international since their first in 1974. In the same period England had played 80. Over the next nine years India would play 160 ODIs while England played a mere 117.

The Indian team was changing too. Few people saw the 1983 victory coming but maybe they should have done. Three months earlier amid the sugar plantations of Guyana they had beaten West Indies in a one-dayer for the first time. The team was young and led by a feisty captain in Kapil Dev.

It contained a number of all-rounders and had an opening batsman, Krishnamachari Srikkanth, who played with the sort of carefree aggression that was way ahead of its time. In three one-dayers against Sri Lanka in 1982–83 he scored 244 runs off 195 balls. The modern master blaster Virender Sehwag would probably consider that slow going but back in the early 1980s this was mould-breaking behaviour.

Before Sehwag: Krishnamachari Srikkanth was a big-hitting opening batsman who was ahead of his time.

The post-World Cup euphoria did not last long for India. They barely won a match in either form of the game over the next 18 months until a remarkable clean sweep in an Australian one-day tournament grandly called the World Championship of Cricket arranged to celebrate the 150th anniversary of the state of Victoria.

There were twice-yearly one-day tournaments staged at a new stadium in Sharjah in the United Arab Emirates. The money rolled in but many of these matches and series had little context.

In 1986 India won their first Test series in England since 1971 and caused the sacking of England captain David Gower in the process. It was certainly an improvement for India on the previous series between the sides 18 months earlier when England had become the first team to win a series in India after falling behind.

Dev-astating: Kapil Dev during his 175 not out that rescued India against Zimbabwe at Tunbridge Wells in the 1983 World Cup. He put on 126 for the ninth wicket with Madan Lal, whose contribution to the stand was 17. India made 266 for eight and won by 31 runs.

Dilip Vengsarkar, a tall, elegant right-hander, was India's batting star of the series, making two centuries including his third in as many appearances at Lord's. No batsman has a hit-rate at the home of cricket quite like Vengsarkar, who finished his career with three hundreds in four Lord's Tests. Sachin Tendulkar never made one.

Straight after the England tour India hosted a rebuilding Australia in a three-Test series that finished 0-0 but that unpromising scoreline does not begin to tell the story.

Only one of the previous 1,051 Test matches had finished in a tie: where the fourth innings was completed and the scores were level. Around

Around 30,000 spectators in broiling humidity saw the second-ever tied Test

30,000 spectators in the broiling humidity of Chennai were about to witness the five-day game's second deadheat.

Australia batted first and their total of 574 for seven declared contained an astonishing act of batting endurance from the maverick right-hander Dean Jones, who made 210. With the

King of Lord's: Dilip Vengsarkar made three Test hundreds in four appearances at Lord's. His third in 1986 (126 not out) was described by Wisden *as an innings of 'classical elegance, charm and responsibility' and set up India's first Test win at Lord's.*

thermometer touching 40°C and humidity at 80 per cent, Jones was, by his own admission, 'a mess'. He said: 'On about 170 I wanted to go off because I was stopping every over to be sick. And [captain] Allan Border said, "You weak Victorian. I want a tough Australian out there. I want a Queenslander." So I stayed.

'When I came off the ground they put me in an ice bath. I thought I was OK. Then I got out of the bath and passed out. I woke up in hospital at one o'clock in the morning.'

Kapil Dev made a hundred for India and an Australian declaration in their second innings left India needing 348 to win the first Test. 'The last day started with about 10,000 fans in the ground' recalled Indian all-rounder Ravi Shastri. 'By the end there were 50,000.'

At tea India were 193 for two, needing 155 from 30 overs. Then they lost three wickets for 13 runs. They needed four from the last over with one wicket left and Shastri facing the spinner Greg Matthews, who had bowled unchanged for the entire final day. With one needed to win, last man Maninder Singh tried to turn the ball to leg and was given out lbw.

As the Australians left the field Border handed Jones the match ball and said: 'I think you've earned this.'

Kapil Dev

India had had fast bowlers before but not since independence and the partition of 1947. Indeed, had Kapil Dev's parents not moved south to Chandigarh from Rawalpindi at partition, he might have opened the bowling for Pakistan.

He remains India's greatest all-rounder, their first modern fast bowler and still their greatest. He was the leading wicket-taker in Test history for a while, breaking Richard Hadlee's record. Kapil captained India to the 1983 World Cup, a shock victory over the champion West Indies side that redefined the country's relationship with cricket forever. In 2002 he was voted Indian cricketer of the century.

He took 219 of his 434 Test wickets on the slow, mostly unresponsive pitches in India, testament to his marathon runner's lungs and capacity for thankless toil. His action was rhythmic and athletic with a touch of wristy artiness that was almost a homage to the great spinners who had preceded him as India's dominant bowlers.

His seventh Test at Chennai against West Indies in 1979 was something of a turning point. *Wisden* reported: 'The match exploded into a bumper war on the third day, during which 15 wickets fell. The Indians for once gave as good as they got.' India won the Test and Kapil took seven wickets in the match.

In the following match he made his first Test hundred. It was his cavalier batting that brought people through the turnstiles and his rivalry with other great all-rounders – Ian Botham, Hadlee and Imran Khan – was a defining narrative of the era.

His innings tended to be explosive rather than elongated. Substantial cameos like 75 from 51 balls in a one-dayer at Brisbane in 1980 against New Zealand that had the Kiwi bowler Jeremy Coney waving a white handkerchief in mock surrender. At Lord's in 1982 he smashed 89 from 55 balls. Four years later he returned to captain India to their first Test victory there, hitting the winning runs in the process: three fours and a six off Phil Edmonds.

In the 1990 Lord's Test, which was famous for Graham Gooch's 333, Kapil saved the follow-on for India by hitting four successive sixes off the spinner Eddie Hemmings.

'He was a great asset to India. He played like a champion and was a great leader' – Clive Lloyd

None of those Lord's feats, though, can compare with what happened on 25 June 1983 when he lifted the World Cup for India and broke the hold that West Indies had on the competition. His key contribution to the final was his over-the-shoulder catch to dismiss Viv Richards and start a remarkable West Indies collapse.

Earlier in the tournament he had saved India from embarrassment against Zimbabwe with 175 not out off 138 balls including six sixes, then a world-record one-day score. India were nine for four when he came in.

Full name: Kapil Dev Nikhanj
Born: 6 January 1959, Chandigarh
International career span: 1978–94
Role: Right-arm fast bowler; right-hand middle-order batsman
Notable numbers: 131 Tests, 5,248 runs at 31.05, eight hundreds; 434 wickets at 29.64; became leading wicket-taker in Test history in his penultimate Test v. Sri Lanka in 1994; also finished career as the world's leading ODI wicket-taker with 253 in 225 matches
Extras: Coach of India 1999–2000; broke down live on TV in May 2000 while responding to match-fixing allegations from an ex-teammate; in 2002 chairman of the national academy

Leading man: spinner Anil Kumble, India's leading wicket-taker, appeals unsuccessfully for lbw against England's Nasser Hussain in 2002.

SACHIN AND FRIENDS

It was the Saturday of a Lord's Test, the highlight of an English cricket summer but the attentions and affections of much of the home crowd were elsewhere. The England football team were playing Spain a few miles away at Wembley in the quarter-final of the 1996 European championship.

On the field this drawn Test was a farewell match for the umpire Dickie Bird. But for India the match was notable for the debuts of Sourav Ganguly and Rahul Dravid, two very different characters who would have a profound impact on their country's cricketing fortunes over the next decade and beyond.

Dream debut: Sourav Ganguly raises his bat to the Lord's crowd after his century in his first Test at Lord's in 1996.

India were assembling a batting line-up that would last them for 15 years

To make 1996 even more of a momentous year for Indian cricket, they hosted the World Cup in an Asian collaboration with Pakistan and Sri Lanka that redefined the way the game was administered in India. The tournament was considered a logistical nightmare for the teams but a commercial success, a feather in the cap of the controversial secretary of the Indian board Jagmohan Dalmiya. It was the first of the five World Cup tournaments to be exploited on a serious commercial basis.

Dalmiya came from Kolkata and by the end of the 1990s there would be an axis power based in the capital of Bengal when Ganguly took over as captain from Tendulkar, who himself had taken the reins briefly from Mohammad Azharuddin.

Azharuddin (*below*) was a stylist in the ancient tradition of Ranji and Duleepsinhji, a wristy batsman who made the game look easy. At Lord's in 1990, when Graham Gooch made 333, Azhar played a gem of an innings. He made 121, many of those runs flicked outrageously through the leg side down the famous Lord's slope towards the Tavern boundary.

His glittering career ended in disgrace, though, when he emerged as a leading part of the match-fixing scandal that brought down the South African captain Hansie Cronje in 2000. Azharuddin was given a life ban by the Indian board which was lifted in 2006.

The left-handed Ganguly made 131 and Dravid 95. Had the latter made five more runs it would have been the first instance of two debutants from the same country both scoring hundreds on their Test debuts. So dominant was the football in the minds of the media that Ganguly, a Manchester United supporter, was asked to comment on England's penalty shoot-out victory as well as his debut hundred.

Both men looked entirely at home on the big stage, Ganguly displaying confidence and flair, Dravid the stoical qualities of patience and concentration that would become his hallmarks.

A few months later VVS Laxman made his debut against South Africa and India had assembled a batting line-up that would by and large still be serving their needs 15 years down the line. Sachin Tendulkar was a veteran by this point, having made his debut in late 1989 in Pakistan and a maiden Test century at Manchester in 1990 while still only 16.

Delhi delight: Kumble celebrates dismissing Pakistan's Inzamam-ul-Haq in 1999. He took all ten wickets in the second innings.

almost medium pace, using his height to extract bounce from slow pitches and deceiving batsmen with changes of pace more than sideways spin.

Few bowlers have been as tireless and dedicated as Kumble. He finished his career with 619 wickets, the most by an Indian and third behind the two great modern spinners, Shane Warne and Muttiah Muralitharan. Fourteen times he helped bowl India to victory in the final innings of a Test.

Kumble's most famous and productive fourth-innings finish was against Pakistan at Delhi in 1999. It was India's first series against Pakistan for nine years and the first in India since 1986–87. Only one of the previous 16 Tests between the two countries had yielded a positive result yet this series produced three in three, a revelation for this contest where fear of failure and political sensitivities always weighed heavy.

In the first Test at Delhi Kumble bowled India to victory by becoming only the second man in history after Jim Laker to take all ten wickets in an innings. Set 420 to win Pakistan had reached 101 without loss when Kumble took two wickets in two balls.

Once he had reeled in six for 15 in 44 balls he thought he might have a shot at the full house. He had to wait a while for his seventh as Salim Malik and Wasim Akram put on 58. With nine wickets down, Azharuddin instructed the seamer Javagal Srinath to bowl wide of the stumps in his next over.

Wasim was the last man to go, caught at short leg by Laxman. Kumble was chaired from the field by his teammates. 'My first reaction is that we have

The other mainstay of this new Indian team that emerged during the 1990s was the studious leg-spin bowler Anil Kumble (*right*). Before he faced England at home in 1993 the England coach Keith Fletcher spoke disparagingly of Kumble's qualities, having been on a pre-series spying mission. 'I didn't see him turn a single ball from leg to off', Fletcher said. 'I don't believe we will have much problem with him.' Kumble took 21 wickets at 19 in the three Tests, all won by India. What Fletcher had failed to appreciate was Kumble's unusual style, a throwback to Bhagwath Chandrasekhar from the 1970s. Kumble bowled at

Few bowlers have been as tireless and dedicated as Anil Kumble

Main man: Sachin Tendulkar, who made his Test debut in 1989, on India's tour of England in 1990 when he made his maiden century.

won,' he said afterwards. 'No one dreams of taking ten wickets in an innings because you can't.' Kumble's dream day was shared also by an English spectator, Richard Stokes, who had seen Laker take some of his ten wickets at Manchester in 1956 and was in Delhi to see Kumble's feat.

The Indian team of the late 1990s was long on star quality and worshipping fans but often short on delivering meaningful results. They won plenty of one-day internationals but tended to fall at the final hurdle in a triangular or quadrangular event.

Expectations were high for the 1999 World Cup in England but they departed in the Super Six stage, the second phase of the competition before the semi-finals. There were highlights, though, most memorably a rabble-rousing second-wicket stand of 318 in 45 overs between Dravid and Ganguly against Sri Lanka at the small Taunton ground. It was the highest partnership for any wicket in a one-day international, though the record stood for less than six months until Dravid and Tendulkar posted 331, also for the second wicket against New Zealand.

India's Test tour of Australia in 1999–2000, under the captaincy of Tendulkar, was a harrowing experience for all concerned. All three Tests were lost and seven of eight one-dayers too. They even lost to the Prime Minister's XI, a team of youngsters.

Tendulkar gave up the captaincy and with the appointment of the feisty Ganguly as his replacement and the arrival of the dogged New Zealander John Wright as coach, Team India was about to move figuratively as well as physically into the 21st century.

SACHIN TENDULKAR

When Sachin Tendulkar goes to work the rest of India downs tools. Only Don Bradman had command of a nation's collective psyche like Tendulkar. But the size of his congregation, around one billion obsessives, dwarfs the Australia of the early 20th century that Bradman inhabited.

At times in the past two decades since the arrival of the cherubic teenager with the mop of curly hair it has seemed that his fellow countrymen cared more for his fortunes than those of their team. Sachin-worship is a cult of personality that would fatally distort the values of most mortals. Yet Tendulkar has carried his burden with such patience, dignity and humility that one frequently wonders if he is indeed of this world. He has disguised himself to go to the cinema and he can only indulge his love of fast cars in the middle of the night when the roads are clear.

Tendulkar was the ultimate schoolboy prodigy. At 14 he and his friend Vinod Kambli compiled a partnership of 664 in a schools match, a world record for any level of the game as far as anyone could tell. It has since been beaten by a pair from Hyderabad.

He made a century on his first-class debut, aged 15, and at 16 he was playing Test cricket in Pakistan, wearing Sunil Gavaskar's moulded foam pads and looking – but not playing – like a boy in a man's world. Hit in the mouth by Waqar Younis, he wiped the blood away and made 57. Months later, at Manchester, he scored his maiden Test century, displaying all the attributes of compact technique and mental discipline that would be the constants of his stellar career.

It has been presumed at various points in his career that he had a weakness against the short ball. Yet possibly his greatest innings was his brave and daring 114 on a bouncy pitch at Perth in 1992 when he was a couple of months short of his 19th birthday. The quality of the knock was such that in the Australian dressing room afterwards the fast bowler Merv Hughes turned to his captain Allan Border, later to become the world's leading Test run-scorer, and said: 'This little prick's going to get more runs than you, AB.'

And he has done. His appetite for the game and for scoring runs is as bewildering as his ability. There have been blemishes. In 1992 he had an unsuccessful stint as Yorkshire's first

> ## 'You can't just run up and bowl. You have to plan a week ahead' – Allan Donald

overseas player. In 2001 he was fined and given a suspended ban for ball-tampering. In the mid-2000s a tennis elbow injury diminished his powers and seemingly his hunger.

But he re-emerged better than ever and, having become the leading Test run-scorer in history, became the first man to score 200 in a one-day international in 2010.

He owns almost every batting record going and, after just over a year of waiting, he made his 100th international hundred in March 2012.

Full name: Sachin Ramesh Tendulkar
Born: 24 April 1973, Mumbai
International career span: 1989–
Role: Right-hand batsman (middle order for Tests, opener in ODIs); occasional leg-spin bowler
Notable numbers: 188 Tests, 15,470 runs at 55.44, 51 hundreds, 65 fifties; 455 ODIs, 18,161 runs at 45.06, 48 hundreds, 95 fifties (up to 9 Feb 2012). He holds the all-time record for all categories other than batting averages.
Extras: Married to a doctor Anjali; two children Sara and Arjun; waved the chequered flag at the inaugural Indian Formula 1 Grand Prix in 2011

Tired and emotional: VVS Laxman (left) and Rahul Dravid leave the field after batting for an entire day, scoring 335 runs, during the second Test against Australia at Kolkata's Eden Gardens, the Test India won after following on.

VERY VERY SPECIAL

Only twice before in the history of Test cricket had a team managed to win a game after being made to follow on. England did it against Australia back in 1894 and then again in Botham's Ashes at Headingley in 1981. And Australia were the victims again when India pulled off an astonishing turnaround at Kolkata in 2001.

That Australia, under Steve Waugh's hardboiled captaincy, were pursuing a record 17th successive victory, having disposed of India comfortably in the first Test, made events all the more remarkable. He has since described the Kolkata Test as 'the best in the game's history'. For Waugh and his relentless quest for

excellence, India represented, in his words, the 'final frontier' for his side since Australia had not won a series there for 31 years.

India had created opportunities with the ball in the first Test at Mumbai but their batting had let them down.

In the second Test at Kolkata Australia posted 445 despite the young off-spinner Harbhajan Singh taking a hat-trick. Their last two wickets added 133 with Glenn McGrath, every inch the epitome of a No.11, making 21 not out. McGrath the bowler then suffocated India's batsmen with four for 18 in 14 overs. Only VVS Laxman, the tall, elegant batsman from Hyderabad, offered any

Laxman's stroke had Warne shaking his head, looking for explanation

resistance with a feisty half-century that earned him promotion three places up the batting order to No.3. In the second innings he would write himself into Indian cricket history and produce an innings that has defined his career.

Laxman was not a mainstay of India's side. Before Kolkata he had played 20 Tests over five years, averaging only 27. His batting average jumped eight points after Kolkata, such was the magnitude of his performance.

In front of a huge, baying crowd at Eden Gardens Laxman and Rahul Dravid, who had been laid low with a fever before the Test, broke a host of records. On the fourth day of the Test the two batted all day, scoring 335 in the 90 overs. In all they put on 376 for the fifth wicket. Laxman's 281, made off 452 balls over ten hours, was the highest Test score by an Indian batsman.

Laxman scored runs all round the wicket but one shot sticks out above all others. Having just reached his double hundred he was facing Shane Warne who was bowling round the wicket, pitching the ball outside Laxman's leg stump. Laxman deftly manoeuvred himself inside the line of the ball, his back foot almost off the cut strip, and drove the ball with a flick of the wrists through extra cover.

It was a stroke that had Warne standing, shaking his head, arms folded looking around for explanation or inspiration.

Soon afterwards Dravid (*right*) reached his hundred with an equally audacious on drive against the spin of Warne. Dravid's normally calm exterior was broken as he removed his helmet and thrust it and his bat passionately in the direction of the Indian dressing room. Warne applauded, frustrated but willing to acknowledge the skill in front of him.

India v. Australia 2001
(† denotes team winning toss; * not out)

1st Test, Mumbai, 27 February–1 March India 176 (SR Tendulkar 76; SK Warne 4-47) and 219 (Tendulkar 65); †Australia 349 (ML Hayden 119, AC Gilchrist 122; Harbhajan Singh 4-121) and 47-0. Australia won by ten wickets.

2nd Test, Kolkata, 11–15 March †Australia 445 (Hayden 97, JL Langer 58, SR Waugh 110; Harbhajan 7-113) and 212 (Hayden 67; Harbhajan 6-73); India 171 (VVS Laxman 59; GD McGrath 4-18) and, following on, 657-7 dec (Laxman 281, R Dravid 180). India won by 171 runs.

3rd Test, Chennai, 18–22 March †Australia 391 (Hayden 203, ME Waugh 70; Harbhajan 7-133) and 264 (ME Waugh 57; Harbhajan 8-84); India 501 (SS Das 84, S Ramesh 61, Laxman 65, Tendulkar 126, Dravid 81) and 155-8 (Laxman 66). India won by two wickets.

India won the series 2-1

So, having been 274 behind, India were able to declare and set Australia 384 to win. This was the moment for Harbhajan, whose 32 wickets in the series were only three short of the record for a three-match rubber.

Having taken a princely 13 wickets at Kolkata, he took 15 more at Chennai in a Test that was a thriller in its own right but inevitably overshadowed by the Kolkata comeback.

Steve Waugh became only the sixth batsman in Test history to be given out handled the ball, a dismissal that sparked an Aussie collapse. India were 110 for two needing 155 to win but only just prevailed against Waugh's indefatigable side. The final frontier remained unbreached.

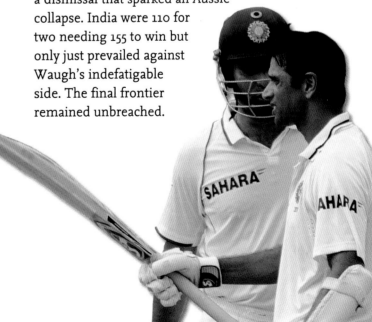

Shot in the dark: Mahendra Singh Dhoni launches a six to win the 2011 World Cup for India against Sri Lanka at Mumbai.

DHONI DELIVERS

The first decade of the second millennium was when India started to transform star turns into stellar results.

The new captain Sourav Ganguly was a talented player for sure, a left-handed attacking batsman, particularly adept at the one-day game, and a useful medium-pace bowler. But his real qualities lay elsewhere. India had had plenty of tough cricketers over the years but they tended to be stoic, dedicated types. Ganguly introduced a haughty, brash aggression that had never been seen before from an Indian side.

That he got under the leather-bound skin of Steve Waugh, his Australian counterpart, is a badge of honour for him, though outside his home state of Bengal he divided opinion.

The remarkable come-from-behind victory over Australia in 2001 was the greatest achievement

Ganguly was the first Indian captain to win more Tests than he lost

under his captaincy but he also led India to the 2003 World Cup final at Johannesburg where they crumbled against Australia.

At a sun-kissed Lord's in 2002 as India completed a thrilling one-day victory over England, Ganguly stood bare-chested on the dressing-room balcony waving his shirt about his head in a mixture of celebration and mocking. Earlier in the year Andrew Flintoff, briefly a county teammate of Ganguly's at Lancashire, had ripped his own shirt off after winning a one-dayer at Mumbai. The traditionalists blushed, youngsters roared.

At Adelaide in late 2003 India won their first Test in Australia for a generation and only their fourth overall. An amazing match in which both sides slugged out 500-plus totals turned on the medium-paced swing of Ajit Agarkar. Rahul Dravid, who made 233 in the first innings, steered India home by four wickets with an unbeaten 72. India lost the next Test at Melbourne and the series was drawn 1-1. They still had not won a series in Australia.

Ganguly's reign ended in 2005 after a fall-out with the coach Greg Chappell. He was the first Indian captain to win more Tests than he lost.

The emergence of Mahendra Singh Dhoni in 2005, with a blistering one-day 148 against Pakistan, was indicative of a breakthrough in India's talent sourcing. More than ever before players were coming from country villages rather than through the traditional urban centres.

Fast bowlers emerged too. The Test series victory in England in 2007, India's first there since 1986, was founded on the left-arm swing of Zaheer Khan (*right*) and RP Singh.

Then came the inaugural World Twenty20 tournament in South Africa. It was a form of the game to which

A day in the sun: Sourav Ganguly expresses his joy at India's thrilling one-day shirt-off victory over England at Lord's.

India had been indifferent until Dhoni, by now the limited-overs captain, led his side to the title. Just like the 1983 World Cup win, this triumph changed everything. In a matter of months the Twenty20 Indian Premier League launched in a blaze of Bollywood money and glamour.

Dhoni took over the Test captaincy in 2008 and by the end of 2009, following four successive series victories, India were ranked No.1 Test side in the world.

After a mid-2000s' dip in form Sachin Tendulkar was back to his best with a one-day double-hundred against South Africa and an inexorable drive towards the unprecedented milestone of a century of international centuries.

Their No.1 status did not last long, though. After the ecstasy of home victory in the 2011 World Cup they were trounced 4-0 in a Test series in England, who took over their top Test spot. They were also whitewashed 4-0 months later in Australia. The stellar batting line-up was failing and Tendulkar's quest for a hundredth international hundred had become an obstructive sideshow.

VIRENDER SEHWAG

It is odd that, for all the craft and patient determination of Indian batsmen through the years, no one until 2001 had made 250 in a Test innings.

Virender Sehwag has broken barriers in more than one sense. One would not wish to be a boundary fence when he is batting such is the ferocity with which he clatters the ball, especially square through the off side. Although it was the languid stylist VVS Laxman who broke that 250 seal, it is Sehwag who has raised the bar higher with two triple hundreds and a 293. He owns India's top three highest Test scores.

'When Viv retired I thought it was the end of entertainment. But then came Sehwag' – Ramiz Raja

A short, stocky and powerful man, Sehwag comes from the outskirts of Delhi where his parents ran a flour mill. He has an uncomplicated, almost non-existent, technique. He stands still at the crease and contrary to the coaching manual does not get into line with the ball. He prefers to give himself room outside the off stump so he can pump the ball to the fence.

Initially, it was presumed he was another Tendulkar but he quickly became a much more brutal, unpredictable presence. His is a unique combination of scoring-speed and volume of runs. He has scored his Test-match runs at 82 per 100 balls, or almost five per over, faster than anyone in history who has scored 2,000 runs or more.

He made a century on his Test debut in South Africa in 2001, having been called into the team only the night before because of illness. He batted at No.6 in that innings but has since become a fixture at the top of the order and would open the batting in most people's World XI.

On the first day of the 2003 Boxing Day Test at Melbourne he smashed 195 and was out trying to bring up his maiden double-century with a six. Three months later he made 309 at Multan, the first triple-hundred by an Indian, in their first Test victory in Pakistan.

He was dropped in 2006 after a bad tour of South Africa but returned re-energized to continue his single-minded quest to bully the world's bowlers into submission. He scored his second Test triple against South Africa at Chennai in 2008. It is the fastest 300 of all time, taking only 278 deliveries.

In late 2009 he broke a raft of records against Sri Lanka at Mumbai. Having scored one boundary in the first 45 minutes of his innings, he launched into an orbit of 40 fours and seven sixes in an innings of 293 from 254 balls. Only Don Bradman has made more than his four scores of 250-plus.

Compared with his colossal Test stats his one-day record is merely excellent rather than extraordinary. But in December 2011 he set a new world-record score with 219, made off 149 balls with 25 fours and seven sixes, against West Indies at Indore.

Full name: Virender Sehwag
Born: 20 October 1978, Delhi
International career span: 1999–
Role: Right-handed opening batsman; occasional right-arm medium-pace bowler
Notable numbers: 96 Tests, 8,178 runs at 56.79, highest score 319, strike-rate 81.99, 22 hundreds; 244 ODIs, 8,060 runs at 35.19, 15 hundreds, strike-rate 104.51 (up to 9 Feb 2012)
Extras: *Wisden*'s leading cricketer in the world 2009 and 2010; ICC leading cricketer in the world 2010; captain of Delhi Daredevils IPL side

EDEN GARDENS

Every international cricketer has three dots on his map that he wants to have ticked of in his career: Lord's, Melbourne and Eden Gardens.

The nature of modern cricket administration in India means that this great venue in Kolkata, formerly Calcutta, does not have a guaranteed slot on the fixture list because matches are spread further and wider than ever before across this vast country. It is a vast, noisy stadium, a little like the MCG and very much unlike Lord's. Eden Gardens hosted the 1987 World Cup final and has held crowds of up to 100,000.

Built in 1864, it staged one of the three Tests in India's inaugural home series against England

It is a vast, noisy stadium, a little like the MCG and very much unlike Lord's

in 1934. Until 1984 it hosted football as well as cricket. It is the home ground of Bengal and more recently the IPL's Kolkata Knight Riders.

In 2001 it was the scene of India'as astonishing victory over Australia after following on. 'Today was one of those days when every pressman felt like abandoning his seat and rushing out to join the chanting, hooting, yelling crowds,' reported www.espncricinfo.com.

There was crowd violence during Tests against West Indies and Australia in the 1960s. The 1996 World Cup semi-final between India and Sri Lanka was abandoned when spectators started a fire in one of the stands.

Let Us Pray For the West Indies team
Dear Heavenly Father, you are the Father
of all captains, please place Brian Lara
under your captaincy, guide, and protect
him and his team through out the I.c.c.
tournament and beyond. Father you alone
have the victory in your hands. "If it be thy
holy will can we not get a surprise?
The   answer and the power is Yours. Amen.

Let us pray for our
country Barbados
Dear Father Lord, in the
Name of Jesus, at this
time of year we have
the unusual activities
in Barbados. Please
Lord, guide our little
Rock from dangerous
occasions, and help
us to understand in all
our doings, do it to your cont. ho...

WEST
INDIES

Pioneer: George Headley, the Black Bradman, batting against Surrey at The Oval in 1939. Previous page: a house in Bridgetown, Barbados, photographed the day before the 2007 World Cup final held in the city.

CRICKET, LOVELY CRICKET

George Headley was the first great West Indies batsman, a player of the highest class who established the credibility of the black man in a sport still dominated by the white establishment.

Indeed, Headley became known worldwide as 'the Black Bradman' although in the Caribbean many preferred to refer to The Don as the white Headley. He was born in Panama, where his father was helping to build the canal, and taken to Jamaica as a ten-year-old to learn English.

In 22 Tests Headley scored 2,190 runs at an average of 60 and never had a bad series. He was not a man for steady consistency but once he was in he was impossible to get out. He passed 50 on 15 occasions and converted ten of those scores into centuries. He was the first man to score a hundred in each innings of a Lord's Test and on his home ground at Sabina Park in Kingston, Jamaica, he scored 270 not out in 1935 to help West Indies to their first series victory over England.

Wisden said the tied Test was 'The Greatest Game ever played with a ball'

Next in the line of succession of Caribbean greatness from Headley is not one man but a trio of Barbadian batsmen known collectively as the three Ws. The slim, languid Frank Worrell was the first black captain of West Indies, the stocky, affable Everton Weekes was the most prolific and the imposing Clyde Walcott was also a wicket-keeper and later president of the ICC.

Throughout the 1950s the three Ws comprised the West Indies' middle order and made their team a credible Test force. They were struggling to win matches consistently but they made their mark boldly in England in 1950 with a victory at Lord's, their first in England, and a series win.

Two spinners Alf Valentine (*right*) and Sonny Ramadhin were the heroes and their deeds inspired the famous *Victory Calypso* sung by Lord Beginner that begins 'Cricket lovely Cricket/At Lord's where I saw it', followed by the chorus 'With those two little pals of mine/Ramadhin and Valentine'.

In 1959 Worrell became West Indies captain and in 1960 he took his team to Australia. Despite losing the series they played a huge part in reinvigorating interest in cricket there after an insipid decade. The catalyst was what *Wisden* called 'The Greatest Game ever played with a ball', also known as the first tied Test match.

Australia had been set 233 to win the first Test of the series at Brisbane and had collapsed to 57 for five and then 92 for six in the face of Wes Hall's sustained pace. But the all-rounder Alan Davidson and

Leaders: Frank Worrell with England's Ted Dexter.

captain Richie Benaud put on a century stand to leave 27 required in the final half-hour. Davidson was then run out for 80 by a direct hit from Joe Solomon. With one over (eight balls in those days) left, the equation was six runs to win and three wickets in hand.

The final over was as improbably eventful as the unprecedented result. Off the second ball Benaud was out, caught behind trying to hook Hall who, three balls later, dropped a catch off his own bowling.

With three to win off three balls Ian Meckiff heaved the ball into the leg side. He and his partner Wally Grout had run two and gambled on a third run. But the throw from Conrad Hunte in the deep was uncommonly accurate and Grout, despite a desperate dive, was run out.

One to win, two balls left. Lindsay Kline was the batsman now and he played the ball towards square leg. He set off but Solomon, with only the width of one stump to aim at, threw down the wicket. The West Indies fielders cavorted in triumph, thinking they had won. The Australian batsman Meckiff thought likewise.

But they had tied, a first for Test cricket and an unimaginable, much needed shot in the arm for the game.

GARRY SOBERS

To master all the various cricketing skills is an achievement that few can claim. To master them all with such outrageous flair is unique to Sir Garfield Sobers.

Don Bradman is the greatest batsman of all time but Sobers is unquestionably the greatest all-round player the game has seen. He could bowl quick or slow, seam or spin and was a high-class fielder. But it was his batting that made the headlines and broke the records.

The collar was upturned, the sleeves buttoned to the wrist and the swagger unmistakable. Sobers took his time to mark his guard as if setting the stage. Nothing was rushed until suddenly the bat would whoosh from shoulder height and dispatch a ball to the boundary.

He was born with an extra finger on each hand which were removed at birth. Initially a bowler, he made his debut for Barbados at 16 and played for West Indies at 17.

His first Test century, as a 21-year-old in 1958, was 365 not out, then the highest score in any Test innings. He was the first man to hit a six off each ball of an over when, playing for Nottinghamshire against Glamorgan, he smashed Malcolm Nash out of the ground at Swansea.

But his greatest innings was not even in an official Test match. He was playing for a Rest of the World XI in Australia after the scheduled tour by South Africa had been cancelled. After a poor showing in the first two matches of the series, Sobers made 254 at Melbourne against the full ferocity of Dennis Lillee, whom Sobers had angered by bowling bouncers at him in the Australian innings.

Bradman described it as the best innings he had ever seen in Australia. Richie Benaud said: 'It was the most amazing innings in terms of timing and power. He had such rubbery arms and wrists, and the power he could get through those wrists was extraordinary.' The great cricket writer Neville Cardus wrote in 1967 that Sobers 'maintained the art of cricket' at a time when the game was turning into an industry.

He captained West Indies in 39 of his 93 Tests and led them to a second successive series win in England in 1966. Having made a match-saving century in the Lord's Test, he produced an epic all-round performance at Leeds. He took eight wickets and scored 174 not out, including the

'Life is for living. I played hard and drank reasonably hard on occasions' — Garry Sobers

unusual feat of a hundred between lunch and tea. In the process he became the first man to pass 5,000 runs and take 100 wickets in Tests.

He was one of English county cricket's first overseas professionals, performing a starring role for Nottinghamshire from 1968–74.

In retirement he has been in constant demand as an after-dinner speaker or tourism ambassador for his native island Barbados. He has always been a keen golfer and follower of horse racing.

Full name: Garfield St Aubrun Sobers
Born: 28 July 1936, St Michael, Barbados
International career span: 1954–74
Role: Left-hand middle-order batsman, left-arm seam or spin bowler
Notable numbers: 93 Tests, 8,032 runs at 57.78, 26 hundreds; 235 wickets at 34.03. Leading Test run-scorer until Geoff Boycott overtook him in 1982. Highest Test score 365* (1958) broke Len Hutton's 364 (1938) and stood until Brian Lara's 375 (1994)
Extras: Football, golf and basketball for Barbados; one of Wisden's five Cricketers of the Century 2000; knighted 1975

Who's grovelling now? West Indies celebrate the wicket of England captain, Tony Greig, bowled by Michael Holding, at The Oval in 1976.

SETTING THE PACE

Great teams are not built overnight but sometimes a moment, a match or a series can be a turning point that changes the course of history. For West Indies, such a series was their 5-1 defeat in Australia in 1975–76.

They had won the inaugural World Cup in England in 1975 but crashed back to earth months later. Brutalized by the menacing pace of Dennis Lillee and Jeff Thomson, racially abused by the crowds and harshly treated, they felt, by Australian umpires, Clive Lloyd's side vowed 'never again'. Lloyd, who had been captain for only a year, felt the scoreline did not reflect the closeness in ability of the two sides. There was indignation and hurt. Michael Holding wept that

'anyone could play the game of cricket so hard'. But the result was to provide inspiration for this new West Indian side to emerge as a crack outfit ready to take on all-comers.

At the start of the decade the signs were not promising. An impressive era was coming to a limp end. Garry Sobers had lost interest in the captaincy and their pair of match-winning quicks Wes Hall and Charlie Griffith were finished too.

Sometimes it was beautiful, sometimes brutal, always compelling

The chastening tour of Australia in 1975–76 signalled the end of another great career, the spinner Lance Gibbs, then the world's leading wicket-taker. To this day West Indies have not possessed a spin bowler of remotely similar stature or class. And for much of that time they did not seek to nurture or select one.

The Jamaican fast bowler Holding said: 'Two fast bowlers, a medium pace and spinner: that was the way teams were supposed to be. We changed all that and people were not accustomed to it.'

Fast bowlers were nothing new but to have a quartet of them was. Most teams were happy with one. A pair, like Lillee and Thomson or Larwood and Voce, was a dream ticket. But West Indies doubled the trouble for batsmen. Sometimes it was beautiful, sometimes it was brutal. It was always compelling and more often than not comprehensive.

There is a misconception that pitches in the Caribbean are uniformly fast and bouncy. There are some, particularly in Barbados and Jamaica. Sometimes they have been uneven, dangerously so at times but in the main they are flat and good for batting. The only way for bowlers to make life hard for batsmen is to hurry them. The pitch won't do it for them.

After a barren period from 1968–73 when West Indies did not win a single Test (out of 18) in four series, fortunes changed with a series win in England. Around the same time their players were taking advantage of a 1968 rule-change that made it easier for county sides to hire overseas players. Foreign professionals had been rattling up runs and shattering wickets for decades in amateur league cricket, especially in Lancashire where the Caribbean connection went all the way back to Learie Constantine in the 1930s.

Most of West Indies' players of the 1970s and 1980s had spells in county cricket, developing long-term associations with their clubs. They became heroes on and off the field, inspiring many a British youngster to play or follow the game.

History makers: Andy Roberts (left) and Viv Richards, the first Antiguans to play Test cricket for West Indies.

But what county cricket did for them and West Indies cricket cannot be underestimated either. The opportunity to play full-time through the Caribbean off-season in a competitive environment with a variety of pitch conditions was of lasting benefit to Lloyd and his up-and-coming West Indies side.

Two of those young men were Andy Roberts and Vivian Richards (*right*), who would make such impressions with Hampshire and Somerset, respectively. Both came from the tiny island of Antigua that has, so the tourism blurb claims, a different beach for every day of the year. The island had never produced a Test cricketer before. By the end of 1974 they had two and both, in their different ways, would provide the cutting edge with which they would tear opponents apart.

Whispering Death: Michael Holding in full flow against England at The Oval in 1976 when he took 14 wickets in the match.

'We wanted to prove to the world that we were the best' – Michael Holding

off in a way this very conservative of games was simply not used to. Their ground-fielding too was of a speed and quality that most Test sides simply could not match. The athletic ability of many of the players was awe-inspiring and it was only enhanced by the influence of Kerry Packer's rebel World Series Cricket in the late 1970s.

All the top West Indies players signed up and they were assigned a fitness trainer, Dennis Waight, a hard-drinking, tough-talking Aussie who made his charges do 500 sit-ups a day. Captain Lloyd saw the benefits of Waight's work and kept him on after the Packer circus had finished. West Indies were the fittest, as well as the most talented, side around.

The great manifestation of this fielding panache was the World Cup final of 1975 when five Australian batsmen were run out, including two direct hits from square leg by Richards.

That final, played in glorious weather on the longest day of the English summer, showcased this relatively new form of the game – the one-day international – to perfection.

Lord's had never seen anything like it. West Indies fans, first-

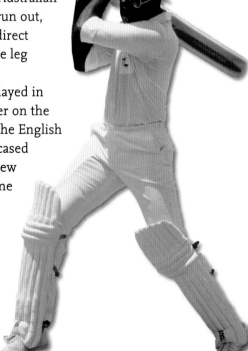

Roberts came first. He was an intelligent and intimidating quick bowler with a poker face. He had tremendous variations in pace, not least with his bouncer of which there were two kinds: sharpish and invisible. He would set the batsman up with a slower (all things are relative) one and then nail them with the both-barrels version.

Roberts had played a single Test before touring India in late 1974, a trip that also welcomed the 22-year-old Richards to the fold. West Indies won the series 3-2 and the Indian journalist Dicky Rutnagur wrote in *Wisden*: 'The 1974–75 team gave a strong a hint of future greatness.' Roberts took 44 wickets in the series on slow subcontinental pitches while Richards announced himself in his second Test at Delhi with a monstrous 192 not out, blazing five of his six sixes after reaching his century.

There was nothing sedate about this new West Indies side. The bowlers bowled at a hundred miles an hour and the batsmen attacked from the or second-generation immigrants to the UK, cavorted on the boundary's edge, and sometimes inside it, in a carnival of infectious, joyful noise.

They would be celebrating again a year later when West Indies returned for a Test-match tour of England and proved that they had learned from their Australian nightmare.

'Our experiences in Australia did serve one useful purpose. It demonstrated to the younger players who were to form the nucleus of our teams for the next few years how tough and demanding Test cricket can be,' wrote Lloyd.

'It was the first time they had tasted the bitterness of defeat. It might have been difficult to take at the time but it did prepare them for the arduous assignments which lay head.'

'We wanted to prove to the entire world that we were the best,' said Holding. They had another motivation too. Before the series started England's South African-born captain Tony Greig gave an infamous television interview in which he questioned the true quality of the West Indies side and said that their players would 'grovel' when things went against them.

'Whether Greig realized it or not, the word "grovel" is guaranteed to raise the blood pressure of any black man,' Lloyd wrote. 'It conjures up hated images of hundreds of years of slavery and servility.'

It was England who did the grovelling in a 3-0 defeat, played in a heatwave summer made famous by the run-scoring feats of Richards, who made 829 runs at an average of 118 despite missing one of the five Tests, and the destructive fast bowling of Holding and Roberts.

There was sourness at the bouncer barrage directed at Brian Close, the England batsman recalled at the age of 46, in poor light during the third Test at Manchester.

Accusations of intimidation and excessive use of short-pitched bowling were a constant part of the narrative as West Indies built the most explosive, dominant and fearsome international team the game had ever seen.

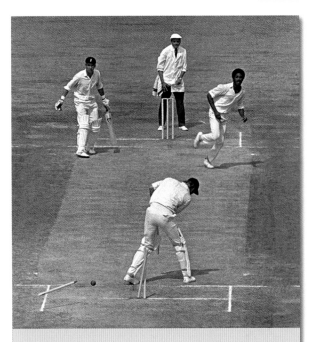

Demolished: Tony Greig's stumps rearranged by Holding.

England v. West Indies 1976
(† denotes team winning toss; * not out)

1st Test, Nottingham, 3–8 June †West Indies 494 (IVA Richards 232, AI Kallicharran 97; DL Underwood 4-82) and 176-5 dec (Richards 63; JA Snow 4-53); England 332 (DS Steele 106, RA Woolmer 82; WW Daniel 4-53) and 156-2 (JH Edrich 76*). Match drawn.

2nd Test, Lord's, 17–22 June †England 250 (DB Close 60; AME Roberts 5-60) and 254 (Steele 64; Roberts 5-63); West Indies 182 (CG Greenidge 84, CH Lloyd 50; Snow 4-68, Underwood 5-39) and 241-6 (RC Fredericks 138). Match drawn.

3rd Test, Manchester, 8–13 July †West Indies 211 (Greenidge 134; MWW Selvey 4-41) and 411-5 dec (Fredericks 50, Greenidge 101, Richards 135); England 71 (MA Holding 5-17) and 126 (Roberts 6-37). West Indies won by 425 runs.

4th Test, Leeds, 22–27 July †West Indies 450 (Fredericks 109, Greenidge 115, Richards 66, LG Rowe 50; Snow 4-77) and 196 (CL King 58; RGD Willis 5-42); England 387 (AW Greig 116, APE Knott 116) and 204 (Greig 76*). West Indies won by 55 runs.

5th Test, The Oval, 12–17 August †West Indies 687-8 dec (Fredericks 71, Richards 291, Rowe 70, Lloyd 84, King 63) and 182-0 dec (Fredericks 86*, Greenidge 85*); England 435 (DL Amiss 203, Knott 50; Holding 8-92) and 203 (Knott 57; Holding 6-57). West Indies won by 203 runs

West Indies won the series 3-0

CLIVE LLOYD

As West Indies cricket declined so painfully in the new millennium most people wanted to know why. Few asked the reverse question: how was it that a disparate group of tiny islands, all individual nations with diverse ethnic origins and little in common apart from their colonial history, became one of the greatest sports teams ever to walk on to a playing field?

The answer is complex, of course, but a major part of that answer is Clive Lloyd, the captain who set West Indies on their way to an unprecedented 20-year period of global domination from the mid-1970s.

Lloyd grew up fast. He lost his father when he was nine and damaged his eyes breaking up a fight at school when he was 12 which necessitated the wearing of spectacles. He was an imposing man, standing 6ft 5in with slightly stooping shoulders to match his famous drooping moustache.

He used a heavier bat than most of his generation and added several rubber grips to the handle to make the bat seem lighter. At the crease he shuffled into line before carving bowlers of all kinds to the boundary 'from a spot on the blade so sweet it was a danger to diabetics' as former England bowler Mike Selvey wrote.

Lloyd made two fifties on his debut to help win a Test in India and also showed off his fielding skills that would become a major plank of his reputation. In his first Test against England he scored his first Test century and then made one at Brisbane in his first Test against Australia.

Like many West Indies players of the time, he planted deep roots in English county cricket. Choosing Lancashire over Warwickshire, he helped the county become the game's first great limited-overs side. Manchester remains his home.

He became West Indies captain in late 1974 and within a few months was showing his big-game temperament with a match-winning century at Lord's in the inaugural World Cup final against Australia. Later in 1975 the same opponents delivered an almighty – and era-defining – 5-1 Test series thrashing. Lloyd reassessed West Indies' capabilities and the all-out pace attack was born. He improved as a batsman as captain, averaging over 50 compared with 38 beforehand.

'We trusted Clive. Because we respected him so much, we were ready to follow him' – Viv Richards

He retired in 1985, having administered the 5-0 'blackwash' to England and a 3-1 victory in Australia. He was the first West Indies player to appear in 100 Tests. He led the side 74 times, securing a run of 26 Tests without defeat and a record-breaking 11 successive victories.

Known affectionately by teammates and opponents alike as Hubert (his middle name), he has been much in demand since his retirement in 1985 for his wisdom and calm authority. He has managed the West Indies team and had a number of ICC roles including match referee.

Full name: Clive Hubert Lloyd
Born: 31 August 1944, Georgetown, British Guiana (now Guyana)
International career span: 1966–85
Role: Left-hand middle-order batsman, very occasional right-arm medium-pace bowler
Notable numbers: 110 Tests, 7,515 runs at 46.67, highest 242*, 19 hundreds. 74 Tests as captain, won 36, lost 12
Extras: Cousin of great West Indies spinner Lance Gibbs; ICC match referee, chairman of ICC cricket committee; awarded CBE; Order of Australia 1985; son Jason plays in goal for the Guyana national football team

Complete bowler: Malcolm Marshall, who died tragically young aged 41, was arguably the greatest of the West Indies champion pace bowlers.

WHEN THEY WERE KINGS

Such was the antiquated relationship between the West Indies players and their governing body there was little hesitation by the top players to sign up for Kerry Packer's rebel World Series Cricket in 1977.

The absence of the leading players meant the West Indies side had an unfamiliar look in the late 1970s. But that meant opportunities for young, emerging talent. One such new boy was the 20-year-old all-rounder Malcolm Marshall, picked

Wes Hall, fast bowler turned preacher, said the final prayers for Marshall

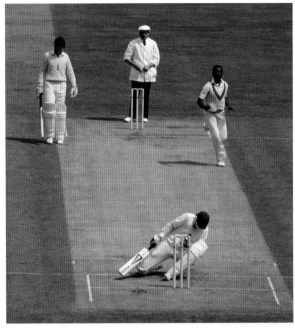

Immediate impact: England debutant Andy Lloyd is hit on the head by a ball from Marshall at Birmingham in 1984.

to tour India in 1978 with only one first-class match for Barbados behind him. He was different from the other fast bowlers. He was noticeably shorter for a start and, fittingly for someone who hailed from the same Barbados village as Garry Sobers, he could bat.

Although he did not make an immediate impact, he was snapped up by Hampshire as a replacement for Andy Roberts. Marshall's long-term association with Hampshire helped him to develop and refine a range of skills that would serve him well at international level.

Because he lacked the height or physical power of many of his colleagues, he had to use other methods. And it was his ability to out-think batsmen, to swing the ball both ways at pace and to cut the ball off the pitch that made Marshall the complete bowler. If you had to pick one from the Caribbean quicks hall of fame, you could do worse than plump for 'Maco'. His death in 1999, aged only 41, from colon cancer was mourned across the world but nowhere more acutely or tearfully than in Barbados itself where Wes Hall, the great fast bowler turned preacher, delivered the final prayers at Marshall's bedside as he passed away.

He was the most prolific Test bowler of the 1980s, taking 297 wickets at an average of 20 and a strike-rate of a wicket every seven and a half overs.

Because of the depth of bowling talent in the West Indies line-up once all the top men returned from Packer, it took Marshall five years to get his hands on the new ball. The next time he would do anything other than open the bowling was 1989, by which time Messrs Ambrose and Walsh had filed off the production line.

It took Marshall no time to make an impact on the 1984 Test series in England. After half an hour of the first Test at Birmingham, England's debutant opener Andy Lloyd was hit on the side of the head as he attempted vainly to avoid a waspish short-of-a-length ball from Marshall. Lloyd's Test career had lasted 17 balls and England lost the Test by an innings and 180 runs.

England knew the chances were slim when, in the one-day series that preceded the Tests, Viv Richards (*left*) played one of the great limited-overs innings of all time at Manchester. His 189 not out pulled West Indies out of the mire of 102 for seven to 272 for nine and a 104-run victory.

Marshall took eight wickets in the second Test at Lord's where West Indies went 2-0 up with a last-day run-chase that elevated Gordon

Perfect finish: West Indies supporters at The Oval in 1984 celebrate their side's 5-0 demolition of England – the first 'blackwash'.

Greenidge, a fellow Bajan and Hampshire man, to super stardom. England, in the unaccustomed situation of parity or even partial dominance, were able to set West Indies 342, the highest total of the match, to win on the final day. They won by nine wickets with 11.5 overs to spare, their one loss being Desmond Haynes run out.

Greenidge (*right*) scored 214 not out from 242 balls. It was Sehwag-style a generation ahead of its time. England did not bowl well but Greenidge was merciless, his cut shot a breathtaking axe of destruction. He made a second double-century in the fourth Test at Manchester that West Indies won by an innings.

On the first morning of the third Test at Leeds Marshall fractured his left thumb in two places fielding a ball in the gully. He was advised not to play for ten days. Instead, he came out to bat one-handed with his left forearm in plaster. He helped Larry Gomes to his hundred and even

Gordon Greenidge's cut shot was a breathtaking axe of destruction

scored a four, edged as he swung at the ball like a tennis player. Then with the ball he took seven for 53, his best Test figures.

In the final Test at The Oval West Indies made their lowest total of the series, 190. But Marshall, with a spell of five for 35 that *Wisden* called an 'almost brutal display of fast bowling', turned the match West Indies' way and put them on track for a 5-0 'blackwash', as one banner put it.

West Indies had now won eight consecutive Tests, matching Australia's record of 1920–21. By the end of 1984 they would stretch their run to 11 straight wins with victories in Australia. It was West Indies' first five-Test tour of Australia since the 5-1 debacle of 1975–76 and a sweet triumph for those players from that trip still around.

As well as their obvious class West Indies continued to display exceptional powers of resilience, regularly posting scores of 400-plus after losing their first five wickets for under 200.

And, as in England, their fielding was outstanding and on a different plane from their opponents'. While slip catches were gobbled greedily the Australians shelled around 30 catches.

West Indies also confirmed their status as kings of the limited-overs format with 12 wins from 13 matches in the tri-series with Sri Lanka and Australia. Their loss to India in the final of the 1983 World Cup was a bizarre aberration.

The 3-1 Test victory in Australia marked the end of Clive Lloyd's career. Viv Richards took over and, while he did not display Lloyd's patriarchal abilities, the results kept coming.

In 1986 West Indies inflicted a second 'blackwash' on England, this time in front of their own adoring fans across the Caribbean. England were blown away in a storm of injury, incompetence and innuendo about off-field misbehaviour. On an uneven pitch in Jamaica Mike Gatting had his nose broken when he top-edged an attempted pull off Marshall into his face. Gatting was asked by a journalist where the ball actually hit him. With a neat row of stitches visible amid the purple bruising, Gatting's reaction was deadpan: 'I think X marks the spot.'

X marks the spot: Mike Gatting, aided by physio Lawrie Brown, leaves the field in Jamaica in 1986 after edging a ball into his face.

West Indies had a new bowler in their armoury. The Jamaican Patrick Patterson did not have the accuracy of his peers but he was as fast as any and more frightening than most, particularly on spicy pitches. No England batsman made a century in the five Tests and, as the series went on, they seemed to lose their appetite for the contest.

In the second innings of the fifth Test Richards, on his home ground in Antigua, made the fastest century in Test history off 56 balls despite England having anything between six and nine men on the boundary. In all Richards scored 110 not out in 83 minutes out of the 146 scored while he was at the crease.

West Indies had won ten consecutive Tests against England whose despondent supporters wondered if they would ever beat the kings of the Caribbean again.

MICHAEL HOLDING

Never has a nickname been so chillingly yet gracefully evocative as 'Whispering Death', the label attached to Michael Holding by umpires to describe his long, barely audible approach to the wicket.

To the batsman he was a speck in the distance, setting off, it seemed, from the boundary's edge. With huge, athletic, rhythmic strides he reached the crease before delivering the ball, apparently effortlessly, at bone-crunching speeds.

He was the fastest of the West Indies pace bowlers who came to dominate world cricket through the 1970s and 1980s, though injury meant he played only 60 Tests.

Two spells in his Test career define the brutality and the brilliance of Holding. In 1976 at Manchester he bowled a viciously hostile spell to the 46-year-old England batsman Brian Close, the very essence of impassive Yorkshire toughness, that eventually prompted an intervention from the umpire Bill Alley. The footage is YouTube gold as the ball fizzes past Close's bare, balding head that just sways out of the way in time and then takes blows on the body, which he reacts to with, carefully managed wince.

In 1981 in Barbados Holding bowled an over to England's Geoff Boycott that the batsman himself and most observers considered to be one of the fastest, most brilliant ever bowled. It was the second over of England's first innings of the series. Each ball stretched Boycott to the limit and the final one clattered into his stumps.

At The Oval in 1976 he produced one of the great examples of sustained fast bowling to take 14 English wickets on a pitch that yielded two double-centuries and more than 1,500 runs.

As famous as the sight of Holding cruising in to bowl is the image of him kicking a stump out of the ground in a Test against New Zealand at Dunedin in 1980, boiling over in frustration at a series of bad umpiring decisions.

He was not a noted batsman but he had big-hitting capabilities down the order and holds the record for most sixes (36) by any Test batsman who has scored fewer than 1,000 runs.

He played also for Tasmania in Australia, Canterbury in New Zealand and Lancashire and Derbyshire in English county cricket. In retirement he has developed into a respected and much loved television commentator, his deep,

'If I were you I'd try and get down the other end'
— Len Hutton to Bob Woolmer on how to best to face Holding

warm Jamaican voice instantly recognizable to viewers around the world.

Holding has been an outspoken critic of the contemporary administration of West Indies and world cricket. In 2008 he resigned from the ICC's cricket committee in protest at a decision to change the result of the 2006 Test between England and Pakistan at The Oval that had originally been forfeited by Pakistan in protest at a five-run penalty from umpire Darrell Hair for ball-tampering.

Full name: Michael Anthony Holding
Born: 16 February 1954, Kingston, Jamaica
International career span: 1975–87
Role: Right-arm fast bowler, right-hand tail-end batsman
Notable numbers: 60 Tests, 249 wickets at 23.68, 13 five-wicket innings, two ten-wicket matches; 910 runs at 13.78, highest score 73, 36 sixes; 102 one-day internationals, 142 wickets at 21.36
Extras: Mainstay of Sky Sports' TV commentary team; huge horse-racing fan and close friend of the Barbados-born champion flat-racing trainer, Sir Michael Stoute

Dynamic duo: Courtney Walsh (left) and Curtly Ambrose celebrate during South Africa's maiden Test in West Indies at Bridgetown in 1992.

LAST DAYS OF EMPIRE

Although West Indies continued their phenomenal record of undefeated series, that had begun in 1980, until their momentous home loss to Australia in 1995, there were signs of decline towards the end of the 1980s.

A three-day defeat in 1987 at Christchurch, their first over such a short period since 1965, allowed New Zealand to level a three-match series. They still managed to inflict their customary humiliation of England in 1988. It was only 4-0 this time but England were so undermined they went through four different captains.

There was a shock to the Caribbean system, though, when England won the first Test of the 1990 series in Jamaica and were close to winning the third. In the end West Indies prevailed after a burst from their new giant fast bowler, Curtly Ambrose, in the fourth Test at Barbados. At the start of the final Test in Antigua, which West Indies won easily, the captain Viv Richards confronted an English journalist. He had objected to comments made about Richards' sportsmanship, or lack of it, while claiming a dismissal in Barbados. These were tetchier times.

'Curtly talk to no man' was the refrain. He preferred bowling and guitar-playing

Staying power: no fast bowler sent down as many overs as Courtney Walsh, here at The Oval in 1991.

A year later Richards called time on his glorious international career at the end of a drawn series in England. His replacement was a fellow Antiguan, the smiling, relaxed Richie Richardson who, like Richards, never wore a helmet.

The bowling cupboard was not bare but there was an increasing reliance on the Antiguan Ambrose (*right*) and his equally tall partner Courtney Walsh from Jamaica. Through the 1990s until March 2001, when Walsh retired, the pair took 719 Test wickets, more than all the other West Indies bowlers during that period put together.

Walsh's longevity defied belief. No fast bowler in history bowled as many as his 5,003 Test overs, not to mention his 11 seasons for Gloucestershire in English county cricket. He had a long apprenticeship, making his debut in the 1984 series in England and spending years as backup to Holding, Marshall et al.

With his wide-eyed, slightly quizzical demeanour Walsh played good cop to Ambrose's silent assassin. 'Curtly talk to no man' became a refrain as Ambrose turned down every interview request that came his way. He preferred to express himself through his world-class bowling and his guitar-playing in a band that has also numbered Richie Richardson among its members.

Because West Indies did not have the fast-bowling depth to dominate from first to last as they had in the previous generation, opponents were often lulled into a false sense of security. And that was when Curtly was at his most dangerous.

At Port of Spain, Trinidad, in 1994, England had secured a first-innings lead and were set a modest 194 to win the Test. Mike Atherton was lbw to Ambrose's first ball of the innings and by the close of the fourth day England were 40 for eight, demolished by a rampant Ambrose who finished with six for 24. Walsh completed the rout the following morning and Ambrose was carried off the field on his teammates' shoulders.

The final Test of the 1994 series was a high-scoring draw that barely reached beyond the first innings and would normally have been forgotten about as soon as it had finished. But this was the match in which Brian Lara made 375, breaking Garry Sobers'

Raising the bar: Brian Lara leaves the field under a guard of honour after his world record 375 in Antigua in 1994.

West Indies won that series in Australia 2-1 but the sides' next meeting, in the Caribbean in 1995, was very different. It was the moment when the crown slipped and was snaffled by the Aussies.

It was West Indies' first Test series loss since 1980, a run of 29 rubbers undefeated. It signalled the end of the glory days though the swiftness of decline shocked and saddened fans all over the world, not just in the islands of the Caribbean where success was expected and demanded.

Defeat by the minnows of Kenya in the 1996 World Cup was followed by a 3-0 Test series defeat in Pakistan in 1997. But it got worse a year later with a 5-0 whitewash in South Africa. The leading figures on and off the field resigned, Chaos and discord reigned with golden child Lara never far from the action, for good and ill.

The tour to England in 2000 marked the end of the Ambrose-Walsh axis that had been holding the West Indies side together, though Walsh would play on for a few months more. More shockingly for West Indies supporters it was the first series defeat by England since 1969. Four years later England routed them in the Caribbean, their first series win there since 1968. The surprise victory in the 2004 one-day Champions Trophy final at The Oval against England was a brief shaft of light in a dark time for Caribbean cricket.

Lack of succession planning during the good times and lack of grass-roots investment has been exposed in recent years.

Relations between the governing body and the leading players are rarely cordial with the lure of the Indian Premier League

world record set in 1958. Sobers was at the ground when Lara passed the milestone against a wilting England attack and the game was paused for a moment of Caribbean cricketing theatre as the great all-rounder strode out to the middle to congratulate his young successor.

Sobers' 365 not out had been his maiden Test hundred and Lara's epic was only his third. His first came only 15 months earlier, a monumental 277 at Sydney against Australia. The next Test of that series at Adelaide was a thriller, West Indies winning by a single run after the Australian tail had rallied in pursuit of 186. It was the narrowest margin of victory in Test history.

Ambrose took ten wickets in the match but it was Walsh who clinched victory when a short ball brushed the glove of the Australian No.11 Craig McDermott on its way through to the keeper.

Gayle force: Chris Gayle celebrates reaching a Test century against England at The Oval in 2004.

Gayle has openly admitted an indifference towards Test cricket

compromising West Indies' ability to get their best side on the field. This conflict is embodied by Chris Gayle, the powerful and flamboyant Jamaican batsman whose destructive abilities have brought him a Test triple-century, the fifth-fastest Test hundred of all time and a memorable flaying

of Australia in the 2009 World Twenty20 at The Oval when he demolished Brett Lee.

Yet Gayle has openly admitted to an indifference towards the future of Test cricket and a contractual dispute with the West Indies board led to his absence from the Test side in 2011.

West Indies' hard-fought 1-0 Test series victory over England hinted at better times ahead. Though progress has been slow, they do possess some young talented individuals: batsmen like Darren Bravo, Lendl Simmons (*left*) and Adrian Barath and the fast bowler Kemar Roach.

Brian Lara

With an appetite for run-getting matched only by Don Bradman and the flair of Garry Sobers, Brian Lara was one of the greatest modern batsmen. While Sachin Tendulkar churned out runs modestly and methodically, Lara was all flamboyance and flourish, with controversy never far behind.

His distinctively high backlift hinted at some great explosion of power to come. He was utterly compelling to watch.

The tenth of eleven children, Lara grew up playing all manner of sports in northern Trinidad and became close friends with the island's leading sportsmen like the footballer Dwight Yorke. He was captain of Trinidad at 20 and made his Test debut in the same year.

His first Test hundred was a colossal 277 against Australia in 1993. He named his daughter after the venue where it occurred, Sydney. He was only 24 when he broke Garry Sobers' record for the highest individual Test score, making 375 in Antigua against England in 1994.

Having been catapulted into world stardom by that innings, he proceeded straight to England for a season with Warwickshire. The summer began with a string of centuries and another mind-blowing record: the highest score in first-class cricket, 501 not out against Durham (*right*). But Lara was a vulnerable figure, struggling to adjust to his new-found celebrity and open to commercial exploitation.

For much of his career he was the nugget in a pan full of grit, a situation that brought challenge and confrontation. He was on the losing side in 63 of his 131 Tests, for a long time a record until his long-suffering teammate Shiv Chanderpaul stole the unwanted record.

Allied to his talent was an iron will. If he set his mind to achieve something, he generally did. When the Australian Matthew Hayden broke his record with 380 against Zimbabwe in 2003, Lara raised the bar six months later with an unbeaten 400, again on the featherbed pitch in Antigua, again against England.

In 1999, when he was captain, he single-handedly won two Tests against Australia to secure a drawn series only months after the 5-0 drubbing in South Africa, a tour that had been overshadowed by an acrimonious pay dispute.

'He played my bowling better than anyone, including Tendulkar'
— Muttiah Muralitharan

West Indies had been bowled out for 51 in the first Test and seemed set for another humiliation. Yet in the second Lara made 213 to set up a ten-wicket victory. There were only three other scores over fifty in the match.

Somehow he bettered that performance in the next Test in Barbados. With 153 not out he marshalled a gripping run chase, leading West Indies to a one-wicket victory. The next top score was 38. Steve Waugh, the Australian captain, said he had never played in a better match.

Full name: Brian Charles Lara
Born: 2 May 1969, Santa Cruz, Trinidad
International career span: 1990–2007
Role: Middle-order left-handed batsman
Notable numbers: 131 Tests, 11,953 runs at 52.88, 34 hundreds, 48 fifties, highest 400 not out (world record); 299 one-day internationals, 10,405 runs at 40.48, 19 hundreds, 63 fifties; became leading Test run-scorer of all time in 2005 until Tendulkar broke the record in 2008; highest first-class of all time (501 not out)
Extras: In 2010 made a comeback after two years retired to play in Zimbabwe's domestic Twenty20 competition

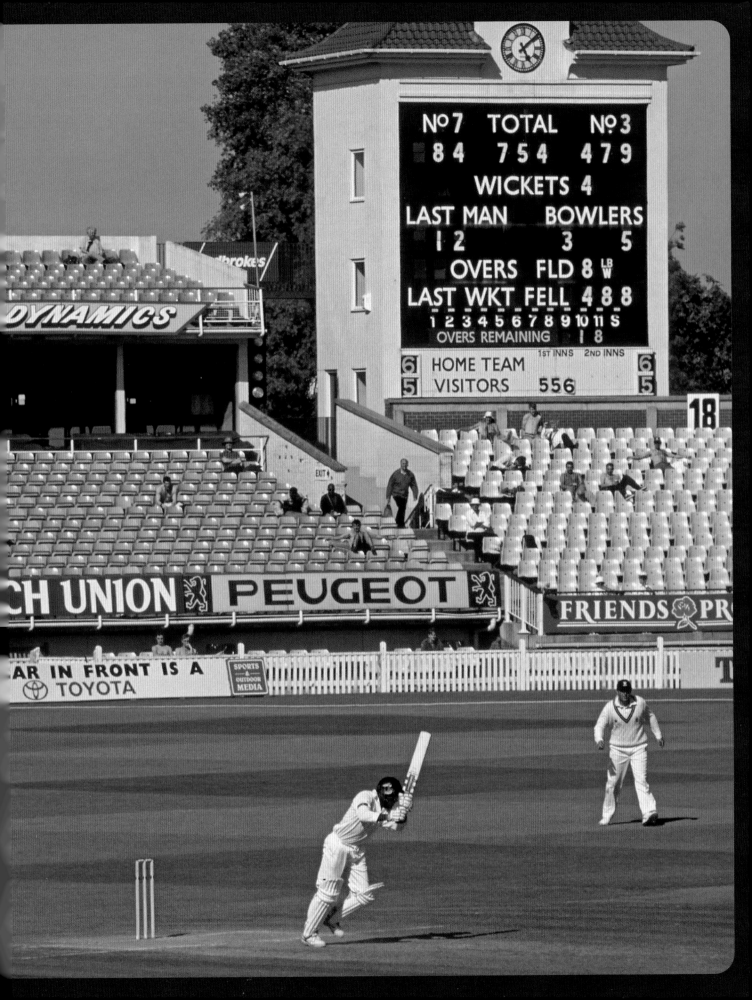

KENSINGTON OVAL

Jamaicans and Trinidadians would doubtless disagree but Barbados has traditionally been the beating heart of cricket in the Caribbean.

The island has produced more Test players than any other and a Barbados all-time XI is a tasty side: Gordon Greenidge, Desmond Haynes, Everton Weekes, Frank Worrell (capt), Clyde Walcott (wk), Garry Sobers, Malcolm Marshall, Joel Garner, Sylvester Clarke, Wes Hall, Charlie Griffith.

The Kensington Oval, in the west-coast capital Bridgetown, was for decades a fortress for the West Indies team. After losing to England in 1935 they did not lose any of their next 27 Tests on the ground until England beat them in 1994.

Between 1978 and 1986 they won six successive Tests by margins of nine wickets, 298 runs, ten wickets three times and an innings and 30 runs. Pitches tended to be hard, true and bouncy,

Kensington's notable numbers (to 9 Feb 2012)

Capacity: 28,000
No. of Tests: 47 Tests (1930–2011)
Highest team score: 749-9 dec, West Indies v. England 2009
Lowest team score: 81, India v. WI 1987
Highest individual score: 337, Hanif Mohammad for Pakistan v. West Indies 1958
Most Test runs: 1,339, Brian Lara (West Indies), 1992–2005
Best individual bowling: 8-38, Lance Gibbs for West Indies v. India 1962
Most Test wickets: 53, Courtney Walsh (West Indies), 1988–2001
Highest ODI team score: 313-6, Sri Lanka v. West Indies, 2003
Highest ODI individual score: 149, Adam Gilchrist for Australia v. Sri Lanka, 2007

For decades it was a fortress. West Indies did not lose a Test here between 1935 and 1994

giving the quick bowlers the perfect conditions to wreak their havoc, though the best batsmen could score plentifully too. In the 1978 Test Australian Graham Yallop made history by becoming the first batsman to wear a protective helmet in a Test match.

Until a $135 million redevelopment ahead of the 2007 World Cup, the Oval, which hosted the final, was a charming mixture of constructed stands and open 'bleachers', allowing spectators to move freely and celebrate noisily.

In recent times, as the West Indies side has struggled and the Caribbean has become a more affordable holiday destination, the ground has often seemed like an away game for West Indies. In 2004 when England played there the ground was a sea of red-and-white cross of St George flags to witness a Matthew Hoggard hat-trick.

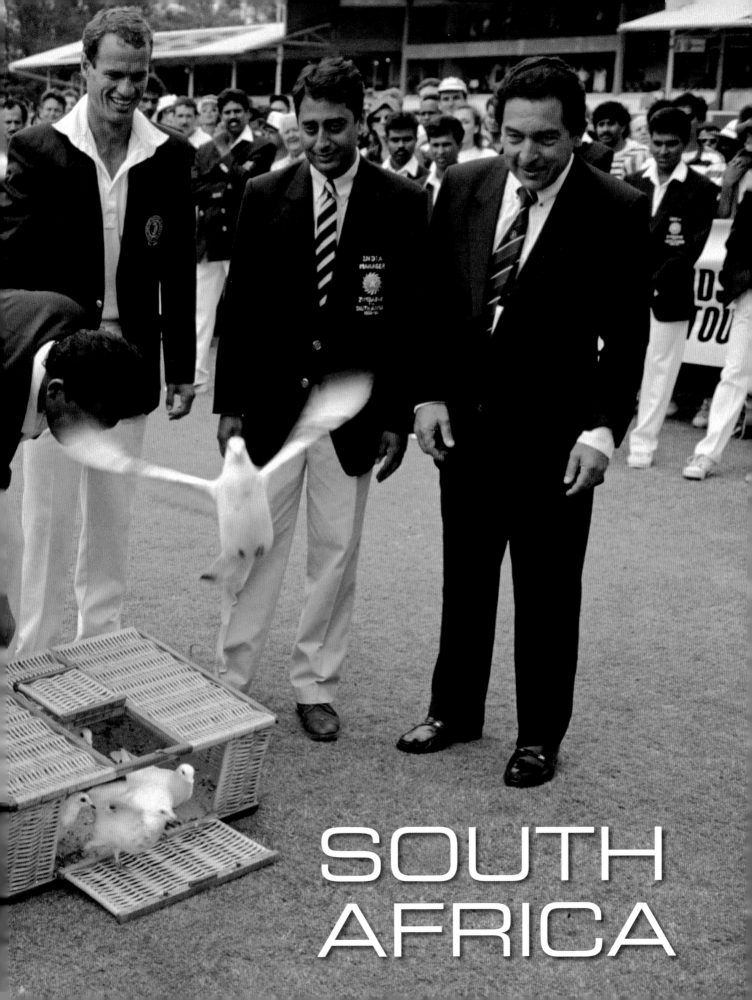

SOUTH
AFRICA

Catalyst: Basil D'Oliveira, batting for England against Australia in 1972, was the central figure in the controversy that led to SA's isolation. Previous page: doves are released before South Africa's first Test since readmission, against India at Durban in November 1992.

BRILLIANCE BEFORE BAN

As a last hurrah it takes some beating. South Africa had not played a Test series for three years. The door was closing on their international participation because of their government's apartheid policy of racial discrimination.

The catalyst for the international boycott was the controversy surrounding the selection, or non-selection, of England's all-rounder Basil D'Oliveira for their tour of South Africa in 1968–69. D'Oliveira had been born in South Africa and was categorized by the apartheid system as Cape Coloured. The South African government had made it clear he would not be welcome and the country's cricket officials tried to exert pressure on MCC, who selected the England team, not to pick him. He was not chosen in the original party, a decision that only increased the pressure on English cricket authorities to sever ties. When he was drafted in after an injury the political heat intensified and the tour was cancelled.

South Africa's final Test series before entering a 22-year period of isolation was one of the

When cricketing heaven is discussed, Barry Richards' name is there

Opposition: anti-apartheid protests before a South Africa v. Barbarians rugby match at Twickenham in 1970.

game's most memorable contests, or more properly no-contests. In the first three months of 1970 Australia were beaten 4-0, all four Tests conceded by huge margins.

South Africa's side contained players who would be regarded as among the best not only from their country but from anywhere in the world. And while the deprivation of international competition for South Africa was a perfectly right and proper decision, a number of high-class players were cut off in their prime.

Mike Procter, a burly all-rounder with an extraordinarily awkward-looking bowling action, took 26 wickets in the series and would find a home from home with Gloucestershire. He had played only seven Tests. Indeed, English county cricket would provide havens and talent outlets for others like the all-rounder Eddie Barlow, with Derbyshire, and the opening batsman Barry Richards with Hampshire.

These were the only four Tests of Richards' career. He made the most of them scoring two centuries and averaging 72. He would form a fantasy opening partnership with the West Indian Gordon Greenidge at Hampshire. When old players congregate to discuss a cricketing heaven, when push comes to shove in the arguments about true greatness, Barry Richards is never far from the lips.

In a glittery line-up perhaps the most notable star was the powerful left-hander Graeme Pollock. In the second Test at Durban, the city of his birth, he smashed 274, the highest individual score by a South African.

The captain of that great side was Ali Bacher (*below*) who would become a central figure in South African cricket for the next generation and beyond. He won the toss in each of the four Tests against Australia and it was a golden touch that would not desert him. In the 1980s he organized a series of highly controversial and divisive rebel international tours to South Africa by teams from England, Australia and, most eyebrow-raisingly of all, West Indies and Sri Lanka.

Despite the stigma attached to these excursions, Bacher skilfully reinvented himself as the man to run the rehabilitated version of South African cricket when the United Cricket Board was formed, to bring together the black and white cricketing authorities. South Africa were formally welcomed back into the fold in 1991 with a one-day international in India. Bacher would later mastermind South Africa's hosting of the 2003 World Cup.

GRAEME POLLOCK

Don Bradman said that, alongside Garry Sobers, he was the best left-hander he ever saw and accolades do not resound any more than that. His batting average of 60.97 is second only to Bradman's among those who have had 20 or more Test innings.

Graeme Pollock was the middle-order batting powerhouse of South Africa's world-class side of the late 1960s that annihilated Australia in 1970 before being taken apart themselves by their country's international sporting isolation. His 274 at Durban is regarded as one of the great innings. Although tall and a brutal destroyer of bowling he was also a great timer of the ball, especially driving through the off side.

Pollock was moderately better off than some of his younger teammates. He had played 23 Tests before the boycott but he bore no bitterness over it – a mark of the unassuming decency that made him such a hero to a generation. 'I wasn't angry. Something had to be done,' he said recently. 'The ruling people wouldn't show the world that we'd got it all wrong and were prepared to change it. What South Africa got was deserved. Unless you're a total hypocrite, you have to ask on what grounds were we eligible to play international sport?'

Pollock chose not to pursue a professional playing career overseas like many of his teammates but devoured bowling attacks in South Africa's highly competitive Currie Cup competition. He also played 16 unofficial Tests against the touring rebel sides.

As a nine-year-old at the renowned Grey High School in Port Elizabeth he took all ten wickets and scored a century. In 1961, as a 16-year-old, he was the youngest South African to score a first-class century and at 19 he was the youngest to score a double-century. He was also the youngest South African to score a Test century, at Sydney against Australia when he was still 19.

In 1971 in a match to celebrate the tenth anniversary of the formation of the Republic of South Africa he and other players walked off after one ball in an anti-government protest.

Late in his career he moved teams, swapping Eastern Province for Transvaal and their famous Mean Machine. He was as productive as ever, scoring almost 5,000 runs and averaging 55. He bowed out with an unbeaten half-century in the Currie Cup final in 1987 at the age of 43.

'Graeme is a gentleman and what I always liked about him was his modesty' – David Richardson, ex-South Africa wicketkeeper

He remained a national treasure of South African cricket and was voted the country's top cricketer of the 20th century.

Along with Sobers, he presented the match awards at the 2003 World Cup final at Johannesburg. He was a national selector from 2000 to 2002.

Full name: Robert Graeme Pollock
Born: 27 February 1944, Durban
International career span: 1963–70
Role: Middle-order left-handed batsman
Notable numbers: 23 Tests, 2,256 runs at 60.97, highest score 274, seven centuries; has second-highest batting average (minimum 20 innings) of all time behind Don Bradman; first-class average of 54.67, 64 centuries, 99 fifties
Extras: Played for Rest of the World v. England in 1970; brother of SA Test bowler Peter Pollock and uncle of SA all-rounder Shaun Pollock

Giant step: South Africa reached the semi-finals of their first World Cup in 1992. Here skipper Kepler Wessels is dismissed by Ian Botham in the semi against England. This tournament was the world's first sight of super-fielder Jonty Rhodes.

WELCOME BACK

'I know how Neil Armstrong felt when he stood on the moon,' said an emotional South African captain, Clive Rice, after his team's first official international match for almost 22 years.

It was November 1991 and South Africa had just lost a one-dayer by three wickets to India in front of 90,000 at Eden Gardens in Kolkata. The South Africans were understandably not yet attuned to the special rigours of international competition. They were either too old – Rice was 42, batsmen Jimmy

Cook and Peter Kirsten 38 and 36, respectively – or too young and naïve. They were also too white. The squad contained two black players, diplomatic as much as cricketing selections.

But there was great interest in the novelty of South Africa's re-emergence. At Delhi 75,000 watched them win their first match, an eight-wicket victory underpinned by a third successive fifty from Kepler Wessels, the rhino-tough opener who had also played for Australia during isolation.

Stretched to the limit: Jonty Rhodes, who made fielding fashionable, goes airborne against India in the 1992 World Cup.

Wessels captained South Africa in their first major assignment, the 1992 World Cup, where they reached the semi-finals and lost out to England only via a farcical finish when a rain interruption mutated their target from 22 off 13 balls to 21 off one. The tournament was the world's first sighting of Jonty Rhodes, a jack-in-the-box athlete who would set new fielding standards. In their match against Pakistan, he ran out Inzamam-ul-Haq with a breathtaking, fully airborne dive at the stumps.

Hot on the heels of the World Cup came their first Test back, also their first-ever Test against West Indies, in April 1992. It was a great match in Barbados in which South Africa, not for the last time, would pass up a winning opportunity. South Africa lost every match on the tour but the political significance transcended on-field performance. The team contained only one non-white player, Omar Henry, but they were welcomed throughout the Caribbean. The only unrest was a bizarre domestic protest in Barbados at the omission of local fast bowler Anderson Cummins (*right*), a controversy that gave rise to the immortal banner: 'No Cummins, no goings.'

South Africa dominated the match and were 123 for two chasing 201 to win in the final innings

There were no easy victories to be had against the new South Africa

when Courtney Walsh ripped out the middle order with four for eight in 11 balls. They lost by 52 runs.

But there was no need for a settling-in period. They would prove themselves to be a fiercely competitive outfit with intensely gutsy batsmen and hard-nosed fast bowlers. Style played second fiddle to substance. Their only serious deficiency was in the spin-bowling department.

They matched Australia home and away, securing 1-1 draws, including a classic five-run victory at Sydney in the New Year's Test of 1994 after conceding a first-innings lead of 123. Australia needed only 117 to win and were 51 for one in pursuit until Fanie de Villiers, a lively, canny medium-pacer, intervened. He took six wickets in the innings and ten in the match, including the match-winning scalp of Glenn McGrath caught and bowled.

There were no easy victories to be had against the new South Africa but nor could they quite seal the deal. They drew also in England in 1994, their first tour there since 1965. They achieved a crushing 356-run victory at Lord's in a Test overshadowed by the 'dirt in the pocket' controversy when Mike Atherton, the England captain, was seen on television to be rubbing soil on the ball.

In the third and final Test at The Oval they were blown away by a career-defining nine wickets for 57 by England's wayward fast bowler Devon Malcolm. It was a performance of remarkable venom and hostility inspired to an extent by being hit on the helmet by de Villiers. Malcolm, famous for his poor eyesight and schoolboy fielding, was supposed to have said to the South African fielders as they gathered to check on his health: 'You guys are history.' It was a tall tale but it made a good title for his autobiography.

Fall from grace: Hansie Cronje was a successful and respected captain until the shocking revelations of match-fixing in 2000.

THE CRONJE YEARS

The five-run victory over Australia at Sydney in January 1994 was achieved under the temporary captaincy of a 22-year-old all-rounder Hansie Cronje, who filled in after an injury to Kepler Wessels. Cronje would have a profound effect on his country's cricket – for good and evil – over the next half-decade.

He took over officially from Wessels later that year and developed, in conjunction with the innovative coach Bob Woolmer, an aggressive and fiercely competitive team. Those who played for him considered him an inspirational leader. They ran the supreme Australian side close but never quite got over the line, either at Test level or, infamously, in the 1999 World Cup semi-final when a meltdown between the batting partners

Lance Klusener and Allan Donald led to a tie and Australian progression to the final.

At Adelaide in 1998 Shaun Pollock's seven for 87 had secured South Africa a first-innings lead of 167 in a Test they had to win to level the series. But they dropped ten catches and were three wickets short of victory. Mark Waugh, the Australian batsman who made an unbeaten century to save the game, was put down four times and given not out when he trod on his stumps as he staggered away after being hit by a ball from Pollock. Cronje's frustration boiled over afterwards when he stuck a stump through the door of the umpires' dressing room.

Cronje's almost reckless aggression as a batsman was in contrast to some of his captaincy

Cronje did it for money and the prize of a leather jacket from a bookie

that veered into deep conservatism. They lost the 1998 series in England by two Tests to one despite being 1-0 up and being a single wicket away from going two up with two Tests to play. The response to frustration was often to try to bore the opposition out with a line of attack relentlessly wide of off stump. Cronje had few tricks up his sleeve, just brute force and containment.

Their one touch-player, the middle-order batsman Daryll Cullinan, sadly became entangled in Shane Warne's web. In seven Tests against Australia he averaged only 12 and was dismissed by Warne four times. Yet overall he averaged 44 and in 1999 broke Graeme Pollock's 29-year-old record for South Africa's highest individual score. But the Test, against New Zealand at Auckland, typified Cronje's safety-first approach. Even allowing for a desperately slow pitch, his side batted too long: he declared their first innings after an hour of the third day once Cullinan had got his record. The match was drawn after an unusual record achieved by New Zealand's No.11 Geoff Allott whose 101-minute innings was the longest nought in Test history.

One achievement that Cronje's side managed that Australia could not was victory in India, ending the home side's run of 14 series without defeat. But the 2-0 triumph was overshadowed in the most disturbing way imaginable just over a month later when Cronje confessed in a 3 am phone call to the South African board chief executive, Ali Bacher, that he had been involved in match-fixing.

It emerged that Cronje had tried to manipulate the performances of his own players with financial inducements while in cahoots with illegal bookmakers and fixers. He pocketed

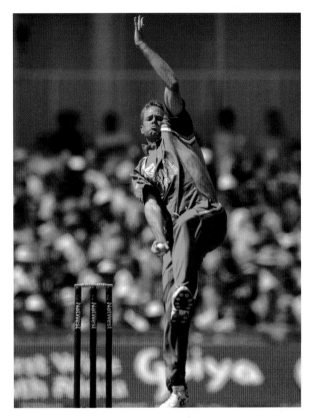

Pretty Polly: fast bowler Shaun Pollock, here bowling against England in 2003, shows off his high, classical, textbook action.

hundreds of thousands of dollars for providing privileged information to the bookies as well as the attempts to corrupt his teammates.

The revelations shed new light on the remarkable finish to the final Test against England at Centurion Park in January 2000. A heavily rain-affected match was destined for a draw until Cronje approached his opposite number, Nasser Hussain, with an offer to set up a final-innings run chase, a commonplace tactic in the league format of county cricket but unheard of in the Test arena. At the time it was thought Cronje was doing the game a great service, trying to provide entertainment for the paying public. In fact, he was doing it for money and the prize of a leather jacket from a bookie.

Cronje's tragic downfall took a macabre twist two years after his shaming. He was killed when a plane he was travelling in crashed into the Outeniqua mountain range in the Western Cape.

ALLAN DONALD

He was the first South African bowler to take 300 Test wickets, testament to his strength of mind and body as well as searing speed that earned him the nickname 'White Lightning'.

It was accepted without argument that he was the fastest white bowler in the world during the 1990s when West Indians and Pakistanis were the speed merchants par excellence.

He was instrumental in South Africa's first Test victory since readmission. On a slow pitch at Port Elizabeth he took 12 wickets against India in only his fourth Test. They were the fourth-best figures by a South African and were a sign of things to come. There was never any let-up from Donald. He had power, pace and a relentless determination.

One of his most famous spells was one in which he had to concede defeat but only after several slices of bad luck and a wrong umpiring decision. At Nottingham in 1998 he was trying to force a breakthrough in a run-chase by England. He had Mike Atherton given not out, caught off a glove, and Nasser Hussain dropped by the wicketkeeper Mark Boucher. That drop provoked a primeval roar from Donald, who had flung everything at the batsmen over a sustained period. Yet during the next over, Donald ran from his fielding position at fine leg to apologize to Boucher for his outburst.

An Afrikaaner with an English name and an accent that developed a West Midlands nuance to it, he remains a hugely popular figure inside and outside South Africa. Nowhere is he regarded with more affection than Birmingham where he made his home and became a match-winning stalwart for Warwickshire in county cricket for over a decade.

When Shaun Pollock emerged in 1995 he and Donald formed a premier new-ball partnership. While both were quick, Donald was the more outwardly aggressive, angling the ball, after his huge, big-effort delivery stride, into the batsman and then shaping it away. Pollock was the classic, side-on bowler who got so close to the stumps when he bowled he often flicked the bails off as his arm came over. In 1998 they were the two leading bowlers in Test cricket, Donald taking 80 wickets (the fourth most in any calendar year) and Pollock 69.

'Sometimes I had to over-step the mark to put the batsman on his guard'
– Allan Donald

In the 1999 World Cup semi-final on his home ground at Edgbaston, Donald set up what should have been a South Africa victory with four wickets, twice taking two in an over. But he will forever be cursed by the batting meltdown when he, the No.11, was run out after his partner Lance Klusener instinctively set off for a winning run with two more balls still remaining. The match was tied and South Africa were eliminated because of their defeat by Australia in an earlier match.

Full name: Allan Anthony Donald
Born: 20 October 1966, Bloemfontein
International career span: 1991–2003
Role: Right-arm fast opening bowler, right-hand tail-end batsman
Notable numbers: 72 Tests, 330 wickets at 22.25; strike-rate 47.0 is third best all-time of bowlers with 300 or more Test wickets; 164 ODIs, 272 wickets at 21.78. SA's third highest Test wicket-taker, second-highest in one-dayers
Extras: Has been an assistant coach with Warwickshire, bowling coach with England and South Africa and also a television commentator

Man for all seasons: AB de Villiers is the ultimate all-rounder – demon fielder, capable wicketkeeper and top batsman in all formats.

RISE UP THE RANKINGS

The post-Cronje recovery was a major project for South Africa. Shaun Pollock was the first man charged to take on the captaincy and it ended unfortunately.

South Africa hosted the World Cup in 2003, a source of immense pride – and inevitable expectation – for a sport-obsessed nation keen to show the rest of the world a transformed society.

Yet they were eliminated in the first phase of the competition after an embarrassing miscalculation in a rain-affected match against Sri Lanka. The revised target that they reached resulted in a tie and not the victory they required.

The man South Africa turned to next was young, only 22, but mature beyond his years. He was big, brash (nicknamed Biff) and unpopular with opponents. It was a huge burden for a young man to shoulder but Graeme Smith's appointment in 2003 was inspired.

He had made his Test debut only a year earlier against Australia and invited ridicule by revealing details of the verbal abuse he received by the Aussie fielders: what goes on the field stays on the field being the unwritten code that Smith seemed to have broken. On the 2003 tour of England, his first high-profile series as captain, Smith was

Graeme Smith delivers under pressure. His runs make a difference

mistakenly called Greg by the England captain, Nasser Hussain, an indication perhaps that opponents were taking him too lightly.

There was no danger of that after he scored 277 in the first Test at Birmingham, the highest Test score by a South African, and then 259 at Lord's, the highest score on the ground by a foreign batsman. His brutal style, with a heavy leg-side bias, offended the purists and won few admirers initially, though his longevity and success have won plenty over. No batsman in history has scored more runs than Smith in successful fourth-innings run-chases. In other words, he delivers under pressure. His runs make a difference.

In 2008, at Birmingham, he played one of the great pressure innings, making an unbeaten 154 out of 283 to steer South Africa to an unassailable 2-0 series lead over England. It was their first series victory in England since 1965 and another milestone on their quest for the top Test ranking.

They moved closer to that goal later in 2008 when they won a series in Australia, their first in nine attempts. In the first Test at Perth, South Africa were set an improbable 414 (only one team in history had successfully chased a larger total) having been outplayed for much of the match. Smith, with an injured elbow, made his sixth century of the year and passed 6,000 career Test runs. When AB de Villiers was joined by the debutant JP Duminy, a stylish but seemingly fragile left-hander, they still needed 108 to win with six wickets left. Much could go wrong, particularly given the South Africans' nervousness against Australia. They did not lose another wicket.

Duminy starred in the next Test at Melbourne where his ninth-wicket stand of 180, the third-highest in history, with the fast bowler Dale Steyn turned a heavy first-

Heavy duty: Graeme Smith has led South Africa from the front with crucial runs in successful run chases.

innings deficit into a sizeable lead. The dispirited Australians collapsed and South Africa won by nine wickets, Smith's inevitable contribution a mere 75. It was Australia's first home series defeat in 16 years.

When Australia conceded the Ashes to England in August 2009, South Africa, who were in their off-season, assumed top spot: the No.1 Test team in the world. They were a very fine side. Their batting had a combination of substance – Smith and the relentless Jacques Kallis – and style provided by Hashim Amla. They possessed the best new-ball attack in the world. Steyn, with his intimidating sneer, swung the ball at express pace while the tall Morne Morkel (*left*) bounced from the other end. They even had an effective spinner, the unheralded left-armer Paul Harris, with his boyishly tinted hair, proving that appearances can be deceptive.

And master-minding the whole operation, alongside Smith, was Mickey Arthur who, after five years as South Africa coach, would resurface as Australia's top man in late 2011.

Makhaya Ntini

'Is this a joke? I don't believe you,' was Makhaya Ntini's reaction to being selected for South Africa in 1998. Only four years earlier he was herding cattle barefoot in a tiny village in the Eastern Cape.

He was invited to join the South African board's development programme and showed immediate aptitude for fast bowling. In a one-day international against New Zealand at Perth in January 1998 he became the first black African to play for South Africa. It was a big deal for him but an even bigger deal for his country as it sought to make its sporting teams properly representative of its diverse population.

Ntini made a good early impression, made his Test debut two months later and remained a stalwart of South Africa's consistently impressive pace attack until 2009.

His career was derailed after a handful of matches when he was convicted of rape. He protested his innocence and was acquitted on appeal. But he spent almost two years out of the side until a four-wicket, match-winning comeback in a one-dayer against Australia at Durban in 2000.

There were faster bowlers and more technically skilful bowlers but none had a greater appetite for the contest than the superfit, ever-enthusiastic Ntini. Twelve bowlers in history have sent down more international overs than him but only one, the West Indian Curtly Ambrose, played in fewer matches than his 284.

His bowling style was quirky, with a line of attack that came from wide of the crease and angled the ball into the right-handed batsman and across the left-hander.

The meat of his career was between 2002 and 2008 when he took 332 of his 390 Test wickets at an average of just under 27. In 2003 he became the first South African to take ten wickets in a Test at Lord's. His pair of five-wicket hauls condemned England to an innings defeat.

Having picked up 29 wickets and a man-of-the-series award against West Indies, he got to work in the back-to-back, home-and-away series against Australia in 2005–06. His four for 72 helped to set up South Africa's monumental victory at Perth in 2008. But a year later it was

'You have demonstrated that everyone can rise above their circumstances and achieve success'
— letter from Nelson Mandela

clear his powers were fading. He failed to take a wicket as England clung on for a draw at Centurion Park and crucially could not dislodge the last pair of batsmen after being preferred to the talented newcomer Friedel de Wet, who had taken four wickets, to bowl the final over.

When he went wicketless again in the next Test Ntini was dropped, effectively ending his international career.

Full name: Makhaya Ntini
Born: 6 July 1977, Mdingi, Cape Province
International career span: 1998–2010
Role: Right-arm fast-medium bowler; right-hand batsman
Notable numbers: 101 Tests, 390 wickets at 28.82, 18 five-wicket innings, four ten-wicket matches (SA's second-highest Test wicket-taker behind Shaun Pollock); 173 ODIs, 266 wickets (SA's third-highest ODI wicket-taker behind Allan Donald and Pollock).
Extras: In 2011 named SA cricket's first development ambassador; had to fly home from Australia in 2009 when his wife and two children were involved in a car crash

NEWLANDS

There are few more stunning sights in world cricket than the view from the grassy bank on one side of Newlands as Table Mountain imposes its rocky bulk over the ground.

Some would argue that this perfect vista is somewhat spoiled by the Castle brewery that bubbles and smokes away beneath the mountain.

But all things are relative. There are not many better places to watch cricket than at this sporting hub (the international rugby stadium is a short walk away) in one of Cape Town's leafier suburbs.

New Year is the traditional Test-match time of year for Newlands when the sky is blue, the sun hot and the sizzling braais even hotter.

Newlands' notable numbers (to 9 Feb 2012)

Capacity: 25,000

No. of Tests: 48 (1889–2012)

Highest team score: 651, South Africa v. Australia, 2009

Lowest team score: 35, SA v. England, 1899

Highest individual score: 262, Stephen Fleming for New Zealand v. South Africa, 2006

Most Test runs: Jacques Kallis, 2,098 (South Africa), 1996–2012

Best individual bowling: 8-11, Johnny Briggs for England v. South Africa, 1889

Most Test wickets: Makhaya Ntini, 53 (South Africa), 1998–2009

No. of ODIs: 35 (1992–2011)

Highest team ODI score: 354-3, South Africa v. Kenya, 2001

Highest individual ODI score: 131*, Neil McKenzie for South Africa v. Kenya, 2001

For the New Year Test the sky is blue, the sun hot and the braais even hotter

The pitch is a rare beast in South Africa in that it offers some help to the spin bowlers. Few Tests are drawn and the home side like playing here. Only five Tests of 24 have been drawn since South Africa were readmitted to the international arena in 1991. And they have lost only three of those Tests, all to Australia.

Newlands hosted the opening match of the 2003 World Cup between South Africa and West Indies. It also hosted matches in the inaugural World Twenty20 in 2007 and in the Indian Premier League when the tournament temporarily relocated to South Africa because of security concerns in 2009.

PAKISTAN

One-day wonder: Javed Miandad, Pakistan's finest batsman, batting against India at Melbourne in 1985. Previous page: Saqlain Mushtaq bowls to England's Matthew Hoggard at Manchester in 2001. All 11 Pakistan players are in the picture.

STYLE AND SUBSTANCE

Pakistan joined the Test arena in 1952, five years after the nation had been formed through the partition of India. They lost their first series to India but did have a triumphant tour of England in 1954 when the medium-pacer Fazal Mahmood took six wickets in each innings of the final Test at The Oval to level the series. Mahmood was Pakistan's first star bowler – one his successors, Shoaib Akhtar, called him 'the torch-bearer'.

Hanif Mohammad paved the way for the batsmen, playing the longest innings in Test history at Bridgetown in 1958, his 337 not out lasting 970 minutes. A year later, playing for Karachi, he made 499 (he was run out going for the 500th run), which remained the highest score in first-class cricket until Brian Lara broke it in 1994. Hanif was part of a fine cricket dynasty: his brothers Mushtaq and Sadiq made significant impacts and his son Shoaib opened the batting for Pakistan.

For 13 years from 1959 to 1972 Pakistan did not win a single Test and it was only with the emergence of Imran Khan and then, in the mid-1970s, of Javed Miandad that they forged sustained credibility on the international stage. Miandad was a unique character. Feisty, fearless

Some of the planet's most talented players emerged from this young nation

and innovative in the middle order he remains Pakistan's greatest batsman. He balks at the Karachi streetfighter image that is his broad-brush portrait, only because he thinks it implies social inferiority to the likes of the westernized Imran who would happily be seen in morning coat at Royal Ascot.

He was not one to back down, a trait most publicly exhibited at Perth in 1981 when a collision with Australian fast bowler Dennis Lillee turned into a full-blown incident with Miandad raising his bat as if to strike Lillee.

Miandad was spotted by Abdul Hafeez Kardar, Pakistan's first Test captain, who labelled him 'the find of the decade'. Kardar was not wrong. Miandad adapted to all conditions whether it was the pace of Australia or the swing of England. He made 163 on his Test debut against New Zealand but his high water mark came in 1987–88. His 260 at The Oval set up a huge Pakistan total of 708 and ensured they secured their first series victory in England.

Then in the Caribbean he took two hundreds off the West Indies pace attack, including a second-innings 102 in Trinidad that took Pakistan agonizingly close to what would have been a series-clinching victory.

For many Pakistan fans Miandad's finest hour – or even few seconds – would be his last-ball six to beat India in the final of a one-day tournament

The long game: Hanif Mohammad, seen here in England in 1967, scored 337 not out in 970 minutes against West Indies in 1958.

in Sharjah. Miandad made an unbeaten 116 out of 248 as Pakistan won with only one wicket standing. Needing four to win off the last ball, Miandad swiped a low full-toss from Chetan Sharma over mid-wicket for six and instantly became a national hero. Pakistan lost only two games to India in the next five years.

Miandad was an exceptional batsman in one-day cricket. His unorthodox style meant he would hit the ball in unexpected areas, maybe tickling the ball from outside off-stump down to fine leg or reverse-sweeping at a time when the shot was still shunned by traditionalists. He was also an aggressive runner between the wickets and a terrific scamperer of singles.

Through the 1980s Pakistan were becoming a world force, thanks to the brilliant leg-spin of Abdul Qadir (*left*), Miandad's mastery and the leadership and fast bowling of Imran. Some touring sides, England mostly, chuntered about alien food, ball-tampering and biased umpiring – Miandad was not given out lbw in Pakistan until 1985, nine years after the start of his career – but it was clear that some of the most talented players on the planet were emerging from this young nation born out of bloody post-imperial conflict.

Imran Khan

Suave, sophisticated and stunningly gifted, Imran Khan was one of the greatest all-rounders ever to play the game and a remarkable leader who made Pakistan into a Test force and one-day world champions. In later life he has embroiled himself first in fund-raising for a cancer hospital and then in the unpredictable world of Pakistani politics.

Imran was born into an educated, wealthy Lahore family that also had exceptional cricketing pedigree. Former Pakistan captain Javed Burki and the great batsman Majid Khan are cousins.

And like Burki, Imran attended Oxford University, having been schooled in England also. He made his name playing county cricket for Worcestershire and then Sussex. Initially, he was a medium-pacer with a whirly action who swung it big but with little control. Over the years he honed his skills to become one of the world's best fast bowlers, the equal of some of the champion West Indians of the same era.

While his contemporary Ian Botham peaked early and then went into gradual decline, Imran simply got better and better. His batting average climbed and the bowling average slimmed down to world-class levels.

As a batsman he transformed himself from a happy-hitting tail-ender into a serious player of substance. The turning point came in his first Test as captain at Birmingham in 1982 when he was caught behind trying to hook England quick Bob Willis.

'I realized that if I was going to lead by example I would have to cut out this kind of shot,' Imran wrote in his autobiography. He did. He averaged 53 in that three-match series and in his 48 Tests as captain he averaged an astonishing 52, 15 runs above his overall career average.

He followed on from that tour of England with a staggering all-round performance over six Tests at home to India. Pakistan won the series 3–0 with Imran averaging 61 with the bat and taking 40 wickets with the ball.

As age, and a shin injury, claimed their restrictions, so Imran adjusted his methods. Any reduction in pace was mitigated by a constant increase in nous and skill. He was one of the first bowlers to use reverse swing, an innovation that few understood yet now is an everyday part of the quick bowler's armoury.

'When I retired I left the greatest Pakistan team in its history' – Imran Khan

In 1987, aged 34, he took 21 wickets in Pakistan's first Test series victory in England. A year later he took 23 in three Tests in West Indies.

Then in 1992, when he was almost 40, came his finest moment, leading Pakistan to their first and so far only World Cup title. After the thrilling win over England at Melbourne, Imran gave a speech that became instantly famous for his explanation of how he had urged his young team to play like 'cornered tigers'.

Full name: Imran Khan Niazi
Born: 25 November 1952, Lahore
International career span: 1971–92
Role: Right-hand middle-order batsman, right-arm fast bowler
Notable numbers: 88 Tests, 3,807 runs at 37.69, highest 136; 362 wickets at 22.81, best eight for 58; 175 ODIs, 3,709 runs, 182 wickets. One of only five players to have scored 3,500 Test runs and taken 350 wickets
Extras: Married to English socialite Jemima Khan 1995–2004; in 1996 founded the political party Movement for Justice in Pakistan; member of National Assembly 2002–07

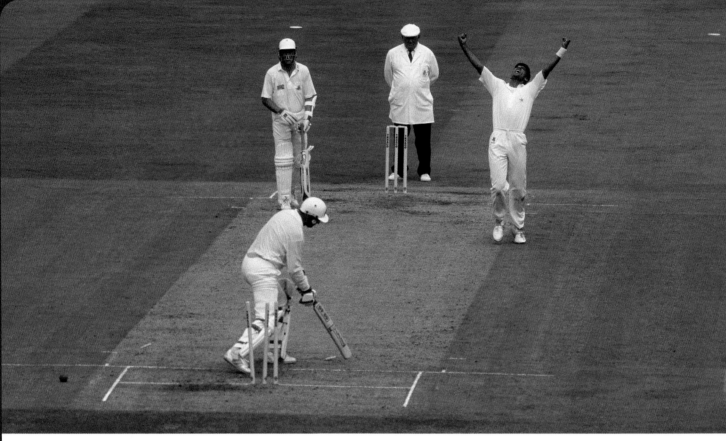

Waqared: England captain Graham Gooch is bowled and bewildered by Pakistan's Waqar Younis at Nottingham in 1992.

MAGIC AND MADNESS

The stereotype of Pakistan as a super-talented yet disparate bunch of individuals began to attach itself through the 1990s. It was a decade of high achievement but ended with a cloud of suspicion following a judicial investigation into match-fixing.

Their triumphant World Cup campaign was pure Pakistan: they won only one of their first five matches but then had a run of five straight wins culminating in a 22-run victory over England in the final at Melbourne. Imran's 'cornered tigers' speech afterwards left no one in any doubt as to who was in charge. His was an autocratic reign that galvanized a team containing up-and-coming stars like batsman Inzamam-ul-Haq, all-rounder Wasim Akram and leg-spinner Mushtaq Ahmed.

One man absent from the final was pace bowler Waqar Younis, who missed the tournament through injury. But Waqar had already made a

Crowning glory: Imran Khan gives his post-match speech after leading Pakistan to victory in the 1992 World Cup at Melbourne.

stunning impression, taking 55 wickets in his first 11 Tests and a remarkable 113 wickets in the 1991 English county season as Surrey's overseas star.

Waqar preferred crushing toes to shaving chins like the West Indians but such was his pace that he prompted the gifted New Zealand batsman Martin Crowe to attach a protective grille to his helmet for the first time in his career. Waqar took 28 wickets in three Tests against the Kiwis in 1990 on the dead pitches and in the extreme heat of Pakistan. It was a sign of things to come.

Pakistan arrived in England in 1992 as one-day world champions but they left as a major five-day power, having won a controversial series 2-1 and rewritten the conventions of Test-match bowling in the process.

England suffered four shocking batting collapses because of Wasim, Waqar and the spin of Mushtaq. The traditional expectation was that the quicker bowlers could use the new ball to good effect until it lost hardness and shine, then the spinners would take over. Wasim and Waqar blew this orthodoxy apart with reverse swing whereby an old, dry, scuffed ball swings in the opposite direction to how one would expect.

England's players, press and public, for whom this was an uncomfortable novelty, cried foul and accused Pakistanis of tampering with the ball. These claims only heightened the bad feeling between the two countries following the sour tour of 1987 when Mike Gatting went nose to nose with umpire Shakoor Rana.

Imran predicted that Pakistan would never return to England after 1992 yet they did four years later, as scheduled, for a tour that needed to spread some love. They did that with their stunning, explosive cricket and the charm and calm of the captain Wasim Akram. He was already

Cover-up: Wasim Akram in full flight with his right hand over the ball so the batsman cannot predict which way it will swing.

into his second spell in charge and had been vilified when the side lost to India at the World Cup earlier in the year.

In between those two victorious tours of England, Pakistan beat the re-emerging Australians in an epic contest at Karachi in late 1994. Wasim and Waqar blew away Australia's second innings, then on a wearing pitch Inzamam made 58 not out against Shane Warne, who took five wickets, and put on 57 with Mushtaq Ahmed for the last wicket as Pakistan sneaked home.

Pakistan played electric cricket in the 1999 World Cup to reach the final but then produced a frustratingly limp display in the big match against Australia at Lord's, where the crowd were on their way home by mid-afternoon.

Wasim Akram was suspended after the tournament following allegations of match-fixing and there began a seemingly never-ending period of political upheaval, uncertainty and indeed under-achievement. Mercurial was not even the half of it.

There was political upheaval, uncertainty and under-achievement

WASIM AKRAM

A pioneer of reverse swing and master of deception, Wasim Akram is the best left-arm pace bowler in history.

He would mask the ball as he ran in to bowl by covering his ball-carrying left hand with his right before unfurling a graceful, whippy action and leaving the batsman hapless and helpless. According to Brian Lara, he was 'the most outstanding bowler I have faced'.

In partnership with the right-handed Waqar Younis he formed one of the most feared new-ball partnerships in the game and introduced a level of subtlety to the fast bowler's art that had rarely been evident when West Indies had a monopoly on pace. He was also a useful lower-order batsman who had a capacity for destruction, though that facet of his game remained unfulfilled. However he does hold the record for the highest score by a Test No.8, 257 not out against Zimbabwe in 1996, an innings that contained the most sixes (12) in a Test innings.

Imran Khan was his mentor and explained the need for top fitness levels as well as constant improvement and development of his bowling. Fitness became an even greater priority when he was diagnosed as diabetic late in his career. He had suffered plenty of injuries too, notably to groin and shoulder.

YouTube is a mine of Akram artistry, none better than the second-innings dismissal of Rahul Dravid at Chennai in 1999 during the first Test between Pakistan and India for nine years.

Bowling over the wicket he nipped back a couple of in-swingers at Dravid, one of which was perilously close to lbw. Then he delivered an outrageous away-swinger that started well outside leg-stump but veered late across Dravid and clipped the top of his off-stump. Only Shane Warne has created such bewilderment. Equally magical was the ball from around the wicket that

he bowled to the England spinner Robert Croft at The Oval in 1996. Delivered from a wide angle, the ball fizzed in towards Croft from outside off-stump before straightening up and slapping the bottom of Croft's pads with a very late burst of away swing, too late for umpire Mervyn Kitchen, who gave Croft not out. Replays showed that the vicious late swerve made it a cast-iron lbw.

'He was a once-in-a-generation cricketer who lifted fast bowling to new levels' – Kumar Sangakkara

It was Wasim's timely intervention that turned the 1992 World Cup final Pakistan's way. Having helped his side add 52 from the final six overs, he took two wickets in two balls to halt England's chase in its tracks. He broke a crucial fifth-wicket stand by bowling Allan Lamb with an in-swinger that then seamed away from the batsman and clipped the top of off-stump. Lamb's look of disbelief was common to many batsmen who had been sacrificed at the altar of Akram.

Full name: Wasim Akram
Born: 3 June 1966, Lahore
International career span: 1984–2003
Role: Left-arm fast opening bowler, left-handed lower-order batsman
Notable numbers: 104 Tests, 414 wickets at 23.62, 25 five-wicket innings, 5 ten-wicket matches; 2,898 runs at 22.64; 356 ODIs, 502 wickets at 23.52. Second highest ODI wicket-taker of all time
Extras: Childhood passion for table tennis; modelling; regular TV commentator; his wife died in 2009, aged 42, of multiple organ failure; played for Lancashire from 1988–98

Costly mistake: Mohammad Amir bowls a pre-arranged no-ball to Jonathan Trott at Lord's in 2010, evidence of spot-fixing that landed him in jail.

TALENT TO BURN

Only one thing can be said for certain of contemporary Pakistan cricket: it's never dull. There was a brief period of unity and common purpose in the mid-2000s when the coach Bob Woolmer forged a heavyweight (in more ways than one) relationship with the captain Inzamam-ul-Haq. But before and since a seductive chaos has reigned, populated by maverick, headstrong personalities and punctuated by performances sublime and lamentable in equal measure.

Woolmer's appointment was preceded by a watershed visit by India in 2004, their first tour to Pakistan for 14 years. Despite the last-minute uncertainty about whether it would actually go ahead and all the post-9/11 political sensitivities the tour was a public-relations triumph. The Indian players were welcomed with exceptional warmth that mocked the tense and dangerous stand-off between the two governments.

The tour kicked off with a cracking one-dayer that India won by five runs despite a magnificent century from Inzamam, who made another ton in the fourth game which Pakistan also lost. They lost the one-day series 3-2 and the Tests 2-1, all three games sadly one-sided. Pakistan's bowling was a disappointment, notably Shoaib Akhtar, the quick bowler who revelled in the label of the Rawalpindi Express and could lay claim to being the fastest bowler in the world. He took only seven wickets at an average of 42 and fell out with the captain Inzamam.

A year later Pakistan were afforded a similarly fraternal welcome in India. Indeed, a banner at the first Test at Mohali read: 'It is not India versus Pakistan, it is bonds between brothers.'

The series was tied 1-1 with Pakistan drawing level in the final match at Bangalore. The win was founded on a huge stand between Younis

Waiting game: umpires Darrell Hair and Billy Doctrove wait in vain for Pakistan to return to the field at The Oval in 2006.

Khan (267) and Inzamam (184) and finished off by Shahid Afridi, the maverick's maverick, who set up a declaration with a 34-ball 58 and then took three for 13 from 17 overs with his leg-spinning varietals.

Batting alongside Younis and Inzamam in an outstanding middle order was Yousuf Youhana, a stylishly understated right-hander and only the fourth Christian to play for Pakistan. In late 2005 he converted to Islam and became known as Mohammad Yousuf. Coincidence or not, his batting in 2006 was astonishing. By scoring 1,788 runs in 11 Tests he broke Viv Richards' record for the most runs in a calendar year.

A run of five Test series without defeat was shattered in England in 2006. With a depleted and under-performing bowling attack, Pakistan had already lost the series by the final Test at The Oval that ended in rancorous and bizarre scenes.

The Australian umpire Darrell Hair had penalized Pakistan five runs for ball-tampering. The Pakistanis were outraged by the accusation and also by, as they saw it, a lack of explanation from Hair. They refused to emerge after the tea interval and consequently forfeited the match. In

Yet hope emerged from the rubble with Saeed Ajmal and his *doosra*

the fall-out of this extraordinary incident Hair was effectively dismissed by the ICC and for a period the result was changed to a draw.

It was a major controversy to match any in the game's history but was made to look trivial a few months later when Pakistan's shock defeat to Ireland in Jamaica at the 2007 World Cup was followed within hours by the death of Woolmer in his hotel room. He had suffered a heart attack though a swirl of conspiracy theories initially offered ghastlier suggestions.

Since then Pakistan cricket has lurched from crisis to scandal, stopping at every point between. They reached the final of the inaugural World Twenty20 in 2007 and won the tournament two years later with Afridi to the fore. But the terrorist attacks on the touring Sri Lanka team at Lahore in 2009 put paid to Pakistan hosting any team for the foreseeable future. In 2010 in England there emerged a world-class talent in the teenager left-arm swing bowler Mohammad Amir. Crushingly for Pakistanis and neutrals alike, Amir was brought down by the spot-fixing scandal that broke, via a newspaper investigation, during the Lord's Test. Just over a year later Amir (*right*), his older bowling colleague Mohammad Asif and the captain, Salman Butt, were all jailed in London for corruption.

Misbah-ul-Haq, an unflappable middle-order batsman, was the latest man to be entrusted with the hot potato of captaincy. And happily, hope emerged from the rubble, as a calmly led Pakistan demolished No.1-ranked England in Abu Dhabi and Dubai with the off-spinner Saeed Ajmal man of the series and his *doosra* unfathomable.

SRI
LANKA

*Champions: Sri Lanka's captain Arjuna Ranatunga receives the 1996 World Cup trophy after beating Australia in the final at Lahore.
Previous page: England taking on Sri Lanka at Kandy in 2001.*

SUCCESS STORY

It took Sri Lanka only three years to win their first Test yet it took 20 for England to grant them the honour of a full tour that contained more than one Test match.

By the time they came to England in 2002 for a three-Test series, after four single-Test tours, they were already one-day world champions. Theirs is a remarkable and joyous success story, against a background of lengthy and bloody civil war and a highly politicized cricket administration.

They lost their inaugural Test at home to England in 1982 but shocked their complacent hosts two years later when they had the better of a draw at Lord's. England were lifting themselves off the canvas after a 5-0 drubbing by West Indies and doubtless hoping for some light relief after a torrid summer. But, having put Sri Lanka in to

bat, they were confronted by an immovable object in the opening batsman Sidath Wettimuny (*right*) who made 190 in a marathon innings that lasted ten hours and 42 minutes. It was a record score by a batsman on his first appearance at Lord's.

In 1985, 13 months on from that Lord's effort, Sri Lanka had their first victory. It was a convincing one too, by 149 runs, over India at Colombo. Contrary to the regional stereotype it was the seamers who did the damage, principally Rumesh Ratnayake. Tall and strapping, Ratnayake took nine wickets in the match, swinging the ball accurately against an experienced Indian batting line-up.

That victory, though, proved a mirage for Sri Lanka. It was not until well into the 1990s that they won Tests with any regularity. By that stage

Perfect partners: Ranatunga (right) batting with Aravinda de Silva in the 1996 World Cup final against Australia.

Muttiah Muralitharan had emerged from the hills of Kandy. The captain was the canny, stocky, left-handed batsman Arjuna Ranatunga who had made his debut as a teenager in Sri Lanka's inaugural Test in 1982. Aravinda de Silva, a diminutive right-hander, had a full range of classy strokes and was capable of explosive innings. And scheming in the background with Ranatunga was the excellent coach Dav Whatmore, born in Sri Lanka but raised in Australia – an ideal combination.

They won their first overseas Test at the 32nd attempt in New Zealand in March 1995 and their first series victory in Pakistan a few months later. The year ended in hurt and controversy when Murali was no-balled for throwing in Australia. But this was where Ranatunga proved his worth. He backed his man resolutely. Indeed, he backed all his men. When Murali was no-balled again in Australia in a one-dayer at Adelaide in 1999 he threatened to take his players from the field.

If that was a dark moment coming into 1996, the sun was about to shine for Sri Lanka in a World Cup tournament that would open the world's eyes to a new mode of one-day batting.

Gone was the idea that openers were supposed to lay a solid base for the other batsmen to build on. In Sanath Jayasuriya and Romesh Kaluwitharana, Sri Lanka had firestarters at the top of the order who lit the fuse for the rest of

In 1999 Ranatunga threatened to take his players off the field

the innings in spectacular and unprecedented fashion. Pinch-hitting it was called, borrowing baseball terminology. Nowadays it needs no label because it is simply, by and large, the way the game is played.

In the quarter-final against England Kaluwitharana went early but Jayasuriya, a pugnacious left-hander, carved the bowling attack apart. He made 82 from 44 balls and when he was out in the 13th over Sri Lanka already had 113, almost halfway to their target of 236.

The semi-final against India at Kolkata had to be abandoned after a fire was started in the stands with India 120 for eight, chasing 252 to win. The match was awarded to Sri Lanka who went on to win the final at Lahore against a surprisingly sloppy Australian side. De Silva made an unbeaten century, milking Shane Warne and the part-time spinners expertly.

Sri Lanka's triumph was multi-layered. Not only was it a deserved reward for their talented, effervescent cricketers, it came after a bomb blast in Colombo before the start of the tournament that killed 90 people and prevented Sri Lanka fulfilling its role as co-host with India and Pakistan.

Muttiah Muralitharan

For a man who defied biology and geometry throughout his phenomenal, unorthodox career, there was an almost indecent neatness about his retirement as the game's leading Test bowler with precisely 800 wickets.

For almost 20 years Murali, as he was known universally, was indefinable and often unplayable in world cricket. Notionally an off-spinner he was in a category all of his own, turning the ball in ways that only wrist-spinners had been able to dream of. And that was the point – his wrist rotation defied standard biological preconceptions. It was his elbow, and the bending of it, that created a controversy that has never entirely resolved itself.

He was no-balled for throwing by the Australian umpires Darrell Hair and Ross Emerson in 1995–96 and Emerson again in 1999. But at no point did the smile dissipate. His modest, cheery dignity was as remarkable as the power he had to spin a cricket ball.

Murali divided opinion. To Sri Lankans he was their champion, a national ambassador. He was also the only Tamil in the team at a time of bloody ethnic conflict in the country. To sympathetic outsiders he was a fascinating and mesmerizing talent and to many others he was simply a bowler who delivered the ball illegally.

His deformed right elbow that prevented him from fully straightening his arm did not satisfy everyone. He undertook many scientific tests and ICC regulations were even changed to allow a 15-degree flexion in the bowling arm because tests had shown it was basically impossible for anyone to bowl with an entirely straight arm.

He was part of Sri Lanka's 1996 World Cup triumph and showed up England's decision to offer them a single Test in 1998 when he took 16 wickets at The Oval. From the late 1990s through to the mid-2000s he hoovered up batsmen as a child might gobble up sweets at the Muralitharan family confectionery business. He made Sri Lanka unbeatable at home and a tough prospect away too.

He bowled long spells and wore batsmen down as much as working them out. No one bowled more deliveries in Test cricket than Murali and no one took more wickets.

'He was the most difficult bowler I faced. I could never plan against him'
— Virender Sehwag

Murali decided that the first Test against India at Galle in July 2010 would be his last, which meant he needed eight wickets to finish his career on 800. Sri Lanka made India follow on and Murali had made it to 799 with the Indians seven down.

But then he had an agonizing wait: 23 overs and a near run-out of the last pair. Finally, he had Pragyan Ojha caught at slip by Mahela Jayawardene. The crowd erupted and Murali was given a 21-gun salute, a fittingly grandiose gesture for a true legend of the game.

Full name: Muttiah Muralitharan
Born: 17 April 1972, Kandy
International career span: 1992–2010
Role: Right-arm off-spin bowler, right-hand tail-end batsman
Notable numbers: 133 Tests, 800 wickets at 22.72, best nine for 51, 67 five-wicket innings, 22 ten-wicket matches; 350 ODIs, 534 wickets at 23.08, best seven for 30. Leading Test wicket-taker, most five-fors and ten-fors in Tests. Most wickets across all three international formats: 1,347.
Extras: Played county cricket for Lancashire, Kent and Gloucestershire; IPL for Chennai Super Kings.

Too good: England's John Crawley is bowled middle stump by Murali, one of the spinner's 16 victims at The Oval in 1998.

SPIN IT TO WIN IT

In the late 1990s Sanath Jayasuriya represented all that was good about Sri Lankan cricket. He was unusual in that he came from the southern coastal town of Matara, a cricketing outpost compared to the big centres of Colombo and Kandy where Sri Lankan players traditionally emerged through established private schools.

He was the star of the 1996 World Cup and in 1997 against India he added Test-match quantity to his one-day quality with an innings that came close to breaking Brian Lara's world record. But his 340 at Colombo, and a staggering partnership of 567 with Roshan Mahanama, contributed to a team record for Sri Lanka. Their total of 952 for six declared was the highest in a Test innings, beating England's 903 for seven set in 1938.

Jayasuriya's punchy runs gave Murali plenty of time to take his wickets

Jayasuriya (*right*) had started his career as a left-arm spinner who batted a bit in the middle order. That he is Sri Lanka's fifth-leading wicket-taker shows that his bowling played a key part in his success, more so in one-dayers, but his punchy top-order contributions set a template for Sri Lanka and gave Muttiah Muralitharan plenty of time to take his wickets.

When Murali had his most productive five days, at The Oval in 1998, it was Jayasuriya who set up the victory opportunity. England had crawled to a very presentable 445 on a pitch that turned from the first day much to the chagrin of the England coach, David Lloyd. Jayasuriya put England's effort into perspective by smashing 213 off 278 balls as Sri Lanka acquired a lead of 146. Murali, who had taken seven wickets in the first innings, took nine in the second innings to bring England's fragile house crumbling down.

Jayasuriya's powers appeared to be waning at the turn of the millennium but he still helped Sri Lanka reach the semi-final of the 2003 World Cup and the final of the 2007 tournament. In 2003 Chaminda Vaas, the left-arm swing bowler, kicked off their second match with a hat-trick off the first three balls of the match and took four in the first five balls. Brian Lara was one of his four victims a fortnight later in a match-winning performance against West Indies.

Vaas had been around since 1994 and made an immediate impact in Sri Lanka's momentous victory in New Zealand, their first overseas Test win, in 1995. The conditions at Napier were helpful but here was a 21-year-old from the Asian subcontinent utilizing them as if born to them.

The older he got the wiser he got, becoming one of the smartest swing and seam bowlers in the world. He never had express pace but he had clever variations and formed a dynamic double-act with Murali.

Sri Lanka's batting continued to be in safe hands in the form of an elegant and complementary pair of Colombo friends. Mahela Jayawardene is

Smart seamer: left-armer Chaminda Vaas, with his canny variations was the perfect foil for Muralitharan.

a self-effacing right-hander with a hunger for runs and Kumar Sangakkara a more outgoing, flashier left-hander who was a law student when he first played for his country in 2000. In 2006 the two men set a record partnership for any wicket in Test cricket. At Colombo against a South African attack containing Dale Steyn, Makhaya Ntini and Andre Nel, they amassed a scarcely credible 624 for the third wicket, Sangakkara making 287 and Jayawardene 374, the fourth-largest Test score.

Both men captained their country though both felt the strain of the continual political upheaval at board level. Sangakkara's final match as captain was the 2011 World Cup final at Mumbai when Sri Lanka lost to India. It was the dream result for the home side, of course, but Sri Lankans had hoped vainly for Murali, in his final international match, to have the perfect farewell.

GALLE STADIUM

In December 2007 England played a drawn Test at Galle. They would have lost but for the rain. But the result was unimportant. That the match took place at all was a triumph of ambition, resilience and the spirit of cricket.

With the 16th-century Dutch fort at one end and the Indian Ocean behind that, the Galle Stadium is a uniquely scenic venue. But three years earlier the ground had been devastated by the Indian Ocean tsunami that swept away whole villages all down the south-west coast of Sri Lanka between Colombo and Galle.

There was plenty of doubt that the ground would ever be rebuilt and indeed plenty of

Galle's notable numbers (to 9 Feb 2012)

Capacity: 7,500

No. of Tests: 18 (1998–2011)

Highest team score: 600-8 dec, Pakistan v. Sri Lanka 2000

Lowest team score: 79, Zim v. Sri Lanka, 2002

Highest individual score: 333, Chris Gayle for West Indies v. Sri Lanka, 2010

Most Test runs: 1,932, Mahela Jayawardene (Sri Lanka), 1998–2011

Best individual bowling: 7-46, Muttiah Muralitharan for Sri Lanka v. England, 2003

Most Test wickets: 111, Muttiah Muralitharan (Sri Lanka), 1998–2010

No. of ODIs: 4 (1998–2000)

Highest team ODI score: 249-7, Sri Lanka v. South Africa, 2000

Highest individual ODI score: 85, Kumar Sangakkara for Sri Lanka v. South Africa, 2000

In 2004 this uniquely scenic venue had been devastated by the tsunami

opposition to it because of the fear of another such disaster. Days before England's visit in 2007 the outfield was of dubious quality and areas just beyond the boundary ropes there was a muddy mess.

But none of this mattered. Putting a game on was what mattered and it happened in an atmosphere of celebration, relief and solemn remembrance of the terrible events of 2004.

Galle has traditionally been a spinner's pitch and Muttiah Muralitharan, surprise, surprise, devoured batsmen. He took 111 Test wickets in 15 matches at an average of only 18. In March 2004 Shane Warne took his 500th Test wicket here.

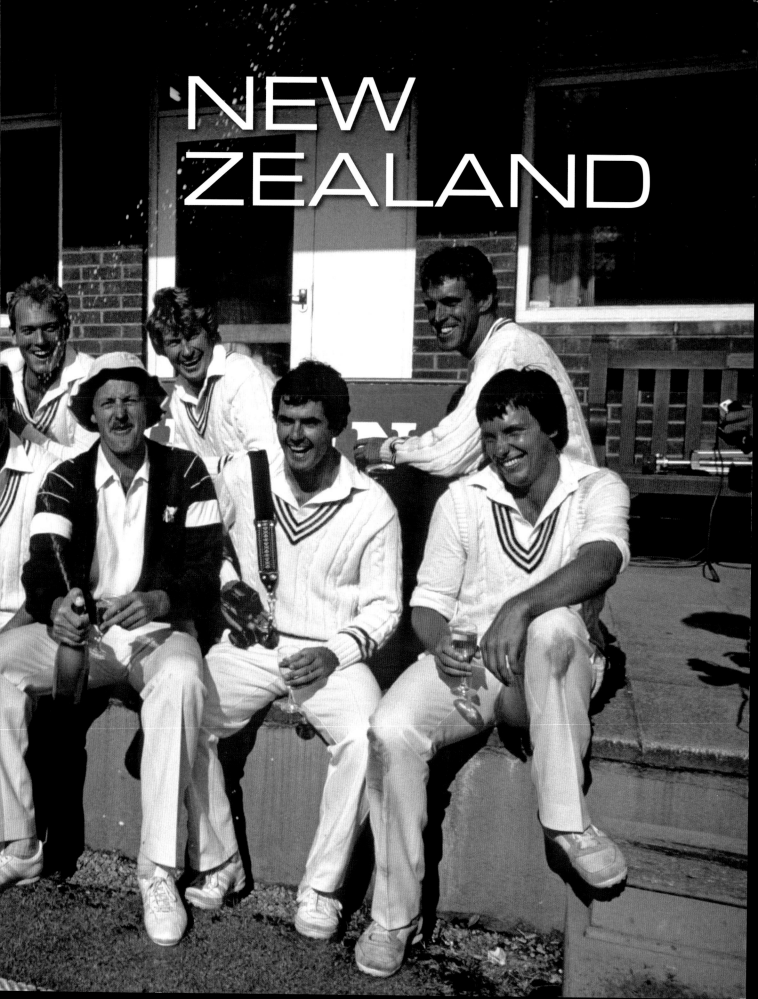

NEW ZEALAND

Heartbeat of the side: John Reid, here batting against England at Leeds in 1965, kept New Zealand afloat in the post-war years. Previous page: New Zealand players celebrate their first Test victory in England at Leeds in 1983.

THE SLOW CLIMB

It took New Zealand 26 long years to register their first Test victory. At last it came on home soil, at Auckland's Eden Park against an admittedly weakened West Indies side in 1956.

This was New Zealand's 45th Test and the catalyst for the success was the new captain John Reid, the all-rounder who replaced Harry Cave in the job after the first Test of the series that New Zealand lost by an innings.

Reid instilled belief into a group of players that had limited talents and resources. Reid, like so many New Zealand cricketers, was a small-town boy but with a big-time mentality. He came from a tiny farming town called Oamaru on the South Island and was the heartbeat of New Zealand cricket for decades whether as player, captain or later as an administrator.

The writer and campaigner Des Wilson, who like Reid came from Oamaru, assessed Reid's contribution thus: 'You have to imagine Ian Botham with no county to play for, only the village team on a Saturday … unpaid with no commercial contracts, with no proper practice wickets and minimal first-class cricket … combining the captaincy of his country with running a local Shell depot and, finally, having no world-class teammates to share the burden of his country's reputation.'

John Reid was a small-town boy but with a big-time mentality

It was Reid's aggressive innings of 84 at Auckland that set up New Zealand's maiden victory, a watershed moment that captured the local imagination as workers deserted offices and shops to head to Eden Park for the climax.

Reid captained New Zealand until 1965, though they won only two more Tests in that time. Both were in South Africa in 1961–62 and the wins secured a drawn series that reflected exceptionally on the team and Reid. In the fourth Test at Johannesburg, that South Africa won by an innings, Reid made 142 out of the 184 scored while he was at the crease. Then in the crucial final Test at Port Elizabeth he squeezed South Africa's second-innings run chase into submission with an epic spell of bowling that yielded the astonishing figures of 45-27-44-4.

Until the emergence of Richard Hadlee in the early 1970s New Zealand were short of bowling resources. They had one or two classy batsmen like the left-handers Martin Donnelly and Bert Sutcliffe. Donnelly played only seven Tests because of World War II but impressed all who saw him with his elegance. Sutcliffe, though, was a star of Reid's team and he too was a stylist, making five Test hundreds including an unbeaten double against India at Delhi in 1955. Sutcliffe's standing in the game can be gauged by the fact that when New Zealand's cricket academy was built at Lincoln near Christchurch the main playing field was called the Bert Sutcliffe Oval.

In terms of productivity, though, both Donnelly and Sutcliffe must bow to Glenn Turner. Like Hadlee, Turner was single-minded and ambitious, out of kilter with New Zealand's amateur administration with whom he would clash often over the years.

The 19-year-old Turner, an insurance salesman by trade, worked nights in a bakery to earn enough money for a trip to England where he thought he was on a promise from Warwickshire. That never materialized but he had to spend only two days in the nets at

Hungry for runs: Glenn Turner cuts Northants' Bishan Bedi for four to bring up 1,000 first-class runs by the end of May in 1973.

their Midlands rivals Worcestershire to be offered a contract.

He began with a reputation for slow-scoring that he refuted verbally and, over time, physically with a growing array of strokes. He made two Test double centuries but his most impressive run-getting came in England where he passed 1,000 runs in a season 15 times from 1968 to 1982. In that last season he made 311 not out, the highest by a Worcestershire batsman until Graeme Hick surpassed it in 1988.

Local hero: Turner batting for Worcestershire against Gloucestershire in the Gillette Cup semi-final in 1973.

All-rounder alert: Richard Hadlee, with his rival Ian Botham fielding at slip, hits out against England at Nottingham in 1983.

KIWIS LEARN TO FLY

The nature of being an all-rounder in New Zealand cricket has generally meant more than just being a batsman and a bowler. Unless you were one of the gilded stars who could make a living from an English county side, your cricket career was recreation rather than profession.

Jeremy Coney was, and is, an all-rounder in the fullest sense. A teacher and a musician, he trained as a theatre lighting director after his playing career was over. These days he combines TV punditry, which he does with distinctive

flamboyance, with theatre work. He is one of the most articulate and imaginative commentators around, once memorably describing the hotch-potch lettering on the scoreboard at Wellington's Basin Reserve as looking like a ransom note.

Tall and skinny with long arms and legs Coney was nicknamed 'The Mantis' and did not give the impression of an elite athlete. But armed with a sharp mind and a big heart, he became a highly effective all-rounder especially in one-day cricket. His greatest contribution to New Zealand cricket,

For much of Hadlee's career New Zealand were a one-man team

Lance's chance: all-rounder Lance Cairns on the way to taking seven wickets against England at Wellington in 1984.

Hadlee's brilliance earned them an innings victory. For much of Hadlee's career New Zealand were a one-man team but here Coney was harnessing some complementary talents. The elegant Martin Crowe, who made 188 at Brisbane, was a batsman at home in the best company. Those were the two world-class performers but there was grit at the top of the order from John Wright and boundless enthusiasm, to add to Coney's, from the wicketkeeper Ian Smith. Then there was the off-spinner John Bracewell, a tough, intelligent competitor who has since become a renowned coach.

Hadlee was at the fore again at Perth with 11 wickets in the third Test when New Zealand sealed their momentous victory. Crowe and his brother Jeff took the Kiwis home to a six-wicket win.

At Nottingham in August 1986 New Zealand completed their first Test series win in England. Fittingly and inevitably Hadlee took ten wickets on a ground that he had made his home for Nottinghamshire. But the barometer of how this team was making everything and more of its talents was the century scored by the No.8 batsman Bracewell, the one Test century of his career.

though, was as the captain who moulded a team of disparate talents and egos in the mid-1980s to seal wins in England and Australia.

He had contributed also to a famous, and highly contentious, victory over the mighty West Indies at home in 1980. This 1-0 victory is remembered for the behaviour of the West Indies bowlers, whose irritation at what they believed was the biased umpiring of Fred Goodall boiled over into violence. But for New Zealand it was only their second series victory in a 50-year Test history and their first at home.

Coney (*right*) was man of the match in a two-wicket World Cup group-stage victory against England in 1983 and was a part of the side that won the country's first Test victory on English soil that same summer. England won the series but they succumbed at Leeds with the burly, big-hitting all-rounder Lance Cairns taking seven wickets in the first innings. Coney did not score a Test hundred until his 25th match against England at Wellington in early 1984. Later in the year he captained the team in Pakistan in the absence of Geoff Howarth whom he would soon replace as full-time skipper.

New Zealand had never even played a Test in Australia until November 1985 when Richard

RICHARD HADLEE

A meticulous, intelligent quick bowler, Richard Hadlee carried New Zealand for much of his outstanding career.

Nicknamed 'Paddles' for his large, splayed feet, he began his career as a tearaway quick with a quirky shuffle at the start of his run-up. But he developed into one of the game's finest swing and seam bowlers and the first to take 400 Test wickets.

For the first five years of his career he was, in his own words, 'erratic, inconsistent and without a great idea of how to get through three days, let alone four or five'.

But with rigorous analysis both of himself and of the Australian Dennis Lillee, whom he admired, Hadlee reduced his long run-up and refined his bowling with devastating effects. His control was impeccable and his knowledge of which type of ball to deliver when and to whom was scientific.

He took ten wickets against India at Wellington when still in his fast phase and, as it happened, lucky still to be in the team. But the legend began in earnest on the same ground two years later when he bowled England out for 64 and brought New Zealand's first victory over them.

His remodelled action was, like Lillee's, a study in graceful perfection but unlike Lillee, whose final approach to the crease was a leap, Hadlee was into his delivery almost without breaking stride.

Statistically, his best Test performance came at Brisbane at 1985 and its significance extended beyond his taking nine wickets in an innings. This was New Zealand's first series win in Australia.

Even though Hadlee did not take all ten he still had a hand in the other dismissal, taking the catch to remove Geoff Lawson. A less scrupulous player might have considered dropping it.

Such were the standards Hadlee set himself, he actually expressed disappointment that he never took all ten in an innings. Alluding to the hat-trick being the bowler's 'ultimate satisfaction', he said: 'The ultimate ultimate must be to take all wickets in an innings and I never did that'.

When New Zealand won their first series in England in 1986 Graham Gooch described the experience as: 'Richard Hadlee at one end, Ilford seconds at the other.'

In February 1990, 18 years after his debut, on his home ground at Lancaster Park, Christchurch, he took his 400th Test wicket when India's Sanjay Manjrekar inside-edged on to his stumps.

'It was Richard Hadlee at one end, Ilford seconds at the other' — Graham Gooch

Because his bowling was so good, Hadlee's batting was often overlooked. He was a dangerous and powerful hitter at No.7 and should have averaged more than the 27 he managed in Tests.

He was a star of county cricket for many years, forming a destructive new-ball partnership with the South African Clive Rice that secured the County Championship for Nottinghamshire in 1981 and 1987.

Full name: Richard John Hadlee
Born: 3 July 1951, Christchurch
International career span: 1973–90
Role: Right-arm fast-medium opening bowler, left-hand middle-order batsman
Notable numbers: 86 Tests, 431 wickets at 22.29, best nine for 52, 36 five-wicket innings, nine ten-wicket matches; 3,124 runs at 27.16, highest 151*, two centuries
Extras: Knighted for services to cricket in 1990; his father Walter captained New Zealand in post-war era and brother Dayle also played Test cricket; since retirement has been a media pundit and also chairman of NZ selectors

The name's Bond: fast bowler Shane Bond in action against Australia at the 2003 World Cup. The Kiwis have reached the semis five times.

SURVIVAL BATTLE

February 1997 was an important month for the modern history of New Zealand cricket. First an 18-year-old, bespectacled left-arm spinner called Daniel Vettori became the country's youngest Test player when he made his debut against England at Wellington. Then for the next Test the captaincy passed to the tall, elegant, left-handed batsman Stephen Fleming who, at 23, was New Zealand's youngest captain.

Fleming captained New Zealand in Tests until 2006 when he passed the flame on to Vettori who himself kept the job until quitting after the 2011 World Cup when he also retired from one-dayers.

Fleming shares a birthday with David Gower and he also shared some of his fellow left-hander's languid strokeplay but it is hard to escape a feeling of under-achievement. Despite averaging 40 in Tests he made only nine centuries in 111 matches.

Vettori (*right*) is only the eighth man in history to take 300 Test wickets and score 3,000 runs. Consistent rather than spectacular he has added huge value to New Zealand in all formats over the years and, with five Test centuries, is the most prolific No.8 batsman in history.

With their calm authority and quiet determination Fleming and Vettori provided

Fleming and Vettori provided stability through a turbulent time

Big shout: all-rounder Chris Cairns appeals in vain for lbw against England's Ashley Giles in 2004.

stability through a period that was intermittently highly successful but turbulent. New Zealand is a small country, New Zealand cricket an even smaller one and the bigger personalities can find the inevitable parochialism stifling.

And when Twenty20 exploded in the mid-2000s, first with the Indian Cricket League (ICL), which was quickly outlawed by the official authorities, and then the Indian Premier League (IPL), the lure of the rupee was strong. Unlike in England, say, where the players can earn decent money for playing for their country, New Zealand fights a constant battle with the Twenty20 purses from around the world. This has affected players' availability and focus on their national duties.

One such player was Shane Bond, a fast bowler of rare talent and pace whose career had already been blighted by injury when he signed up to play in the ICL. When the ICL was black-balled by the officially backed IPL, Bond was banned from playing for his country, a ban that New Zealand were in no position to overturn for fear of offending their global partners, in particular India.

Bond was involved in one of Fleming's finest hours: the drawn three-Test series in Australia in 2001. They survived in the first two Tests, then almost pulled off a remarkable win in the third Test at Perth. Australia were chasing 440 to win and finished 59 short with three wickets standing. But for a couple of umpiring decisions the Kiwis might have done it.

A few months later New Zealand spiked England's guns for the second time in three years by pulling off a last-day heist at

Auckland to level the series. In the first Test at Christchurch, which England won, Nathan Astle launched an audacious assault on an impossible target of 550. With the injured all-rounder Chris Cairns in tow at No.11, Astle scored the fastest Test double hundred, smashing a record set by Adam Gilchrist only three weeks earlier.

In 1999 Cairns was man of the series in one of New Zealand's modern triumphs when they won 2-1 in England having lost the first Test. Emboldened by their tough Australian coach Steve Rixon and inspired by a fit and focused Cairns, they embarrassed England to the point where the crowd at the final Test at The Oval booed the new captain, Nasser Hussain.

Recent years have not been kind to New Zealand's Test side, who play less than most other countries with the one-day game an increasing focus. But they did pull off a shock series-leveller in Australia in late 2011 when Doug Bracewell, a promising seamer and nephew of ex-Test player John, sparked an Australian collapse in a Hobart run-chase.

BASIN RESERVE

In New Zealand cricket mostly plays second
fiddle to rugby union and the cult of the All
Blacks, so venues have increasingly had to become
dual-purpose with cricket pitches cultivated
elsewhere and dropped in ready for match use.

The Basin Reserve, in downtown Wellington
on the southern tip of the North Island, is the
country's only major cricket-only centre (though it
has hosted other sports). One-dayers have moved
to the modern, 48,000-capacity Westpac Stadium,
known as the Cake Tin, that is also home to the
Wellington Hurricanes rugby side.

But the Basin remains a Test-match venue and
also houses the New Zealand cricket museum. It is

It is a stunning venue, in the shadow of Mount Cook and Mount Victoria

in many ways the spiritual home of New Zealand cricket and is the only sporting venue to be part of the country's Historic Places Trust. The first match there was in 1868 between the Wellington Volunteers and the crew of HMS *Falcon*.

a stunning venue, in the shadow of Mount Cook and Mount Victoria, with grass banks providing much of the seating areas.

Wind is always a major factor in Wellington, so provides many challenges for players at the Basin,

Caribbean cheer: Habibul Bashar, the captain who led Bangladesh to wins against India and South Africa at the 2007 World Cup.

BANGLADESH

Officially Bangladesh became a Test nation on 26 June 2000 but it was their qualification for the 1999 World Cup that really fuelled the dream. That they also beat Pakistan in that World Cup only raised the expectations.

For the first time cricketers were national heroes. In terms of location, population and enthusiasm Bangladesh, one of the world's poorest countries, deserved a place at the top table but the lack of long-standing domestic cricket structure has been exposed in the decade or so since their elevation.

They gave a good account of themselves in their maiden Test against India at Dhaka but lost by nine wickets after a second-innings collapse to 91 all out.

Bangladesh lost 22 of their first 23 Tests, 15 of them by an innings, but at Multan in 2003 they thought they had finally broken their duck. Pakistan were 132 for six and still 129 short of victory but Inzamam-ul-Haq played what the former Pakistan opener Ramiz Raja called 'one of the best Test innings of modern times'.

Inzamam made 138 not out and shepherded the tail-enders expertly. He put on 52 for the ninth wicket with Umar Gul, of which Gul's contribution was five. Having been joined by 17-year-old Yasir Ali, on his first-class debut, Inzy sealed the one-wicket win with a boundary.

Bangladesh had to wait another 15 months for their first Test victory. It came against a very green Zimbabwe side but no one in Bangladesh cared. The captain, Habibul Bashar, set the tone with two half-centuries and the slow left-armer Enamul Haque spun the Zimbabweans out with six second-innings wickets.

Later in 2005 Bangladesh toured England for the first time which was mostly as unrewarding as their track record suggested. However, they did claim one notable scalp that was celebrated as heartily in London as it was in Dhaka.

At Cardiff, in a three-way one-day tournament, Bangladesh dumped Australia on their backside with a thumping five-wicket win that gave England increased heart for the epic Ashes series that commenced a month later. The Aussie captain, Ricky Ponting, described the result as 'one of the biggest upsets in history'. The Bangla hero was the 20-year-old Mohammad Ashraful, who four years earlier had become the youngest batsman to make a Test hundred. Ashraful made a run-a-ball century to deliver Bangladesh only their tenth victory in 108 one-day internationals.

Progress has continued to be slow with only intermittent bright spots but progress there is nonetheless. Two players in particular have shone: the left-arm spinner Shakib Al Hasan who became captain at 22, and a hard-hitting left-handed opener, Tamim Iqbal, whose slash-and-dash style bears more than a passing resemblance to Brian Lara.

Tamim Iqbal's slash-and-dash style bears a resemblance to Brian Lara

All-round class: Shakib Al Hasan who became captain at 22 and, in late 2011, the world's leading all-rounder.

Both were at the forefront of Bangladesh's only other Test wins, back-to-back victories over the ailing West Indies in the Caribbean in 2009. In the one-day format improvements were more obvious with Shakib leading his side to 22 wins out of 47 matches before losing the captaincy after the 2011 tour of Zimbabwe.

They were proud co-hosts of the 2011 World Cup with India and Sri Lanka but had wildly contrasting fortunes on the pitch. After a 58-all-out humiliation at the hands of West Indies, supporters turned on their team.

But all was forgiven a week later when they pulled off an unlikely chase against England, after being 169 for eight in pursuit of 227.

'It's a huge victory for us. And for the whole nation, I think,' said a relieved Shakib who, in late 2011, became the No.1 ranked Test all-rounder.

Full bloom: Andy Flower, here batting for MCC against an International XI at Lord's, is Zimbabwe's finest batsman.

ZIMBABWE

Eyebrows were raised when, in early 2012, England's Zimbabwean coach Andy Flower said that the batsmen under his charge were all better players of spin than he had been.

Flower, who helped mastermind England's rise to the top of the world Test rankings in 2011, is Zimbabwe's best batsman by some distance and also one of the most accomplished players of spin from outside the Asian subcontinent.

He kept wicket in Zimbabwe's inaugural Test in 1992 against India at Harare. Batting at seven

the left-hander made 59 and played his part in a big sixth-wicket stand with the captain, Dave Houghton, that took the novice Test nation well beyond respectability.

Flower, whose brother Grant was also a less celebrated mainstay of the side, maintained an astonishing batting record in circumstances that were routinely adverse. Overall he averaged 51 in his career but 53 in Asia.

Zimbabwe won their first Test in 1995 at home to Pakistan but positive results were few and far

Fraternal Flowers: brothers Andy (left) and Grant batting in a one-dayer against England at Lord's in 2000.

England's coach David Lloyd said: 'We flippin' murdered 'em'

between. The talent pool was passionate, small and very white. The political winds of Robert Mugabe's regime were starting to blow.

One of Zimbabwe's greatest triumphs was holding England to a 0-0 draw over two Tests in 1996. It was a nadir for a distracted and unprofessional England side. After the second Test at Bulawayo England's coach, David 'Bumble' Lloyd, made the infamous expression of exasperation: 'We flippin' murdered 'em.'

The series was a moral victory for Zimbabwe who achieved a more material reward by winning all three one-dayers against England, the third of which was illuminated by a hat-trick for Eddo Brandes, a burly seamer whose other life as a chicken farmer summed up the rustic and rudimentary nature of Zimbabwean cricket.

In late 1998 Zimbabwe won their first Test against India and a few weeks later they had their first overseas triumph, at Peshawar against Pakistan. But by the time they toured England in 2000 there was civil unrest at home, the players were in dispute with the cricket board and there was growing global unease about the brutality of the Mugabe government.

Zimbabwe were a co-host, alongside South Africa, of the 2003 World Cup and the politically conscious Flower decided to make a remarkable gesture of defiance. At his side's first match of the tournament against Namibia he and the fast bowler Henry Olonga (*below*), Zimbabwe's first black player, issued a statement mourning 'the death of democracy' in their country and took to the field wearing black armbands.

Over the coming months most of the experienced white players either removed themselves – or were removed – from the team. There was plenty of black talent but without the experience to survive at Test level. All this was set against a toxic background of political and financial corruption.

After a string of massive defeats Zimbabwe effectively suspended itself from Test cricket, a convenient compromise to sidestep the growing stench of scandal and the administration's lack of credibility.

Zimbabwe continued to play one-dayers and by 2011 had returned to the Test arena as the political landscape in the country shifted. Their Test comeback, with a young, multiracial team, was heart-warming. Centuries from Hamilton Masakadza, who made a debut century in 2001, and the 25-year-old captain, Brendan Taylor, set up a 130-run victory over Bangladesh at Harare. Hope had returned.

MOST TEST RUNS

		Tests	Runs	HS	Avge	100s
Sachin Tendulkar (Ind)	1989–2012	188	15,470	248*	55.44	51
Rahul Dravid (Ind/ICC)	1996–2012	164	13,288	270	52.31	36
Ricky Ponting (Aus)	1995–2012	162	13,200	257	53.44	41
Jacques Kallis (SA/ICC)	1995–2012	150	12,260	224	57.02	41
Brian Lara (WI/ICC)	1990–2006	131	11,953	400*	52.88	34
Allan Border (Aus)	1978–1994	156	11,174	205	50.56	27
Steve Waugh (Aus)	1985–2004	168	10,927	200	51.06	32
Sunil Gavaskar (Ind)	1971–1987	125	10,122	236*	51.12	34
Mahela Jayawardene (SL)	1997–2012	128	10,086	374	50.43	29
Shivnarine Chanderpaul (WI)	1994–2012	137	9,709	203*	49.28	24

HIGHEST BATTING AVERAGES (MINIMUM 20 INNINGS)

		Tests	Runs	HS	Avge	100s
Don Bradman (Aus)	1928–1948	52	6,996	334	99.94	29
Graeme Pollock (SA)	1963–1970	23	2,256	274	60.97	7
George Headley (WI)	1930–1954	22	2,190	270*	60.83	10
Herbert Sutcliffe (Eng)	1924–1935	54	4,555	194	60.73	16
Eddie Paynter (Eng)	1931–1939	20	1,540	243	59.23	4
Ken Barrington (Eng)	1955–1968	82	6,806	256	58.67	20
Everton Weekes (WI)	1948–1958	48	4,455	207	58.61	15
Wally Hammond (Eng)	1927–1947	85	7,249	336*	58.45	22
Garry Sobers (WI)	1954–1974	93	8,032	365*	57.78	26
Jacques Kallis (SA/ICC)	1995–2012	150	12,260	224	57.02	41

MOST TESTS AS CAPTAIN

		Tests	Won	Lost	Tied	Draw	Win %
Allan Border (Aus)	1984–1994	93	32	22	1	38	34.40
Graeme Smith (SA/ICC)	2003–2012	88	41	26	0	21	46.59
Stephen Fleming (NZ)	1997–2006	80	28	27	0	25	35.00
Ricky Ponting (Aus)	2004–2010	77	48	16	0	13	62.33
Clive Lloyd (WI)	1974–1985	74	36	12	0	26	48.64
Steve Waugh (Aus)	1999–2004	57	41	9	0	7	71.92
Arjuna Ranatunga (SL)	1989–1999	56	12	19	0	25	21.42
Mike Atherton (Eng)	1993–2001	54	13	21	0	20	24.07
Hansie Cronje (SA)	1994–2000	53	27	11	0	15	50.94
Michael Vaughan (Eng)	2003–2008	51	26	11	0	14	50.98

Top Test Score (how the record has progressed)

Charles Bannerman	165*	Aus v Eng	Melbourne	1877 (1st Test)
Billy Murdoch	211	Aus v Eng	The Oval	1884
Tip Foster	287	Eng v Aus	Sydney	1903
Andy Sandham	325	Eng v WI	Kingston	1930
Don Bradman	334	Aus v Eng	Leeds	1930
Wally Hammond	336*	Eng v NZ	Auckland	1933
Len Hutton	364	Eng v Aus	The Oval	1938
Garry Sobers	365*	WI v Pak	Kingston	1958
Brian Lara	375	WI v Eng	St John's	1994
Matthew Hayden	380	Aus v Zim	Perth	2003
Brian Lara	400*	WI v Eng	St John's	2004

Top Test Scores

Brian Lara	400*	WI v Eng	St John's	2004
Matthew Hayden	380	Aus v Zim	Perth	2003
Brian Lara	375	WI v Eng	St John's	1994
Mahela Jayawardene	374	SL v SA	Colombo	2006
Garry Sobers	365*	WI v Pak	Kingston	1958
Len Hutton	364	Eng v Aus	The Oval	1938
Sanath Jayasuriya	340	SL v Ind	Colombo	1997
Hanif Mohammad	337	Pak v WI	Bridgetown	1958
Wally Hammond	336*	Eng v NZ	Auckland	1933
Mark Taylor	334*	Aus v Pak	Peshawar	1998
Don Bradman	334	Aus v Eng	Leeds	1930

Most Sixes

		Tests	Innings	Sixes
Adam Gilchrist (Aus)	1999–2008	96	137	100
Jacques Kallis (SA/ICC)	1995–2012	150	254	89
Virender Sehwag (Ind/ICC)	2001–2012	96	167	88
Brian Lara (WI/ICC)	1990–2006	131	232	88
Chris Cairns (NZ)	1989–2004	62	104	87
Viv Richards (WI)	1974–1991	121	182	84
Andrew Flintoff (Eng/ICC)	1998–2009	79	130	82
Matthew Hayden (Aus)	1994–2009	103	184	82
Chris Gayle (WI)	2000–2010	91	159	75
Ricky Ponting (Aus)	1995–2012	162	276	73
Clive Lloyd (WI)	1966–1985	110	175	70

MOST DUCKS

		Tests	Innings	Avge	Ducks
Courtney Walsh (WI)	1984–2001	132	185	7.54	43
Glenn McGrath (Aus)	1993–2007	124	138	7.36	35
Shane Warne (Aus)	1992–2007	145	199	17.32	34
Muttiah Muralitharan (SL/ICC)	1992–2010	133	164	11.67	33
Chris Martin (NZ)	2000–2012	65	94	2.38	32
Curtly Ambrose (WI)	1988–2000	98	145	12.40	26
Mervyn Dillon (WI)	1997–2004	38	68	8.44	26
Danish Kaneria (Pak)	2000–2010	61	84	7.05	25
Zaheer Khan (Ind)	2000–2012	83	113	12.37	25
Danny Morrison (NZ)	1987–1997	48	71	8.42	24

TOP OVERSEAS BATSMEN IN ASIA

		Tests	Runs	HS	Avge	100s
Jacques Kallis (SA)	1997–2012	23	2,046	173	60.17	8
Ricky Ponting (Aus)	1996–2012	28	1,889	150	41.97	5
Allan Border (Aus)	1979–1992	22	1,799	162	54.51	6
Matthew Hayden (Aus)	2001–2008	19	1,663	203	50.39	4
Clive Lloyd (WI)	1966–1983	20	1,629	242*	62.65	4
Andy Flower (Zim)	1993–2002	21	1,614	232*	53.80	5
Stephen Fleming (NZ)	1995–2004	18	1,571	274*	65.45	3
Brian Lara (WI)	1990–2006	14	1,530	221	58.84	5
Viv Richards (WI)	1974–1988	24	1,510	192*	44.41	4
Graeme Smith (SA)	2003–2010	19	1,447	232	45.21	3

TOP OVERSEAS BATSMEN IN AUS & NZ

		Tests	Runs	HS	Avge	100s
Sachin Tendulkar (Ind)	1990–2012	31	2,651	241*	51.98	8
Wally Hammond (Eng)	1928–1947	22	2,623	336*	77.14	9
Jack Hobbs (Eng)	1908–1929	24	2,493	187	57.97	9
Colin Cowdrey (Eng)	1954–1975	38	2,289	128*	40.15	5
Javed Miandad (Pak)	1976–1993	25	1,956	271	50.15	5
Rahul Dravid (Ind/ICC)	1998–2012	23	1,932	233	48.30	3
David Gower (Eng)	1978–1991	27	1,893	136	42.06	5
Brian Lara (WI/ICC)	1992–2006	26	1,875	277	40.76	5
Viv Richards (WI)	1975–1989	25	1,837	208	44.80	4
Clive Lloyd (WI)	1968–1985	26	1,784	149	40.54	5

Top Overseas Batsmen in the Caribbean

		Tests	Runs	HS	Avge	100s
Rahul Dravid (Ind)	1997–2011	17	1,511	146	65.69	3
Sunil Gavaskar (Ind)	1971–1983	13	1,404	220	70.20	7
Geoff Boycott (Eng)	1968–1981	14	1,179	116	51.26	3
VVS Laxman (Ind)	1997–2011	16	1,146	130	47.75	2
Alec Stewart (Eng)	1990–1998	15	1,099	143	42.26	2
Steve Waugh (Aus)	1991–2003	14	1,096	200	68.50	4
Colin Cowdrey (Eng)	1960–1968	10	1,025	148	60.29	4
Ricky Ponting (Aus)	1999–2008	8	1,014	206	78.00	5
Polly Umrigar (Ind)	1953–1962	10	1,005	172*	55.83	3
Jacques Kallis (SA)	2001–2010	12	942	147	55.41	3

Top Overseas Batsmen in England

		Tests	Runs	HS	Avge	100s
Don Bradman (Aus)	1930–1948	19	2,674	334	102.84	11
Allan Border (Aus)	1980–1993	25	2,082	200*	65.06	5
Viv Richards (WI)	1976–1991	24	2,057	291	64.28	5
Garry Sobers (WI)	1957–1973	21	1,820	174	53.52	5
Steve Waugh (Aus)	1989–2001	22	1,633	177*	74.22	7
Mark Taylor (Aus)	1989–1997	18	1,584	219	52.80	5
Sachin Tendulkar (Ind)	1990–2011	17	1,575	193	54.31	4
Gordon Greenidge (WI)	1976–1988	19	1,570	223	56.07	6
Ricky Ponting (Aus)	1997–2010	20	1,421	156	41.79	4
Rahul Dravid (India)	1996–2011	13	1,376	217	68.80	6

Top Overseas Batsmen in Africa

		Tests	Runs	HS	Avge	100s
Wally Hammond (Eng)	1927–1939	15	1,447	181	62.91	4
Sachin Tendulkar (India)	1992–2011	19	1,401	169	45.19	5
Stephen Fleming (NZ)	1994–2007	17	1,278	262	44.06	1
Rahul Dravid (Ind)	1996–2011	16	1,099	148	40.70	2
Brian Lara (WI)	1998–2004	11	1,063	202	48.31	3
Inzamam-ul-Haq (Pak)	1995–2007	15	1,033	112	39.73	2
Marvan Atapattu (SL)	1998–2004	12	991	249	49.55	3
Shivnarine Chanderpaul (WI)	1998–2008	15	985	109	39.40	2
Jack Hobbs (Eng)	1910–1914	10	982	187	65.46	1
Ricky Ponting (Aus)	1999–2011	12	968	116	46.09	3

MOST TEST WICKETS

		Tests	Wkts	Best	Avge	SR	5wi	10wm
Muttiah Muralitharan (SL/ICC, OB)	1992–2010	133	800	9-51	22.72	55.0	67	22
Shane Warne (Aus, LBG)	1992–2007	145	708	8-71	25.41	57.4	37	10
Anil Kumble (Ind, LBG)	1990–2008	132	619	10-74	29.65	65.9	35	8
Glenn McGrath (Aus, RFM)	1993–2007	124	563	8-24	21.64	51.9	29	3
Courtney Walsh (WI, RF)	1984–2001	132	519	7-37	24.44	57.8	22	3
Kapil Dev (Ind, RFM)	1978–1994	131	434	9-83	29.64	63.9	23	2
Richard Hadlee (NZ, RFM)	1973–1990	86	431	9-52	22.29	50.8	36	9
Shaun Pollock (SA, RFM)	1995–2008	108	421	7-87	23.11	57.8	16	1
Wasim Akram (Pak, LF)	1985–2002	104	414	7-119	23.62	54.6	25	5
Harbhajan Singh (Ind, OB)	1998–2011	98	406	8-84	32.22	68.1	25	5

BEST BOWLING IN AN INNINGS

Jim Laker (OB)	10-53	Eng v Aus	Manchester	1956
Anil Kumble (LBG)	10-74	Ind v Pak	Delhi	1999
George Lohmann (RFM)	9-28	Eng v SA	Johannesburg	1986
Jim Laker (OB)	9-37	Eng v Aus	Manchester	1956
Muttiah Muralitharan (OB)	9-51	SL v Zim	Kandy	2002
Richard Hadlee (RFM)	9-52	NZ v Aus	Brisbane	1985
Abdul Qadir (LBG)	9-56	Pak v Eng	Lahore	1987
Devon Malcolm (RF)	9-57	Eng v SA	The Oval	1994
Muttiah Muralitharan (OB)	9-65	SL v Eng	The Oval	1998
Jasubhai Patel (OB)	9-69	Ind v Aus	Kanpur	1959

BEST STRIKE-RATE (BALLS PER WICKET – MINIMUM 5,000 BALLS BOWLED)

		Tests	Wkts	Best	Avge	SR	5wi	10wm
Dale Steyn (SA, RF)	2004–2012	51	263	7-51	23.07	40.0	17	4
Sydney Barnes (Eng, RFM)	1901–1914	27	189	9-103	16.43	41.6	24	7
Waqar Younis (Pak, RF)	1989–2003	87	373	7-76	23.56	43.4	22	5
Johnny Briggs (Eng, SLA)	1884–1899	33	118	8-11	17.75	45.1	9	4
Shoaib Akhtar (Pak, RF)	1997–2007	46	178	6-11	25.69	45.7	12	2
Malcolm Marshall (WI, RF)	1978–1991	81	376	7-22	20.94	46.7	22	4
Allan Donald (SA, RF)	1992–2002	72	330	8-71	22.25	47.0	20	3
Mohammad Asif (Pak, RFM)	2005–2010	23	106	6-41	24.36	48.7	7	1
Colin Croft (WI, RF)	1977–1982	27	125	8-29	23.30	49.3	3	0
Fred Trueman (Eng, RFM)	1952–1965	67	307	8-31	21.57	49.4	17	3

TOP OVERSEAS BOWLERS IN ASIA

		Tests	Wkts	Best	Avge	SR	5wi	10wm
Shane Warne (Aus, LBG)	1992–2006	25	127	7-94	26.81	52.6	11	3
Daniel Vettori (NZ, SLA)	1998–2010	20	96	6-28	28.95	68.6	8	1
Courtney Walsh (WI, RF)	1986–1997	17	77	6-79	20.53	45.2	5	0
Derek Underwood (Eng, SLA)	1969–1982	22	73	5-28	26.65	78.9	3	0
Glenn McGrath (Aus, RFM)	1994–2004	19	72	5-66	23.02	54.8	1	0
Richie Benaud (Aus, LBG)	1956–1960	12	71	7-72	19.32	61.9	6	1
Malcolm Marshall (WI, RF)	1978–1990	19	71	6-37	23.05	48.7	3	0
Richard Hadlee (NZ, RFM)	1976–1988	13	68	6-49	21.58	42.7	5	2
Dale Steyn (SA, RF)	2006–2010	13	63	7-51	23.71	39.3	4	1
Shaun Pollock (SA, RFM)	1997–2006	17	60	6-78	23.18	56.8	2	0

TOP OVERSEAS BOWLERS IN AUS & NZ

		Tests	Wkts	Best	Avge	SR	5wi	10wm
Courtney Walsh (WI, RF)	1984–2001	32	104	7-37	30.15	66.8	5	1
Bob Willis (Eng, RF)	1971–1984	31	100	5-32	27.76	64.5	4	0
Ian Botham (Eng, RFM)	1978–1992	25	96	6-78	28.16	60.6	6	1
Wasim Akram (Pak, LF)	1985–1999	16	86	7-119	20.05	48.1	9	3
Curtly Ambrose (WI, RF)	1988–1997	16	83	7-25	19.96	49.4	6	1
Sydney Barnes (Eng, RFM)	1901–1912	13	77	7-60	22.42	55.2	8	1
Derek Underwood (Eng, SLA)	1970–1980	18	74	7-113	25.66	71.6	4	2
Joel Garner (WI, RF)	1979–1987	16	71	6-56	22.28	52.9	3	0
Michael Holding (WI, RF)	1975–1987	18	70	6-21	26.58	56.4	5	1
Lance Gibbs (WI, OB)	1961–1976	17	67	5-66	34.80	101.4	4	0

TOP OVERSEAS BOWLERS IN THE CARIBBEAN

		Tests	Wkts	Best	Avge	SR	5wi	10wm
Angus Fraser (Eng, RFM)	1990–1998	12	54	8-53	20.29	47.4	4	1
Imran Khan (Pak, RF)	1977–1988	8	48	7-80	25.12	45.7	3	1
Anil Kumble (Ind, LBG)	1997–2006	11	45	6-78	31.28	64.4	3	0
S Venkataraghavan (Ind, OB)	1971–1983	13	39	5-95	43.58	101.1	1	0
Stuart MacGill (Aus, LBG)	1999–2008	10	37	5-75	36.62	64.8	1	0

TOP OVERSEAS BOWLERS IN ENGLAND

		Tests	Wkts	Best	Avge	SR	5wi	10wm
Shane Warne (Aus, LBG)	1993–2005	22	129	7-165	21.94	52.3	8	3
Dennis Lillee (Aus, RF)	1972–1981	16	96	7-89	20.56	50.1	6	2
Malcolm Marshall (WI, RF)	1980–1991	18	94	7-22	18.70	45.6	6	1
Curtly Ambrose (WI, RF)	1988–2000	20	88	6-52	20.77	55.8	3	0
Glenn McGrath (Aus, RFM)	1997–2005	14	87	8-38	19.34	39.8	8	0
Courtney Walsh (WI, RF)	1988–2000	21	87	6-74	24.44	58.9	3	1
Terry Alderman (Aus, RFM)	1981–1989	12	83	6-128	19.33	42.9	10	1
Richard Hadlee (NZ, RFM)	1973–1990	14	70	6-53	24.94	58.7	6	1
Clarrie Grimmett (Aus, LBG)	1926–1934	13	67	6-167	29.95	84.1	7	1
Hugh Trumble (Aus, OB)	1890–1902	16	67	8-65	20.35	52.0	5	3

TOP OVERSEAS BOWLERS IN AFRICA

		Tests	Wkts	Best	Avge	SR	5wi	10wm
Shane Warne (Aus, LBG)	1994–2006	13	67	6-86	24.17	59.7	2	0
Muttiah Muralitharan (SL, OB)	1994–2004	13	61	6-39	26.67	67.8	4	1
Anil Kumble (Ind, LBG)	1992–2007	16	59	6-53	31.33	80.3	1	0
Javagal Srinath (Ind, RFM)	1992–2001	12	58	6-76	26.53	56.9	3	0
Sydney Barnes (Eng, RFM)	1913–1914	4	49	9-103	10.93	27.6	7	3

MOST ODI CAREER RUNS

		ODIs	Runs	HS	Avge	100s	SR
Sachin Tendulkar (Ind)	1989–2012	455	18,161	200*	45.06	48	86.27
Ricky Ponting (Aus/ICC)	1995–2012	371	13,688	164	42.50	30	80.55
Sanath Jayasuriya (SL/Asia)	1989–2011	445	13,430	189	32.36	28	91.21
Inzamam-ul-Haq (Pak/Asia)	1991–2007	378	11,739	137*	39.52	10	74.24
Jacques Kallis (SA/ICC/Afr)	1996–2012	319	11,481	139	45.55	17	72.96
Sourav Ganguly (Ind/Asia)	1992–2007	311	11,363	183	41.02	22	73.70
Rahul Dravid (Ind/ICC/Asia)	1996–2011	344	10,889	153	39.16	12	71.24
Brian Lara (WI/ICC)	1990–2007	299	10,405	169	40.48	19	79.51
Mahela Jayawardene (SL/ICC)	1998–2012	360	10,118	144	33.28	15	77.45
Kumar Sangakkara (SL/ICC/Asia)	2000–2012	312	9,936	138*	37.92	12	75.37

Top ODI Scores

	Runs	Balls			
Virender Sehwag	219	149	Ind v WI	Indore	2011
Sachin Tendulkar	200*	147	Ind v SA	Gwalior	2010
Charles Coventry	194*	156	Zim v Ban	Bulawayo	2009
Saeed Anwar	194	146	Pak v Ind	Chennai	1997
Viv Richards	189*	170	WI v Eng	Manchester	1984
Sanath Jayasuriya	189	161	SL v Ind	Sharjah	2000
Sachin Tendulkar	186*	150	Ind v NZ	Hyderabad	1999
Shane Watson	185*	96	Aus v Ban	Dhaka	2011
MS Dhoni	183*	145	Ind v SL	Jaipur	2005

Fastest ODI Hundreds

	Runs	Balls			
Shahid Afridi	102	37	Pak v SL	Nairobi	1996
Mark Boucher	147*	44	SA v Zim	Potchefstroom	2006
Brian Lara	117	45	WI v Ban	Dhaka	1999
Shahid Afridi	102	45	Pak v Ind	Kanpur	2005
Sanath Jayasuriya	134	48	SL v Pak	Singapore	1996
Kevin O'Brien	113	50	Ire v Eng	Bangalore	2011
Shahid Afridi	124	53	Pak v Ban	Dambulla	2010
Sanath Jayasuriya	130	55	SL v Ban	Karachi	2008
AB de Villiers	102	58	SA v Ind	Ahmedabad	2010
Virender Sehwag	125*	60	Ind v NZ	Hamilton	2009

Top T20 International Scores

	Runs	Balls			
Chris Gayle	117	57	WI v SA	Johannesburg	2007
Brendon McCullum	116*	56	NZ v Aus	Christchurch	2010
Tillakaratne Dilshan	104*	57	SL v Aus	Pallekele	2011
Suresh Raina	101	60	Ind v SA	Gros Islet	2010
Mahela Jayawardene	100	64	SL v Zim	Providence	2010

LEADING ODI WICKET TAKERS

		ODIs	Wkts	Best	Avge	Econ
Muttiah Muralitharan (SL/ICC/Asia)	1993–2011	350	534	7-30	23.08	3.93
Wasim Akram (Pak)	1984–2003	356	502	5-15	23.52	3.89
Waqar Younis (Pak)	1989–2003	262	416	7-36	23.84	4.68
Chaminda Vaas (SL/Asia)	1994–2008	322	400	8-19	27.53	4.18
Shaun Pollock (SA/ICC/Afr)	1996–2008	303	393	6-35	24.50	3.67
Glenn McGrath (Aus/ICC)	1993–2007	250	381	7-15	22.02	3.88
Brett Lee (Aus)	2000–2011	205	357	5-22	22.89	4.70
Anil Kumble (Ind/Asia)	1990–2007	271	337	6-12	30.89	4.30
Shahid Afridi (Pak/ICC/Asia)	1996–2011	333	333	6-38	33.27	4.59
Sanath Jayasuriya (SL/Asia)	1989–2011	445	323	6-29	36.75	4.78

BEST ODI BOWLING FIGURES

	Overs	Maidens	Runs	Wkts			
Chaminda Vaas	8	3	19	8	SL v Zim	Colombo	2001
Glenn McGrath	7	4	15	7	Aus v Nam	Potchefstroom	2003
Andy Bichel	10	0	20	7	Aus v Eng	Port Elizabeth	2003
Muttiah Muralitharan	10	1	30	7	SL v Ind	Sharjah	2000
Waqar Younis	10	0	36	7	Pak v Eng	Leeds	2001
Aaqib Javed	10	1	37	7	Pak v Ind	Sharjah	1991
Winston Davis	10.3	0	51	7	WI v Aus	Leeds	1983
Anil Kumble	6.1	2	12	6	Ind v WI	Kolkata	1993
Ajantha Mendis	8	1	13	6	SL v Ind	Karachi	2008
Gary Gilmour	12	6	14	6	Aus v Eng	Leeds	1975

NOTES AND KEY:

All statistics are up to 9 February 2012 and are sourced from <espncricinfo.com>.

ICC = ICC World XI, 2005.

In batting stats, Avge = average number of runs per completed innings; HS = highest score; * = not out.

In bowling stats, Avge = average number of runs conceded per wicket taken; SR = strike-rate, average number of balls per wicket; Econ = economy rate, average runs conceded per over; 5wi = number of five-wicket innings; 10wm = number of ten-wicket matches.

Bowling types: RF/LF = right-arm/left-arm fast; RFM/LFM = right-arm/left-arm fast-medium; OB = orthodox right-arm off-breaks/spin; SLA = orthodox slow left-arm/left-arm spin; LBG = right-arm leg-break and googly spin bowling.

INDEX

First published by Parragon in 2012
Parragon
Queen Street House
4 Queen Street
Bath BA1 1HE, UK
www.parragon.com

ISBN 978-1-4454-9311-4
Printed in China

Photographic credits: All photographs © Patrick Eagar unless otherwise stated.

Getty Images: page 10, 11, 12, 13, 16, 17, 20, 21, 22, 26, 27, 28, 32, 33, 34, 35, 40, 41, 42, 43, 44, 64, 72 (bottom), 84, 85, 86 (top), 88, 95, 101, 108, 114–115, 117, 134 (top), 138, 139, 140, 148, 149 and 178.

The Publishers acknowledge the trademarks of Cricket Australia in these pages and where used note that they have been reproduced with the approval of Cricket Australia.

Picture of Graeme Swann on p78 is reproduced with kind permission of the ECB.